"Lisa Smith gives us a darkly comic, honest, and completely relatable inside look at high-functioning addiction in the world of corporate law—a sort of 'Sex and the Psych Ward.' It's inspiring, informative, and impossible to put down."

—**Jennifer Belle,** best-selling author of _High Maintenance_ and _The Seven Year Bitch_

"Whether she's telling the town car driver to turn around so she can ditch showing up for her niece's birth and meet her coke dealer, or staging her own semi-intervention, Smith takes us into the mind of someone who's completely in control while being radically out of control. This girl may have walked out of a bar, but she's walked into one of the best addiction memoirs I've ever read."

—**Anna David,** _New York Times_ best-selling author of _Party Girl, Bought_, and editor of _True Tales of Lust and Love_

"Raw, naked and unflinching, _Girl Walks out of a Bar_ catapults the reader into the sordid, desperate reality of high-functioning addiction: the booze, the coke, the lies; the denial, the depression, the blackouts. All are on full display as New York lawyer Lisa Smith loses herself in a deep and all-too-human descent into perpetual numbing. A chilling, cautionary tale."

—**Ann Dowsett Johnston,** Author of _Drink: The Intimate Relationship Between Women and Alcohol_

"Smith openly shares the lies, secrecy, depression, and isolation that define a life only made 'livable' by alcohol. Her raw depiction unveils the pressures of her job (20 percent of lawyers have substance abuse problems, she reports) as well as the personal costs of addiction, including divorce, ill health, and self-loathing. Readers will root for this extraordinary woman as she travels the path to recovery, healing, and triumph over addiction; her riveting story will inspire both those who have been there and those who have not."

—*Publishers Weekly*
April 4, 2016

GIRL WALKS OUT OF A BAR

A Memoir by **Lisa F. Smith**

SelectBooks, Inc.
New York, NY

This edition published by SelectBooks, Inc.
For information address SelectBooks, Inc., New York, New York.

First Edition

ISBN 978-1-59079-321-3

Library of Congress Cataloging-in-Publication Data
Names: Smith, Lisa F. (Lawyer), author.
Title: Girl walks out of a bar : a memoir / by Lisa Smith.
Description: First edition. | New York : SelectBooks, Inc., [2016] | Includes
   bibliographical references and index.
Identifiers: LCCN 2015032852 | ISBN 9781590793213 (pbk. book : alk. paper)
Subjects: LCSH: Smith, Lisa F. (Lawyer)--Health. | Substance
   abuse--Patients--United States--Biography. | Recovering addicts--United
   States--Biography. | Recovering alcoholics--United States--Biography.
Classification: LCC RC564 .S5665 2016 | DDC 362.29092--dc23 LC record
available at http://lccn.loc.gov/2015032852

Book design by Janice Benight

Manufactured in the United States of America
10 9 8 7 6 5 4 3 2 1

For CDF, HS, and RLP

Contents

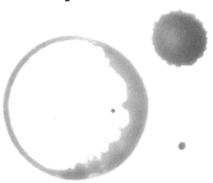

This book is the true story of events to the best of my recollection. Memory isn't perfect, of course, and memory under the influence is worse. I have recreated conversations as accurately as I recall them, and many of the key people included in the story have reviewed the manuscript for accuracy. To protect individuals' privacy, some names, places, and identifying characteristics have been changed.

Acknowledgments

I am grateful to so many people for making this book possible. First, thank you to Jennifer Belle, the leader of the writers workshop that has been the highlight of my week for years, for all of your wisdom, encouragement, and editing. Donna Brodie, Rob Wolf, Nicola Harrison, Barbara Miller, Mike Pyrich, Mario Gabriele, and Aaron Zimmerman, thank you for the insightful feedback, advice, ridiculous laughter, and friendship.

Thanks to my agent and friend, Katharine Sands, for her invaluable guidance. Thank you to my publisher, SelectBooks, especially Kenzi Sugihara, Nancy Sugihara, and Kenichi Sugihara. Thanks also to Jodi Fodor, who has special magic with words and everything else. Sarah Saffian, thank you for your editing and inspiration. Thank you also to Steve Eisner and everyone at When Words Count Retreat.

It's true when I say that I wouldn't be here without my incredible family and friends. Mom, Lou, Andrea, Caroline, and Ben, thank you for all of the love and cheerleading. Dad would have loved this. Thank you to my special cousin-readers, Gail Kaplan, Robert Nussbaum, and the Roethel girls. Gwen Erkonen, thank you for deciding we should try the weekend workshop in Iowa. Kellie Butler, thanks for listening to us ramble about writing.

To my friends who appear in the book and those who don't, I am so grateful to call you my people and love you with all my heart. In the interest of preserving anonymity I won't name names.

And to my husband Craig, thank you for telling me early on that I'd be a cheap date, and then supporting my efforts to write down the reasons why. I wake up every morning wondering how I got so lucky.

part one.

Not
your typical
Monday
morning.

1

Shit. It was 7:00 Monday morning and
I needed wine. In two hours I'd have to be at work, which meant
that I was going to have to steady my shaking hands. I inched
out of bed and walked naked toward the kitchen. After just a few
steps, my stomach lurched with the undeniable rumble of rising vomit, and I dashed to the bathroom with my hand pressed
against my mouth. I vomited violently and then sprawled out
across the cold tile floor and lay there like a deer that had just
been hit by a car. After a few minutes I began to lift my head
upright, slowly, gradually, as if sneaking up on something.
When I had finally reached eye level with the toilet, I saw blood
in the bowl.

Finally steady enough, I went to the kitchen and filled a
dirty glass with wine from an open bottle. Looking down the long
counter at the spoon rest I'd bought in Italy, my fancy tea kettle,
and the slotted spoons in a ceramic pitcher, I could almost convince myself that a normal person lived here, maybe even the successful, thirty-eight-year-old lawyer people saw when they looked
at me. But for that perspective I'd have to hold my hands up like

a photographer framing a shot so I could crop out all the empty wine bottles, the dirty glasses, and the overflowing ashtrays.

My immaculate coffeemaker looked at me in judgment. This would be just another day that I ignored it in favor of the wine bottle. It was a good time for a cigarette.

Still naked, I shuffled to the living room and on hands and knees slapped around under the couch looking for my lighter. All I came up with was a handful of dust and seventeen cents. But there were always matches to be found somewhere in my dark den. I reached into a hand-painted box that sat on my end table and found a plain, white matchbook amid the rolling papers, razor blades, and rolled up dollar bills. I flopped down on the couch and lit a Marlboro Light.

With the cigarette clamped between two fingers, I rested my elbow on my knee and dropped my head. My hair hung over my face like dirty curtains, but the sunlight streaming into the room still stung my eyes. I got up and opened the window to let in the fresh air of early spring. It was in April 2004 and the sounds of rumbling trucks and honking horns on East 20th Street flooded my apartment. Everybody shut up, I thought.

I took a few more slugs of wine and went back into the bedroom where I examined the small baggie of cocaine in my nightstand drawer. Thank God there was still some left. Dumping the remains on the top of my antique dresser, I crushed it into a fine powder with the back of a spoon. Careful not to lose any as I moved my hand across the white streaks in the marble top, I cut a few thick lines with a razor blade. There wasn't nearly enough to get me through the workday. Fuck.

Save it for later, I thought. You're definitely going to need it. But in four quick snorts through a rolled up dollar bill, the coke disappeared, leaving only a burning in my nose and a chemical-tasting drip down the back of my throat that managed to be both disgusting and delicious. My relief was countered by familiar feelings of dread about not having more—the untenable reality of an addict.

Just go—move, move, I thought. I lumbered toward the shower. Catching a glimpse of my bloated face in the bathroom mirror, I let the bath towel drop and rested both of my hands on the bathroom sink. It was hard to hold my head up. I looked like a haggard witch at least twice my age. What had I done to myself? And fuck, how was I going to get through today?

I gulped another big glass of wine as I dug through my closet for a suit. My work wardrobe was ratty. All of my suits, like most of my clothes, were black because black hid the wine stains and cigarette ash. Black also matched my general outlook and helped me disappear in a crowd.

After my obsessive ritual of brushing my teeth and gargling with Listerine at least three times before chomping Orbit gum, I began to feel more like my version of normal—steady enough to get through my workday without people seeing me violently shake or stumble and just barely confident that no one near me would smell the wine that pulsed through my veins.

I slid my laptop into its case. I had spent most of the weekend working on a business proposal that my law firm was submitting to a major power company. The prospective client represented millions of dollars in new business. Nonstop drinking and dozens of lines of coke had fueled my efforts from Friday evening through 3:00 Monday morning. No question that my work was better when I was high than when I was hungover. After drinking I was a three-toed sloth; on cocaine I was a stallion.

With my bag, phone, laptop, and keys together, I looked in the mirror, checking my nose for blood and stray coke and my teeth for smeared lipstick. Then I stepped out into the hallway and locked the door behind me.

5

But something felt wrong, unusually wrong. Anxiety seized me. I felt sicker than usual. My head was heavier and murkier. The shakes were deeper. I could feel them in my guts and in my bones. I even seemed to hate myself more than usual.

Was this it? Was this the end? Was it possible that my body could take no more and I might just drop dead right there? One of the senior citizens on my floor heading to the diner for breakfast would find me in the hall, dead on my back, my eyes and mouth gaping, one hand gripping my laptop and the other holding the *New York Times*. When the police insisted it was an overdose, the horrified old lady would whisper to my parents, "But she seemed like such a nice girl." The thought made me sicker. I'm going to die, I thought. I've killed myself.

Standing in front of the elevator, I stared at the "down" button. My heart was thumping like an angry bass drum, and my neck, back, and chest were seeping a strange, cold sweat. A voice in my brain screamed, "GET HELP!"

Get help? Help for what, I thought. For this anxiety attack (or is it a heart attack)? For the addiction that I'd known about but had dismissed for the past ten years? I wasn't clear about what I needed, but somehow I knew that "it" was over, that something had to change. Without knowing what to do next, I turned away from the elevator.

Back in my apartment, I poured another glass of cabernet.

I called Mark, my ex-boyfriend. Two weeks earlier, he had chosen to go back to being just my "downstairs neighbor." When he had insisted that I get treatment for my alcohol and cocaine addiction I told him to get the fuck out of my apartment.

Before he could say "hello," I choked out the words, "I need help."

Mark was the only person who had any idea that I drank in the mornings and used coke regularly. For years, I had managed to hide it from my family and friends by lying my ass off, being extremely attentive to details, and staying away from the people who mattered most. Mark's finding out was a testament to my spiraling sloppiness.

"I'll be right there," he said and hung up. Two minutes later he was at my door, and when I told him, "I think I need help with addiction," his brown eyes gaped.

"You really mean it? You're finally going to do something?" He looked like a bobblehead, bouncing up and down in his blue Puma sneakers, his shoulder-length curls of brown hair flopping back and forth.

"I have to. As in, *today* or I won't do it." He smiled. I looked at him with the focus of a military sniper. "Do not say 'I told you so,' or I'll throw you out of this apartment. I mean it." He bounced over to the couch and sat obediently.

A strange sense of relief began to warm me. Maybe I was actually going to do something about the horror my life had become. Did I really want to stop drinking? Stop using drugs? It was unimaginable—seeming simultaneously too good to be true and my worst nightmare. Even if I wanted to quit, I seriously doubted I could go five hours without booze or coke. I had resigned myself to being an alcoholic and cocaine addict who would eventually drown in a puddle of vomit. Or maybe on a foggy night I'd stumble into the path of a speeding cab. In any case, it was clear that mine wasn't going to be a graceful death. But on that morning, for the first time ever, I wanted to do something to save my life.

"I'm going to call my doctor," I told Mark. I wiped the smeared mascara from under my eyes with the back of my hand. Strange, I didn't remember crying.

"Hi, Dr. Merkin," I said when my internist picked up on the first ring. "It's Lisa Smith. How are you?" I heard my voice crack.

"I'm fine, Lisa. How can I help you?" *Cut the small talk.*

I blurted it out. "I need to go to detox or rehab for alcohol or something, but I don't know what to do or where to go."

"I doubt you need that. We took your blood just a couple months ago. You're fine."

"Um, no. I'm not fine. I'm drinking all the time. I have to drink to get out of bed in the morning. I'm puking blood and I also see it—uh—when—you know . . . when I go to the bathroom." I must have sounded like a child.

"Oh." He sounded confused and paused before saying, "Yes, yes. Then you're right. If that's true, you need to get help, right away. Inpatient help. Do you want to go away somewhere in particular?"

"I can't go away to some big, long rehab place. I can't tell my office. I just need to go somewhere to sort of detox me, or whatever they do, for a few days, just so I'm not so sick all the time. I just feel really, really sick."

"OK. Is your insurance still Oxford?" he asked. I could hear papers shuffling on his end of the phone.

"Yes. I lit a cigarette, but pulled the phone away when I exhaled.

"There are two hospitals that will take your insurance for detoxification treatment in Manhattan. St. Luke's in Hell's Kitchen?" he asked.

"No way," I said. "I'm not going to a hospital in Hell's Kitchen."

"Okay. There's Gracie Square Hospital on the Upper East Side, on 76th Street," he said.

"That one," I said. "I'll go to Gracie Square." It had to be good, I thought. Gracie Mansion was where the mayor lived. Also, it was only a few blocks from Lenox Hill Hospital where Dr. Merkin saw patients, in an expensive Manhattan neighborhood. Maybe it would have a better class of addict. "Who do I call?"

"Just call the main number, and tell them what's happening to you. If you need a referral, tell them to call me."

"Thank you, Dr. Merkin. I'll call right now," I said.

"Let me know what happens. Good luck, Lisa."

Gracie Square made reserving a bed less complicated than booking a hotel room. They took my insurance and said I could arrive any time until eleven that evening. I felt a pang of excitement at the thought of doing something that might relieve my addiction, and also a pang of dread of putting down the bottle. It reminded me of what people said about the most difficult partners at law firms: "He may be an asshole, but he's our asshole." Addiction was my asshole and the devil I knew. After ten years of drinking like a full-blown drunk, I couldn't imagine life without it.

"What'd they say?" Mark asked. I saw that he had poured himself a glass of wine. I always felt better when I wasn't the only one drinking, particularly before 9:00 a.m.

"They'll have a bed for me. They'll give me medicine, something called Librium, for withdrawal." Then I waved him away. "Let me deal with my office now, before anyone gets there."

Mark sat in my overstuffed club chair staring at me as I pulled my laptop out of its case. His knees were bouncing up and down which made me anxious, so I gave him an errand. "Hey, they said 'no cell phones' at this place. But there's a pay phone. Can you go get me a phone card? I think they have them at the bodega on the corner of 18th."

"Yeah, no problem," Mark said. "I'll pick up an egg sandwich while I'm out. Do you want one?"

"No, I definitely do not want an egg sandwich." I said.

9

I lit another cigarette, logged onto my computer, and sent an email to my boss and several partners. I claimed I had come down with a "stomach-related illness," that required "a procedure" in the hospital. Not to worry, I'd be back "in fine shape" next week, but this week I'd be "out of touch." As I passed off my immediate projects for coworkers to handle, I thanked God for the privacy laws that prevented the firm from questioning me about my health.

I could never let them know what was happening. It wasn't just because I was ashamed, which I was, it was also because of the stigma attached to substance abuse by lawyers. If they found out, overnight I'd go from being viewed as hardworking and smart to weak, defective, and untrustworthy. This was the attitude of the entire industry.

But my parents needed to know. They lived in New Jersey and we had always had a close relationship. Still, as far as they knew, I was doing great. I had told them countless happy lies and called only when sober enough to have a normal conversation. But the bubble of deceit now had one breath too many blown into it, and this phone call would draw a clear line dividing line between "before Mom and Dad knew that I had lied to them for years" and "after Mom and Dad knew that I had lied to them for years." The fact that I was an alcoholic would be less upsetting than the fact that I had been a fraud in our relationship. They believed they knew me well. They didn't. The phone felt like a fifty-pound weight.

"Good morning," my mother said. I pictured her sitting at the kitchen table, drinking her coffee and trying to spot birds outside the picture window. It was her favorite time of the day, and she was probably wearing one of her cotton pajama sets with a soft robe and socks. She was a petite, beautiful woman, a mix of Eastern European Jew and Irish Catholic with deep

GIRL WALKS OUT OF A BAR

brown eyes, short and perfectly coiffed reddish-brown hair, a delicate nose, and a smattering of freckles.

"Everything OK?" she asked. I didn't normally call this early. I tugged at my hair and felt sweat break out across my face and chest. There was still time to lie, but I was too tired and sick of it all. I took a swig of wine and spoke.

"Not exactly. Are you sitting down? I have to tell you something." I'd always thought that, "are you sitting down?" was the kind of line that belonged in soap operas and black-and-white movies. But I genuinely wanted her to hear this sitting down.

"Ok. I'm sitting." Then very quickly, "What is it? Are you sick?"

"Um, I'm just going to say it. I'm having a problem with alcohol." I decided to leave out the coke, at least for now. "It's a big problem. I'm going to check myself into a detox today." She was quiet, so I kept talking. "It's OK, though. I'm going to be OK. I just need help."

When she did speak it was in a voice slightly higher than normal. "What? What do you mean check yourself into a detox? What does that mean?"

"I'm going to go to a hospital, here in the city, just for a few days. They monitor you while you detox from alcohol. They give you medicine for withdrawal."

"*Withdrawal*? What are you talking about? How bad is this? You drink too much sometimes, but is it so bad that you have to be *hospitalized*? Couldn't you just stop drinking for a while?" I could picture her face contorting in confusion. She was in that early phase, when you still think you can fix the situation with words. Tears began to stream down my cheeks.

"No. No, I can't just stop drinking for a while," I sniffed. "I would if I could, but I have to drink all the time just to function. I'm sick all the time, my hands shake, my head throbs. I can't concentrate. Drinking is the only thing that makes me feel normal. It sounds backwards, but it's true. It's bad and I need to go somewhere to make me stop. I just *have to*." It was becoming difficult to keep talking through my tears, and I gasped for breath.

"All right, all right, it's OK," she said, in the same voice she used when I was eight years old. By now I was sobbing. She continued, "It's OK. If you need help, you've got to get help. I'll go get dressed. I pictured Mom dumping the rest of her coffee down the drain and pacing in front of the wall phone, eager to hang up so she could start taking action. "Daddy and I will get to your apartment in about an hour. We'll figure this out."

"No!" I half screamed. "No, really. You don't need to come in to the city. I talked to Dr. Merkin and he gave me the name of a place that takes my insurance, and they're already expecting me. It's called Gracie Square." Before she could respond, I tried to comfort her by blurting, "It's on the Upper East Side!" I got off the couch and began pacing back and forth across the living room with my head still down.

"Wait. If you really need this, shouldn't we look at a few places? Peggy's husband went somewhere nice in Connecticut for a month. I'll call her now."

"No. I have to go today or I'll lose my nerve. Plus, I can't go away to one of those one or two-month-long places. I'm going back to work next week. This is detox, just a treatment so I can feel better." The pitch of my voice was rising. "I don't need to go anywhere that long. I'll be fine. I just feel really sick right now and this will fix it." I slumped back onto the couch. Then I was quiet.

"Alright, OK," she took another long pause. "Talk to your father."

There was a mumbling, scraping sound as she covered the phone receiver and then yelled, "HARVEY!" She must have been standing at the bottom of the stairs shouting up to the second floor. Both of my parents had weak hearing, so shouting was the norm in their house. I could hear bits of their back and forth as she relayed what I had told her. "Alcohol." "That's right." "She said 'no.'" "I don't know. I don't know!" Eventually, my dad got on the phone.

"Yessss," he said drawing out the word in his standard greeting. "We've got a little problem, huh?" Dad had never been one to discuss the intimate, emotional details of my life. A brilliant judge who had graduated from high school at sixteen and college at nineteen and had passed the Bar by twenty-two, he was much more comfortable in the intellectual realm. Whenever there was drama at home, Dad would joke that he wanted a t-shirt that read, "Leave Me Alone" on the front and "Buzz Off" on the back. Only once did I ever see him cry, after his best friend, Angelo, died from a brain tumor. My father's face looked bizarrely different to me that day—changed by contortions and grimaces that scared me.

"Yeah, we do. I need to go to detox for booze. It's a problem."

"Alright, OK, so that's what you'll do," he said. Dad was seventy-five, but he looked like a man in his early sixties. He had a semicircle of hair around his head and was tall and trim thanks to his routine of yoga and a diet dominated by fish and vegetables. When I was two years old, I'd wake up when Dad did, so early that just about the only thing on television was a show called *Yoga for Life*. Decades later I would come downstairs at my parents' house in the early mornings to find him standing on his head, balanced against the laundry room door.

My father never doubted my ability to deal with things. When I was five and terrified of having the training wheels taken off my bike, he quietly removed them in our garage, told me to climb on, and gave me a push. But he didn't chase me to make sure that I didn't fall. He said he wasn't worried. When I made the Law Review after my first year of law school, he said, "Of course you did," with a giant smile.

"What are you going to tell your office?" he asked. I knew that he'd be concerned about that.

"It's already done. I emailed everyone to tell them I have a medical issue that came up over the weekend. If they ask me about it, I'll lie. But they're not supposed to ask about medical things. And I'll be back on Monday."

"OK. Good, good. They don't need to know this. Mom said you don't want us to come in. Keep us posted, though. We'll come if you want . . . at any hour . . ."

"Thanks, Dad. I appreciate that." I started crying hard again.

"Hey, hey, don't cry. This is the right thing you're doing. You've got a problem and you're going to take care of it. It's OK."

After we hung up, I took a deep breath and tried to get my composure back. Why hadn't I saved some coke last night?

My friends were next. My inner circle was tight, and we spent a lot of our time together with drinks in hand, but I'd made sure that they had no idea how much booze and coke I pumped into my system when they weren't around. Now that I was doing something as extreme as going to detox, I had to tell them. They were my city family, my urban tribe. I could never just disappear on them. And I wanted to tell them. I didn't want to do this without them.

I flopped on my bed and called Russell first. I had met Russell almost fifteen years earlier through his wife, Jessica, my closest friend from my first law firm. Russell had been my confidant the few times I decided to talk about having gone too far, like when I'd stayed up all night doing coke at my place with a guy I barely knew. "Ro, it was really fucked up. We were just hanging out watching *Goodfellas*, and when the coke was gone, he wouldn't leave. I went over to the door, like, 'Let's go, you've got to go,' and he actually shoved me up against the wall. I almost called the cops. He was like a drug psycho."

"That's not right, Pumpkin," Russell had said. "You have to be more careful."

As my using escalated, I had told him I was thinking about stopping, without elaborating. "That could be really cool," was his response, without elaborating.

Russell picked up his office phone on the first ring. "Hey, Li," he said.

"Hey Ro. Listen, I'm feeling really messed up. Like way worse than usual. I'm going to check into a detox today. I can't do this anymore."

"Wait, what happened? Are you OK?" he asked.

"Yeah, I think. But you know, I'm not normal anymore. I'm not drinking like a normal person. It's too much now. I have to change."

"OK," he said. "You sure?" I imagined him looking out the window of his office at an investment bank in Midtown at the normal people on the street below. Russell looked like a young John Malkovich with titanium-framed glasses and he carried himself with Malkovich's kind of confidence. He never spoke loudly, but whatever he said was firm and usually not open to challenge. Part of his discipline came from his karate practice. He was working toward his black belt and rarely traveled any-where without the gym bag containing his gi.

"Yeah, definitely. Bad. My doctor gave me a place to go on the Upper East Side. I just have to show up there by eleven o'clock tonight."

"OK, let me just clear one thing off my desk and I'll come over. I'll call Jessica, but she's probably going to be stuck home with the kids." Russell and Jessica had two boys, aged six and three. "Just hang in. OK, Pumpkin?" he said. The uncharacteristic urgency in his voice made me realize that I must have sounded scared or strung out, or both. I hadn't planned on his coming over, but it made perfect sense. None of our crew would let any of the others go through something this serious alone.

My next call was to Jerry. He was a banker who had been a drunken pick-up in an East Side bar one night during my second year of law school. Then we started dating. He was handsome in a smart-ass, mischievous, Jewish kid kind of way. With slicked back dark hair that curled at the bottom and a constant smirk, Jerry always looked like trouble, which he was. After I suggested that instead of calling me at three o'clock on Friday afternoon for a Friday night date, maybe he could ask me out on Tuesday or Wednesday, he didn't ask me out again. Then about a year later I randomly ran into him, and he offered to take me to a Grateful Dead show. I couldn't pass that up, and from that point on we become tight friends, just friends. Drinking was our favorite pastime.

"Yo!" Like Russell, Jerry was at his desk early.

"Listen, I've got some news."

"Yeah? You OK?"

"Not really. I'm in bad shape. I'm checking into the tank," I said.

"The drunk tank? Nah! Get out!"

"No, I'm serious," I grabbed an ashtray off my dresser and lit a cigarette. From the next room came the sound of television news and the faint smell of fried egg and bacon. Mark had returned. Jerry inhaled and then pushed out a deep, loud breath. "OK. OK. What tank do you even go to? Harper's friend went to that place in Minnesota. I think I'd go to Betty Ford. Food's supposed to be good."

"No, no, I'm not doing a big thing like that. I'm just going for five or so days to this place on the Upper East Side to detox. Gracie Square. I got the referral from my doctor. I can get there any time before eleven o'clock tonight."

"Yo! This is going down today? Today? Whoa."

"Yeah, yeah. Russell's coming over here to help me get my shit together and take me over."

"He's coming over? Are you drinking?" Jerry asked. "You better drink now before this whole thing goes down!"

"Oh, trust me, I'm drinking."

"I'll be right there. See you in a few." He hung up and I pictured him scrambling around his office getting ready to run out. He might have had to bail out of a big work meeting to come over, but it wouldn't matter to Jerry. He was that kind of friend. And it certainly wouldn't hurt if alcohol were being served. We were known to open the Dublin House on West 79th Street at 8:00 a.m. on St. Patrick's Day. Maybe it wasn't a bad idea for us to finish off any alcohol in the apartment before I left. I had a feeling I'd need to keep booze out of my place after detox, at least for a while.

At last I took off my work clothes and slipped into old jeans and an oversized cotton sweater. I was clammy with sweat and my insides felt like pea soup puree, churning around and around in a slow blender.

Was I really doing this or would the presence of my friends make me realize that I'd never give up my drinking and drugs? The situation was so surreal, I couldn't be sure. It was as if I were hovering over the scene, watching some actress who looked like me telling her friends that she was just hours away from redefining their friendship forever. Wasn't that true? Didn't the decision to dry out threaten to change every relationship I had? Forever? Not the least of which would be the

17

relationship with myself. Jesus, what would I do with myself sober all day? Fuck. This couldn't possibly stick.

Jerry was at my door in minutes. "DOG!" He hugged me hard and I spilled into him. Then he helped himself to a glass of wine and headed into the living room to light a cigarette. "What's up, dude?" he politely asked Mark who was sitting on the club chair. Mark and I spent most of our time together in my apartment, and I usually saw my friends separately, so they barely knew who he was. When they were around, he tended to hang back, maybe because being with us was like being at someone else's family dinner—you'd definitely been invited and they tried to make you feel welcome, but you really weren't part of the family.

"Hey!" Jerry said when Russell knocked shortly after. "Big day, huh? You believe this?" I hugged Russell in the doorway. Jerry sat with his jacket off and tie loosened, his right arm slung across the back of the living room couch. "She's going to the drunk tank!"

"Yeah, I know," said Russell. Then looked at me. "You OK?" I hugged him again and nodded into his chest. "Jess is with the kids," he said. "No babysitter."

"Sure, yeah," I said. "I'm OK." I tried not to sound disappointed.

Russell grabbed a glass of wine and sat on the couch next to Jerry, dropping the bag with his Karate gi on the floor. Sitting cross-legged opposite them, I leaned back against my heavy wooden bookcase.

"So, what's up with this?" Jerry asked me. "What happened, baby? You really think you need this?"

"I have to drink to get out of bed. I'm puking blood. I'm shitting blood. It's really, *really* bad."

Jerry's eyes popped. "Oh my God! Why didn't you say anything? I had no idea!"

"Doesn't matter now," Russell said. "We'll get her in today and she'll get better."

I rocked forward and hung my head over my legs. It didn't seem real for me to be telling everyone the things I'd been so carefully hiding for so long. I felt sick and relieved at the same time.

"Shit. Did you call Devon?" Jerry asked.

Devon, a marketing executive at a financial firm, arrived shortly thereafter and was already crying before she hugged me. She was the kind of woman whose mascara didn't run when she cried. Devon actually looked great in a bikini—from every angle. And she could eat roast beef sandwiches dripping with mayonnaise and never gain a pound. My news had shaken her up, but not one hair in her expertly highlighted blonde bob was out of place. We had met in a shared beach house on Fire Island almost fifteen years earlier and had spent the first night bonding hugely over vodka sodas. Now she was here in my apartment, on a workday, getting ready to send me to detox.

Were it not for me in the crummy clothes I had changed into and Mark in his holey jeans, the room could have passed for a Wall Street happy hour.

"Hey, you guys! What did you know about this?" Devon asked Russell and Jerry, pointing a well-manicured finger in their direction.

Russell was looking at his phone. Jerry spoke up. "We didn't know anything, Dev! What the fuck? Why don't you get some wine and relax?" Jerry knew that Devon hated being called "Dev" and being told to relax.

"Clowns," she said, shaking her head. "Where's the wine?" I pointed to the kitchen. "Here, I got this for you," she said. She tossed me a little white stuffed tiger with black stripes that she had picked up on her way over. It roared three times when you squeezed its middle. "Just in case you need protection." My eyes teared. I never would have thought to do that for anyone.

The same question kept coming up in various forms: "Why didn't you tell us things were so bad?" What was the right answer? The lies had become so free-flowing that I hesitated to say the simple truth, which was, "There's something wrong with me, with the way I think. I've always known it. I'm not like you guys. I'm chasing a happy life, but I don't think I deserve it. I'll never be good enough. Every day I still feel like the fat kid in fifth grade. The only way I can stop that script in my head is by drinking and using coke. But now drinking and using coke have become all I think about, all I care about."

I listened to the chatter that always sounded like family bickering among my friends, mixing in with the Talking Heads CD that played in the background. My mind zipped through the repercussions of what I was about to do. If I detox the booze out of my body, does that mean I never get to put any more *in*? What if I couldn't sit around and drink with these guys anymore? Would I have to just sit there and watch them drink? It was unthinkable. Sure, I was vomiting blood, but how do you live without drinking?

Suddenly I remembered all of us on Fire Island when we rented the beach house for the summer of 1992. The weekends when we could all leave the city for the beach were precious, and this had been a particularly good one, a perfect, clear blue-sky Fourth of July.

We had all congregated on the wooden deck in the back, sitting in a circle of beach chairs around the grill. It was a Saturday, and we had invited some other friends to join us. The sun was setting and the air had that magic twilight quality that emerges right at the beginning edge of a summer night. Most of us had just showered after a long day of laughing and sleeping on the beach. We walked around barefoot, letting our just-cleaned hair dry however the ocean air willed.

Jerry was hovering over the grill watching fresh clams open one by one and bopping along to the Grateful Dead's "Bertha," that played out of the house speakers. As the clams opened, he plucked them off the grill with oversized tongs and dropped them into a large bowl. "Dude. These are amazing!" he kept saying, to no one in particular.

The salty sea air mixed with the smell of garlic powder melting into drawn butter. I could hear the whir of the blender inside as Russell yelled, "Frozen margaritas—two minutes!" Jessica, Devon, and I giggled and cackled as we remembered listening to a bunch of day-tripping teenagers on the beach talking about their evening plans. "We're totally getting into the Albatross tonight. It's gonna be awesome," we heard one of them say. Our cigarette smoke trails crossed and we shook with laughter as we joked about a bunch of seventeen-year-olds with fake IDs trying to use pouty lips and cleavage to get past Bobby, the bar's grumpy, gay bouncer.

That's how it always was when we got together—it was comfortable. It was funny. It was easy. We were happy. And we were usually smoking and drinking. Now I was afraid I'd never fit in with my friends again. I was going off the rails and ruining everything. Another reason to hate myself.

• • •

Snapping back, I realized it was close to lunchtime. "Hey, you guys hungry? Should we order Chinese?" I asked. "Maybe we should eat and I'll take a nap before we go." I was trying to slow the clock.

LISA SMITH

"Yeah, get a bunch of food." Jerry said. "Don't know when you're going to get a decent meal again!"

After a full plate of spring rolls, sweet and sour shrimp, and broccoli with garlic sauce, I needed sleep. "You guys, I'm going down for a nap," I said, staggering into the bedroom.

When I awoke several hours later, it was dark outside. For a moment I forgot the gravity of my situation, but as my eyes began to adjust to the light of my bedside lamp, my mind caught up on current events. I was about to slide back under the covers when Devon padded into the room, having long ago kicked off her Gucci shoes.

"I packed your bag," she said. "You never know who's going to be in rehab, so I put some nice stuff in, too: good bras, a couple of short skirts, high heels. . . There could be rock stars there."

"I doubt it's that kind of place," I said.

Devon shook her head and rolled her eyes. "It's entirely possible, so you and your nice panties will be ready."

I washed my face, brushed my teeth and walked back out into the living room where my support team remained gathered, still sipping red wine from large glasses. It was time to leave. All I had to say was "Let's go," but instead, I flopped my still exhausted body down onto one of the club chairs. My friends stood up and began to put their coats on. They talked about who should share a cab, and I panicked.

"You know what, you guys? I'm feeling way better. Maybe I should just get more sleep and go tomorrow instead." My leg was draped over the oversized arm of the chair, and I avoided eye contact with everyone.

Devon whipped around toward me. She was holding a little bag with my toiletries and pointed a tube of toothpaste at me. "Oh, no, you don't!" she said. "After what we went through

22

today? And what you told us you've been doing? You're going to detox, and you're going right now." I looked to the guys for help, but all three of them were nodding in agreement.

Russell turned to me as we were walking out. "Why don't you give me a set of keys? I'll come back here with Devon and we'll make sure there's nothing lying around when you get back." Russell was always two steps ahead of a situation. It was part of what made him so successful in law and in banking.

"OK, yeah, good idea," I said, watching him drop my spare set of keys into his jacket pocket. Then I said, "Oh wait, you know what else? Take down all the sweaters on the shelves in the walk-in closet. Shake them to see if any stray bags of coke fall out," I paused, thinking through my other stashes. "Oh yeah, and the boxes in the linen closet? You know, like where I keep Band-Aids and hotel shampoos? Better check those, too." His expression didn't change as he nodded slowly, but I swore I could see him start to process the fact that I hid bags of coke between my sweaters and in Band-Aid boxes. "Oh yeah, and there's some really good pot in the box with the votive candles on my bookshelf," I said, as if I had left something off a shopping list. "Give it to Jerry."

There was nothing but support in my friends' eyes, but I felt as if I'd just told them I'd been selling crack to sixth graders.

• • •

We took two taxis to Gracie Square. I sat between Russell and Devon, my head resting on Russell's shoulder. I felt so tired and sick that there was no room left for fear or dread.

The front of the hospital was like none I'd ever seen. No bright lighting, no circular driveway for drop-offs and pick-ups, no fleet of idling ambulances waiting for their next 911 call. In fact, the building looked like the dreary corporate offices of a company that time had forgotten. Russell, Devon, and I exchanged curious looks but no one spoke.

Jerry and Mark arrived in their own cab. "Yo, smoke 'em while you got 'em," Jerry said, handing me a cigarette. "What the fuck is this place? Doesn't look like a hospital."

"No idea. Give me your lighter," I said, grabbing it with a shaking hand.

After stomping out my cigarette, I swung open one of the big glass doors and headed toward the receptionist who sat in a booth behind a panel of protective glass. A young, tired-looking security guard in a blue uniform sat at a wooden desk a little farther back in the lobby. Was he armed? We all looked at each other as if to acknowledge that whatever this place was, it was no New York-Presbyterian.

Devon raised an eyebrow and pursed her lips. "I don't like this place," she said. I shrugged back at her, and she offered, "Why don't you let me call Silver Hill? It's a place up in Connecticut and is supposed to be nice. I think Billy Joel went there."

Starting over didn't sound like a good idea at that point. I shut my eyes and said, "Let me just try it here. If it's terrible, I'll leave."

The receptionist directed us to a large waiting area with hard plastic, burgundy chairs that were linked up in sets. After a few minutes, a tall, middle-aged man in khakis and a faded blue button-down shirt walked into the reception area, looked around, and approached our group. He had thinning brown hair, and he walked with the casual lope of someone unlikely to be surprised by whatever happened next.

"Hi. I'm Brad," he said, clasping his hands together, perhaps an attempt at enthusiasm. "I'm here for Lisa." I gave him a half wave from where I was slouched in a chair and leaning on Russell.

"Hi Lisa. I'm going to get you admitted and up to the detox floor. We need to go to the intake area. Are you folks Lisa's friends or family?" he asked the group.

"We're her friends," Russell said before anyone else could speak. "We'd like to hear what's going to happen." He was using the voice he probably adopted when closing corporate mergers. I nodded at Brad, and he pulled up a chair so that everyone could hear.

"OK, I'm going to explain a few things," Brad said. "Lisa, I understand that you're here because you have an alcohol problem and are seeking a medicated detoxification. If you choose to do that here, you need to understand that this is a locked-down psychiatric facility, not a hospital where you can come and go." I kept my eyes on Brad, afraid to look at anyone else. "If you agree to be treated, you must sign a consent that requires us to keep you here for at least 72 hours. You cannot leave before that, unless a written request is granted."

He seemed like a kind man, but there was no mistaking the seriousness in his tone. "From here, I'll take you to the detox unit where you will be treated with the rest of the detox patients. Now I want you to be prepared: you might see and hear some things you're not used to, but the patients there are all dealing with the same thing you are. They're just getting help, like you. The floor is coed and you'll share a room with another female patient. You will share a bathroom with the patients in the next room. Also, you should know that there are no locks on any of the doors because the staff needs unrestricted access to patients at all times. Do you understand all of this?"

I nodded and tried to keep a calm face but my insides were shouting at me, *Why didn't you research this more thoroughly? Why did you just pick this place? Christ, you give more thought to changing your lip color.* Devon seemed to share my thoughts.

Her expression seemed to say, "I'm not leaving you here with Jack Nicholson in his creepy ass hotel!" But I was so tired, and it had taken so much to come this far—I just wanted to give whatever signatures would let me fall into a bed, any bed. Brad held out a clipboard with a stack of papers, and I started signing with my right hand while Russell held my left hand. Then it was done. I was officially a mental patient.

"OK, Lisa, you won't meet the staff psychiatrist until tomorrow morning. I'm taking you to the night physician now. He'll take some blood so he can run the necessary tests and get you started on Librium."

Hot tears built up in my eyes and I struggled to hold them back as I hugged my friends goodbye. They looked more frightened than I was, but then again, they hadn't made a practice of snorting coke for breakfast followed by vomiting blood. They called out, "We'll visit" and "You'll be OK" as they walked out into the world I couldn't rejoin for 72 hours. I wondered if they were comforting themselves or me.

Then it occurred to me that they were probably going for a drink. My mouth watered at the idea. They'd certainly earned a drink, and surely there would be a download discussion. A big part of me wanted to run after them, but a bigger part was grateful that I'd signed away the option.

2

Brad and I rode the ancient elevator up to the third floor in silence. He clasped his hands behind his back as we both looked up, watching the floor numbers tick higher.

"This is it," he said and pulled open the final door to the detox unit. The door slammed shut behind us. Shit, I thought. I'm really on a locked-down floor of a mental hospital. What just happened? I'm a nice Jewish girl from New Jersey who belongs to MoMA and reads *The Economist*.

The unit looked like a typical hospital floor lined with patient rooms, but it smelled like a combination of antiseptic, piss, and vomit. I became dizzy as we started down the hall and my stomach scrambled as if I might barf.

There was a loud commotion directly in front of us. Two haggard-looking women were screaming at each other. "Fucking cunt! I'll kill you!" It was impossible to tell what they were fighting about because their exchange was nothing but screamed threats and name-calling. They looked middle-aged with their pasty white skin and long, frizzy hair, but something told me that they may very well have been in their twenties. They wore

27

grubby sweatpants and t-shirts, both of which hung off their bodies the way clothes seem to want to escape long-term heroin users and war-weary refugees.

"Keep moving," Brad said as he veered me away from the chaos. Raw fear jolted through my fingers and toes. There would be no need for the lingerie Devon packed.

Seconds later, a tall, angry man stormed toward us. He had what looked like several days of stubble on his face and tattoos on every bit of exposed skin. He looked strong enough and pissed off enough to take down the two battling women with a single swing. But he was staring at me.

I fell behind Brad and looked at the floor, but it didn't help. As soon as we were within twenty feet, the man bellowed, "HEY!" I pretended not to notice.

When I didn't respond, he repeated himself. "HEY!" I couldn't help looking up. He came closer pointed his finger at me, and scowled, "YOU, GIRL. I'M GONNA FUCK YOU UP!"

I looked around, hoping that he'd mistaken me for someone else he intended to fuck up. And that scary freak must have read my mind because as he passed us, he turned back and shouted, "YEAH, YOU."

I looked at Brad in a panic. "That's it," I said. "No fucking way. I'm out of—"

"No, no, no, no," Brad interrupted. "It's going to be fine. I know it looks scary, but really, it's going to be fine." He had his arm around my shoulder and was guiding me forward quickly.

"Did you hear that? That guy said he's going to fuck me up. You have to let me go." I stopped walking and stomped my foot.

"Lisa, take it easy. No one is going to hurt you. You signed yourself in. You're here for 72 hours, and we're legally required to keep you here. It's OK; he's just talking. He's here for the same reason as you, just here to get help." Did Brad believe what he was saying? I didn't trust him. I felt like I had to run away, fast. Was this what they meant by "fight or flight" on those animal shows I watched on the National Geographic Channel at 3:00 a.m., coked out of my head? Was this what a gazelle felt right before a lion's teeth sank into her hindquarters?

"No," I said to Brad. He continued walking, so I had to follow. "No way I'm sleeping here with no locks on the doors and these lunatics running around. No fucking way." The words didn't seem to be coming out fast enough. Brad just kept walking.

We arrived at the examination room where the night physician was waiting to complete my intake process. By now I was near hyperventilating. "Lisa, this is Dr. Maxwell," Brad said.

With his slick black hair, Dr. Maxwell looked a little like my former pediatrician and seemed to have the same cold manner. No one introduced the nurse next to him. Brad turned to the doctor and said, "She's scared. A few people acting up out there." Acting up? I thought. Acting up is a baby tossing Cheerios off his high chair. This was a credible, physical threat and they needed to do something about it.

I fell into the first chair I saw and started bawling. "I want to leave!" I screamed. My fists were clenched into balls.

Dr. Maxwell looked unfazed. "Lisa, calm down," he said. "We're just going to take some blood and then we can give you some Librium. It will help you relax and you'll feel much better. It's okay." I saw him arranging his bloodletting instruments, no longer looking at me.

"NO!" I shrieked, as if they were threatening to pull out a fingernail with a pair of pliers. "I am not letting anyone stick any needles into my arm. I am not taking any Librium or any drug in this place. And I am not staying."

Another argument occurred to me and I tried to sound calm and reasonable. "The conditions here are unacceptable. I am a lawyer. I know my rights." This was a lie. I had no idea what my rights were in this situation. "You cannot keep me here against my will. I do not feel safe." I had heard somewhere that "I do not feel safe," was an effective buzz phrase for when you needed help, but that might have been in a *Vanity Fair* article I read about a dominatrix. "If you don't let me leave, I'm going to call the police!"

As I rocked back and forth sobbing, Brad and Dr. Maxwell stepped out of the examination room.

They returned a few minutes later. "OK, Lisa," said Brad. "We're going to work with you here, but you're going to have to work with us. We understand that you feel uncomfortable, but we cannot let you go tonight. You can write a request to be released, but it can't be reviewed until the psychiatrist arrives in the morning. And then it will be up to him. You're going to have to spend the night here, but we think we can make it a little easier on you. We can put you on the Asian floor."

"The Asian floor?" I asked, still choking back tears. "What do you mean the Asian floor?"

"We have a floor upstairs that's all Asian," Brad said. "Patients, doctors, and nurses. These aren't detox patients. They're patients with other mental illnesses, such as dementia, paranoia, and schizophrenia. They come here because their families want a more comfortable, familiar atmosphere for them. You're still going to see lots of people roaming the halls, talking to themselves, acting in ways you're not used to seeing. But it can be quieter up there." This couldn't be happening. Was I really locked in a mental institution and negotiating which was the most desirable floor? I wanted a drink.

"What do you say?" Brad continued. "You would be right outside the nurses' station. Just give it a try for tonight and we'll get your request for discharge evaluated in the morning."

There was clearly no going home that night. If I got out of reach of the dangerous lunatics on the detox floor and was outside a nurses' station, I thought, I could probably make it until morning. To survive the night, I could sit in a ball on the floor next to the doorway of my room so that if anyone came by to attack me they would see an empty bed and move on to another victim. "All right," I said. "I'll go up there tonight, but just for tonight. Then I'm out."

"Great," Dr. Maxwell said. "Now if you'll just roll your sleeve up, we'll draw that blood and get you started on the Librium."

"No fucking way," I said. "No blood. No drugs. Please give me a piece of paper to write out my request to leave." Brad handed me a pad and pen. I scribbled a short note requesting my immediate discharge and handed it to Brad. "Let's go upstairs," I said.

● ● ●

Just two floors above the detox, looking the same but smelling better, the Asian floor felt like another world. In some ways it was. As described, everyone on the floor was Asian, with the exception of Brad and me. He walked me to the nurses' station. "This is Vivian," he said, as a short, plump Asian woman with a sympathetic smile shook my hand. "She'll help you get settled for the night." I nodded at him and shook the nurse's hand. Then she took my bag from Brad.

"So, you'll be OK here tonight?" Brad asked.

Vivian was setting my bag down on the bed in a small room directly across from the nurses' desk. "Yeah, I can do this," I said. Brad looked relieved.

"Great," he said. "Dr. Landry, the psychiatrist, will come see you tomorrow to discuss your situation and your request to leave."

"Thank you," I said. "I really appreciate what you did."

He shrugged. "It's OK. But remember that people don't usually land in this hospital unless there's a good reason. See how you feel in the morning." As he walked away, I laughed to myself. See how I feel in the morning? I could tell him how I'd feel in the morning: desperate to get out of this place to have a fat cocktail and a smoke.

Vivian had begun to dig into the contents of my bag like a power-drunk TSA agent. What was the worst thing she could find? A bag of drugs I might have forgotten in the lining? Maybe they'd kick me out.

Meanwhile I took a good look at my Spartan accommodations. The room was about twelve feet long and seven feet wide with a cold, speckled linoleum floor. A twin-size mattress half as thin as a telephone directory sat on top of a low, wire frame and was pushed along the side of the wall. No headboard, no box spring. The bed was made up with some scratchy sheets and a stained, thin, white cotton blanket. I was going to need that heavy sweater that Devon had packed.

A wooden chair sat at the foot of the bed, and directly across from it was a small sink with a piece of shiny metal over it meant to function as a mirror. Looking into it, I could make out my image generally, but the details of my face were unclear. When I moved my head, I morphed into another form.

The small window near the head of the bed was embedded with wiring, blocking any view outside. There was no telephone, television, or clock, and I thought of a good question for *Jeopardy*: "In these two places, it's impossible to tell if it's night or day."

"What are a casino and a mental hospital, Alex?"

Vivian looked amused as she picked at my bag, smirking when she came across the negligees, push-up bras, and pair of

32

spiky heels. She let me keep the clothes but removed anything that, in a spy movie or an episode of *MacGyver*, might have facilitated my escape or suicide. She shook her head as she filled a black plastic tray with items that were to be returned to me at the end of my stay: my cell phone, cigarettes, money, credit cards, driver's license, MetroCard, tweezers, razors, and a small glass pot of lip gloss.

"You can get ready for bed now," she said, relinquishing what remained in the bag. "I'll be back in a few minutes to take your blood pressure."

The only thing I had resembling pajamas were the negligees Devon had packed. I didn't even own pajamas. Having something normal to sleep in was just another thing that my alcoholic lifestyle had rendered unimportant to me, like doing laundry and opening mail.

Piles of unopened envelopes would sit on my kitchen counter for months. Although there was plenty of money in my bank account, I almost never paid my bills on time. It was sheer laziness, although I told myself I was just "too busy" to get to it. When I got around to calling the credit card companies, weeks after bills were due, I would pay over the phone, hefty penalties included. The renter's insurance on my apartment was cancelled for nonpayment. I skipped sending in rent checks and made it up the next month. I was a top-bracket taxpayer living like a broke drug addict.

I pulled on a pair of leggings, circa 1988, and took off my bra, leaving on the heavy cotton sweater I had worn all day. The room was cold, so I added thick wool socks.

The bathroom had a thin wood door. No locks, not even on the bathroom doors. I flipped the thick black switch on the metal plate. The fluorescent light that flickered on was dim, and that was fine with me. Out of fear, I never fully assessed the toilet and made a decision never to sit on it; I would squat. In the corner, there was a narrow stall shower with a decrepit white plastic shower curtain hanging from a semicircle shaped rod. *Won't be touching anything in there either*, I thought.

Vivian wheeled in a blood pressure contraption that sat atop a long rod with three wheels at the bottom. The bed creaked as I wrestled my arm out of my sweater, like the first move in a pathetic strip tease. She choked the band around my arm and looked at her watch as she took the reading. She didn't mention that she would do this every three hours of the next twenty-four.

"You know, it's not so bad here," she said. "You'll be OK. You look tough." Tough? I thought. Rough, maybe. Strung out and ancient, sure. But tough? It must have been Vivian's way of psyching me up for what was going to happen the next morning.

"I'm not going to be staying. I already submitted my request to leave. As soon as I see the psychiatrist tomorrow, I'm going."

As she pumped the little rubber bulb, I hoped that my hysteria and anxiety had catapulted my blood pressure to a level that would get me transferred to the cardiac unit at Lenox Hill. There I could relax, safe among bankers, lawyers, and other overachievers who had worked their way into a cardiac vacation. It didn't happen.

She unwrapped the band from my arm, looped the thick, black cord around it, and raised her eyebrows. "Right," she said. "You should think about staying." Then she rolled her machine out of the room.

I sat on the bed looking around and feeling twitchy. Trembling and sweating, I badly needed a stiff drink and a cigarette. I pulled the stuffed tiger out of my bag and slid under the crappy sheet and blanket. The light stayed on and my eyes sat wide open until they finally dropped shut from exhaustion.

• • •

It was unclear when morning arrived because no sunlight streamed through the wire-covered window. When the morning nurse, Jane, stormed into my room, she barked, "Eight o'clock! Everybody up for breakfast *right now*. Time to eat!" Her urgency seemed unnecessary. It wasn't as if anyone here had to rush off to work.

As I lifted my head from the pillow, a more intense, disorienting sickness than I had ever felt came over me. It was as if I had been taken to the rooftop of a skyscraper, turned upside down, and shaken by my feet. I would have sworn that I was throbbing from my bones outward. My head felt split, my palms were thick with sweat, and my gut convulsed as if I were vomiting again.

Remembering that there was no wine next to me to slug and calm everything down, I tried to sit up anyway. It was a bad idea. Oh, shit, I thought. This is withdrawal.

I slid back down and closed my eyes. The morning routine was underway and I could hear people scurrying around. Maybe it was finally safe to get some sleep. I pulled the sheet over my head.

"Come on, Lisa. Rise and shine. Time to eat breakfast!" Jane said.

"You know what?" I said, working hard to form the words. "I really didn't sleep last night and I'm not hungry. I think I'm just going to stay in bed until the psychiatrist comes to see me." Facing the wall, I curled up into the fetal position.

"No, Lisa. Time to get up. Everybody has to get up and eat breakfast. That means you, too. Let's go." She wasn't kidding, and she wasn't leaving. Fuck. I managed to pull myself back up and lower my feet to the floor. There was a good chance I'd throw up, so I dropped my head between my knees. My hair swept the floor. Jane stood silently next to the sink.

"OK, OK," I muttered. I bent into a crouch and then stood up slowly. Jane stepped aside as I approached the sink. I brushed my teeth with my right hand and gripped the sink with my left. At that point, washing my face or changing my clothes seemed as feasible as mountain climbing, so I just slipped my feet into my sneakers, still holding the sink. Then I pulled my hair back into a ponytail and looked dully at Jane. She chirped, "Let's go!"

As I followed her down the hall, I realized that I was about to eat breakfast in a room full of mental patients. My eyes didn't focus well, and it felt as if there were little needles behind them trying to poke their way out. Every inch of me ached. Maybe I could eat in my room? I knew the answer.

When we arrived for breakfast, the other patients were already seated and eating. About twenty faces looked up at me, as if to say, "What's with the white girl?" Jane hustled me to a free seat at one of the round tables. There were mumbles mixing in with the sporadic moaning and shrieking around the room. The patients' ages appeared to range from young adult to very old. It definitely smelled better here than in detox and people seemed to be clean and groomed. I was thankful the three other patients at my table were more interested in their eggs than in me.

A tall metal cart with rows of plastic trays was wheeled into the dining area with each tray labeled for an individual patient. I wasn't sure if this reflected dietary concerns or just quality of insurance coverage. It couldn't have been the latter because my insurance was great and my breakfast sucked.

My plate featured a pile of gray, soggy eggs that at best had been reconstituted from some sort of powder and at worst were real but weeks old. Pass. Orange juice sounded like a good idea because that's what normal people drink in the morning and my mouth felt like it was wrapped in sandpaper. I peeled back the tin foil on the top of the squat, clear plastic container and took a gulp. It could have used some vodka. Vodka. How wonderful it would be right now to be standing naked in front of my freezer drinking vodka out of the bottle! I shuddered as if someone were holding that frosty bottle against the back of my neck. I would have paid just about anything for that vodka.

As I picked at the top of a mini blueberry muffin, I watched the nurses trying to cajole other patients who weren't even pretending to eat. These patients found more compelling uses for cooked eggs, like finger painting and having conversations with them.

Before long, Jane came looking for me. I wasn't hard to spot. "Lisa, Dr. Landry is ready to see you. First we need to look at you," she said.

Happy to have mealtime cut short, I followed her into a small room off the dining area, where she took my blood pressure, temperature, and weight. This once-over seemed meant to confirm that I was the same person who had been left in the room the night before.

Reviewing my file, Jane asked, "Why didn't you give blood or take medicine last night? Don't you want to get better?" Was this the conclusion she drew just because I didn't want to risk physical assault on the detox floor? I felt too sick to talk about it, so I shrugged, grateful to be allowed to return to my room and collapse onto the cot.

A short while later, the doctor appeared. He looked just like an uptown psychiatrist, from his carefully trimmed salt-and-pepper hair and beard to his corduroy pants and sensible, brown walking shoes. "Hi Lisa, I'm Dr. Landry." He was looking at papers in a manila folder, presumably my file. "I understand there was quite a commotion here last night," he said, taking off his glasses as he finally looked at me.

I tried to sit up, but my head felt like a bowling ball on a lollipop stick neck. Get up, I told myself. Get up or he won't let you out of here. He's the only one who can.

I grabbed the side of the metal cot, the heel of my hand digging into the thin mattress. I pushed up from there, and my body slouched into a letter "C." "Yes, I need to be discharged right away," I said, my voice cracking.

He sat on the wooden chair at the end of my bed. "Mmm. Your file says you checked yourself in last night on a 72-hour psych hold on account of alcohol abuse. Is that correct?"

"Yes. But I made a mistake. I want to leave." My voice sounded so small. He didn't respond and continued to flip the papers. "Did they tell you about that man threatening to fuck me up on the detox floor?" I asked.

"They did," he said. "Let's talk a little about your drinking. Signing yourself into a locked down detox is pretty serious business. I find it hard to believe you would do that if you don't need help." I was quiet. "How much do you drink? How often?"

I had to lie or he wouldn't let me out. With a shaking hand, I pushed back my mop of knotted hair and looked Dr. Landry in the eye. "I drink a lot. Every day. I start as soon as I wake up and I can't stop. I can't stop." Wait, *what*? What did I just say? I began sobbing, and it felt surreal that I was the one ratting myself out to this guy. And why did I suddenly feel as if a backpack loaded with lead was being lifted from my shoulders? It was as if some healthy part of my consciousness had taken charge.

Dr. Landry looked like a cop relieved to have gotten a confession without having to beat it out of the suspect. Tears streamed down my face and burned my cracked lips. Were they from relief? Sadness? Fear? I didn't know and didn't care, maybe because by now I was feeling horribly, horribly sick from withdrawal. It was as if someone was trying to pull my head and stomach inside out with their bare hands. A silent scream ripped through my head.

"OK," Dr. Landry said. "Let me be straight. You need a medical detox. If you don't do this, you might die. You can even stay on this floor to be more comfortable. That's all we need to talk about right now. Will you stay and do that?"

I thought about the night before—the strung-out women fighting in the hallway, the screaming from random rooms, no locks on the doors, the guy threatening to fuck me up. I pictured the scratchy sheets and blood pressure readings every three hours. There were the smells of vomit and antiseptic and no communication with the outside world.

"I'll stay," I said, collapsing back onto the smelly cot.

"Great. Let's just get you started on Librium and we can talk more when you feel a little bit better."

My old life was gone. I could never go back to the time when no one knew about my sickness. Every important person in my life now knew me as an addict. I had taken the first step toward staying alive, but all I wanted was that icy cold bottle in my shaking hand.

part two.

How did a nice girl like you become an addict like that?

3

Life hadn't always been about the next drink for me, but it had always been about finding some escape from a world in which I never felt at ease. As a girl, I had no idea how to define the way I felt almost every day and night of my childhood, and I certainly didn't understand it. But I was always anxious and often sad, painfully sad. While I imagined other kids waking up every day to a bluebird of happiness chirping, "You're worthy!" "You're happy!" "Wonderful things are going to happen today!" I felt plagued by a mosquito of doom, a predator I couldn't swat, all day buzzing into my ear, "You're not as good as everyone else—everybody knows it." "Something bad is about to happen." "You're not worthy." "You will fail."

I learned at an early age to pretend to feel fine when I didn't and to act happy when I wanted to shut myself in a dark bedroom and weep. Lying became easy, and habits and substances that brought even temporary relief were my refuge. Little did I know on that wakeup morning in 2004 that my self-hatred had been ingrained from the beginning. It's just how my brain was wired all along. Of course, the good news is learning that you

43

can be rewired. The bad news is that you obsess about all the self-destructive years that led to the discovery.

• • •

In the summer of 1974, I was eight years old and attended the "best" day camp in the northern New Jersey suburbs. My mother said that any kid would love the place. Apparently, any kid but me. I was extremely self-conscious thanks to being overweight. I wasn't obese, but I was big enough to be an easy target for cruel kids, and my nondescript brown hair and small eyes did nothing to flatter my chubby face. Pudgy, unattractive, and miserable—I was a walking ABC Afterschool Special.

To make the childhood years worse, I wasn't athletic. My lack of coordination doomed me year round: nine months in the school yard, one month at camp, and two nebulous summer months when other kids jumped, biked, and ran around like young gazelles. When I threw a football, it sputtered end over end and landed eight feet in front of me. When someone yelled "Race you home!" I'd give it a half-hearted jog for half a block and then gasp my way through the rest of the walk. I was picked last for every team and placed last in every lineup, but when my teams lost, I was the first one blamed.

The camp was located on what felt like a massive property made up mostly of scattershot woods and otherwise undeveloped terrain that would appeal to an aspiring serial killer. I'd seen *Helter Skelter* on my parents' bookshelf and developed a fear of being randomly murdered by hippies.

The focal point of the camp was a giant swimming pool made to resemble a lake and was referred to as the "plake." I thought that if the two words had to be crossed, it was wrong to take one of them in full and just add a letter from the other. It should have been "pake" or "lool." This is the kind of observation that regularly entertained my mind, but whenever I tried to point out the misnomer, the other kids would roll their eyes as if to say, "Nobody cares, Word Nerd."

Each morning, our group of about a dozen eight-year-old girls congregated around Dina, our counselor, to hear the day's schedule. My only reprieve from physical activity was the daily "elective" period that immediately followed lunch. Avoiding sports, I was left with something called "Indian Lore," which involved sitting in a tepee for an hour and a half with a man called "Uncle Jim." He didn't appear Native American in his sleeveless white undershirt, thick, black-rimmed glasses, and black pants with the outline of a hard pack of cigarettes in the pocket, but he wore a colorful headdress fashioned from oak tag paper and cardboard cutouts. Uncle Jim told stories of Native Americans—their lives and traditions. I loved a good story, especially from a seated position, so Indian Lore quickly became the only part of the camp day that I enjoyed.

After several weeks of my finding comfort in the cross-legged tales of tribes long gone, Dina and another camp supervisor sat me down to talk. "Lisa, you've really learned all you can learn at Indian Lore. You need to start choosing other electives. It's supposed to be a time for you to try new things and meet other campers," Dina said.

"But I don't want to go to another elective. I hate sports," I protested, knowing that this was futile. The two of them just shook their heads at me and I fought back tears.

That night, I explained my plight to my mother while she made dinner for my brother, Lou, who was six, and me. "I know you don't want to do it, but it's good for you to try other things," she said, stirring powdered Ore-Ida mashed potato mix into a pot of hot milk, her gold chain bracelets jangling. "And get your hand out of the cookie drawer! Not before dinner!"

Lou and I heard the groan of the garage door opening, and that meant one thing: Dad and his '72 Chevy Nova were home for the night! We squealed as we rushed to the door that connected our living room to the garage.

"DAD! DAD!" We both tried to simultaneously hug and climb up him as he crossed the threshold, still in his suit and carrying his tennis bag. I always wondered why he wore a suit to work when all he was going to do was take off the jacket so he could wear the black robe.

"Yessss. What's going on, kids?" he said, messing up our hair and trying to high-step beyond the little koalas that clung to his pant legs.

"Dad, the idiots at camp don't want me to go to Indian Lore anymore because they think I need to try something else. I hate everything else. I hate that camp," I said.

My dad smiled. He hadn't even had a chance to put his bag down. Then he looked to my mom for help. She shook her head and pursed her coral-glossed lips. "Listen to your mother," he said with a laugh. That was his escape line that signaled the death of the subject. Then he headed for the stairs and said, "I'm going to change out of these clothes." With Dad upstairs and Mom busy stirring instant potatoes, I sneaked into the bread drawer and ate two Yodels.

Back at camp I accepted defeat and searched for the next least physically challenging elective. Although it involved more time on the plake, canoeing appeared to be the best option. It didn't require real strength or coordination, and it didn't seem to involve competition or any of the athletic world's other countless opportunities for failure. Over in a designated area of the plake, canoers practiced in long aluminum two-man canoes. If at least eight people showed up on a given day, I would be out of the water lounging on the grass around the plake at least half the time. It wasn't Indian Lore, but I liked the numbers.

But to my surprise, I wasn't a bad canoer, so I elected canoeing every day. I attributed my non-disastrous learning curve to the fact that canoeing involved more strategy than strength. I worked with a partner, Tim, a nerdy brown-haired boy about my age. Together we learned the most advanced canoe maneuver: tipping the canoe over, righting it, and climbing back in from the water to retake control. We practiced this move over and over, getting every step just right. Before long, I was instructed to man the back of the canoe and lead the "tip overs," the role assigned to the better canoer in each pair. Me. The "better canoer." Incredible.

At the end of the summer, Tim and I were chosen to perform in front of the entire camp at the Water Show, the big performance on the plake featuring the best people in each water skill. "You should be excited! This is a real honor!" Dina said when she heard the news.

"Yeah, it's great. I can't wait," I lied, gnawing my fingernails. The dread in my stomach told me that no good would come of this. I thought about faking illness on the day of the Water Show—the only problem was Tim, who was excited to show the camp what he could do. I couldn't ruin it for him. Dear God, how long until ice cream break?

The day of the Water Show was sticky hot, and I was made even stickier by the Native American gear and headdress that Dina had convinced me to wear. "It's perfect!" she had gushed. "You know—the whole Indian theme with the canoes . . . you'll be so authentic!" Standing at the side of the plake, I turned to look at the hundreds of kids scattered along the grass I felt dizzy and leaned against a tree.

A lifeguard with a bullhorn on the plake's diving platform narrated the show. The counselors cheered and shouted at their protégés from the sidelines, like revved up Little League parents with everything to lose.

When it was our turn on the plake, my stomach rumbled and swirled like an old washing machine during its last days. The feathers in the headdress caught some wind and I worried that the whole thing might blow off. Tim and I climbed into the wobbly canoe, and my bare feet felt colder than usual against the metal bottom of the boat, but we paddled out without incident. The sun shimmered off the water, and the sky was the brilliant blue that every child chose from the Crayola box when asked to "draw a picture of a perfect day." After a few turns and glides by the crowd, we waved to them, smiling, and I thought I might be enjoying myself.

Then came the big move. I lifted my paddle to signal to Tim that we were ready for the tip over. "One! Two!" I called out and we rocked the canoe with our hips, increasing the momentum until we were ready to flip it over. "Three!" And "sploosh!" we were in the water. It was colder than I expected, but the rush of excitement was bigger than the cold. We each made our way under the canoe, and, just as we'd practiced over and over again, we lifted it straight up in unison. Gently, carefully, we placed it back on the surface of the water. Then we set our oars in the boat and climbed back in. I felt my face break out in a huge, genuine smile. I thought, this must be what it's like to hit a home run.

Tim and I smiled at each other in acknowledgement of a job well done, and then I turned to look at the shore and enjoy the applause. But wait. What was that? I didn't hear applause. I heard laughing. And I saw pointing, kids pointing and rolling in the sand in an exaggerated way. Oh my God, I thought . . .

they're laughing at us! Oh *my God*! Those idiots thought we had accidentally capsized our canoe in front of the entire camp. And I was wearing that stupid headdress!

I hated the morons. I hated them all. I could see that the camp leaders were trying to help, explaining that we had just performed a difficult trick, but it was no use. The joke was already on us.

That night, my mother watched from the couch as I dramatically reenacted the catastrophe. In the middle of our den, I swept my arms back and forth to show our canoe paddling and then I rolled on the floor to demonstrate the reaction of the crowd. I looked like someone playing charades where the answer was, "Successful Canoe Maneuver Leads To Abject Humiliation."

"Oh, Lisa. That's terrible," she said. "What can I do to make you feel better?" She scratched my back as I climbed on the couch and put my head in her lap.

I looked up at her with hopeful eyes, "Can I have two bowls of ice cream tonight?" Normally, I was allotted one standard size bowl of my favorite, vanilla fudge.

My mother looked a little disappointed. "You haven't even had dinner yet. How do you know you're even going to want a second bowl?" she asked.

"I know," I said. "I just know."

• • •

Even at that age, I understood that my compulsion to eat wasn't shared by other people I knew. I licked spatulas covered in Duncan Hines Brownie mix and then licked the bowl. I sneaked from cookie jars and hid candy that I could eat later when no one else was around. It was never enough and it was never too sweet. Food, and desserts in particular, just plain made me feel better. Other kids would eat a cookie at recess and run out onto the playground, excited to have the freedom to jump around. I would eat a cookie, sit in the grass, stare at the sky, and wish I had a dozen more cookies.

At my annual visit to the pediatrician that autumn, Dr. Birnbaum ran through all the checks he performed on me year after year: heart, lungs, teeth, height, weight, immunizations, and so forth, and then began scribbling on my chart. Sitting on the exam table, I amused myself by swinging my legs back and forth and twisting my ankles left and right, pointing and flexing my toes the way I saw gymnasts do it. Without looking up from his clipboard, Dr. Birnbaum said, "If you don't stop eating, you're going to be as big as a house." My extended legs and pointed toes froze in place. His words sent a rush of acid shame into my stomach. I felt a flash of heat up my neck and into my face, and I remained silent with my head held down. The only sound was the crinkling of the paper on the exam table.

During the drive home was the first time I ever heard my mother use the word "asshole." "You never have to go back to that asshole doctor again," she said, as she sneaked glances at the tears streaming down my cheeks.

I couldn't look at her, but I nodded. "Can we have Burger King for dinner?"

"Sure," she said.

Lou and I were hunched over our Whopper Jr.'s and large orders of fries at the kitchen table when my dad walked in that night. Fast food was thrilling to us, so much so that on that day we hadn't pulled ourselves away to attack him at the door. "What's the occasion?" he asked. "We're eating like Kings on a Tuesday night?" It was his code for Burger King. If we had Dairy Queen for dessert, we "ate like Kings and Queens," which was a real treat.

"Yes," my mom said. "Lisa had her physical today, and that Dr. Birnbaum is a nasty man." As far as I know, that was her only comment to my dad about the incident. And if they discussed my weight when they were alone, neither of them ever let on. Mom tried to monitor my nutrition and sometimes talked to me about eating habits, but that was about it. Dad never said a word.

My comfort eating was developing into a big, bad habit, and I knew it. After school my brother would take off to play kickball or tag with the neighborhood kids, but for me afterschool time meant free access to food. I knew that spending every afternoon sprawled in front of the ABC *4:30 Movie* with a tub of vanilla fudge ice cream and a spoon was only going to cement my status as the pudgy kid. But for those ninety minutes I felt relief as the sweetness melted on my tongue and slid down my throat. I was calm, and it was the closest I ever came to happy.

● ● ●

My parents were a social couple and social drinkers in the '70s, and it didn't take me long to notice that at the parties they threw, the adults became happier the more they drank. People sometimes talked about the fact that my mother's father had been an "alcoholic," which sounded like a bad thing, but I never saw anything but smiling faces when booze was flowing.

Our house was regularly filled with family and friends on occasions like New Year's Eve, Super Bowl Sunday, and Kentucky Derby Saturday, but even the first day of summer, the anniversary of D-Day, or a full moon offered my parents good enough reason to host another bash. A four-bedroom, tradi tional center-staircase colonial, our house had the distinction of being the only private home in Bergen County with a regulation-size bocce court. It covered an entire side of our massive front lawn.

The court was the brainchild of one my father's oldest friends, whom we knew only as "The Dalai Lama," a nickname that I understood had nothing to do with Buddhism and everything to do with a piece of headgear he wore one stifling hot day on the golf course. If the sun was shining on a weekend, a party broke out around the bocce court. "Harv!" the Lama announced one fall Saturday when I was about ten. He had walked unannounced into the kitchen from the back patio. The Lama smelled of soap and cigarette smoke as he hugged me. "Lisa! Good day for a game!" He had a booming, gravelly voice thanks to decades of smoking, and when he walked he hunched like a much older man.

An air of mystery surrounded the Lama; we never went to his house, but he was a regular fixture at ours. Lou and I didn't know where he lived or how he and our dad became friends, and there was talk of a wife, but we never met her. We heard he did some kind of "accounting," but he didn't seem to work for a company.

It didn't take long for my father's friends and their wives to start appearing, old buddies from Lodi, the working-class, largely Italian town where they all grew up. Dad's parents had owned a candy and newspaper store where he was put to work as a young boy starting at four o'clock in the morning, folding and then delivering the day's papers. My dad was the only Jew in that neighborhood, the youngest of five kids and the only boy in his family. His buddies from Lodi called him "Meyer Lansky," and they always greeted each other with firm claps on the back. Our neighborhood had a mix of families with dads whose occupations ranged from banker to butcher, and they all called Dad "Judge," though he bristled at the formality.

"What are we drinking?" my dad asked each new arrival. No one ever stood empty handed in our house or front yard.

Once the game was set up, I zipped into the kitchen to fetch beers for my dad's friends. But I'd linger in the kitchen because the inescapable smell from the pans of home-cooked lasagna and baked ziti and the fresh bread baked just that morning from "the best" bakery in Hoboken made me delirious. And the desserts!

"Can I have one now? I'm starving!" I asked my mom as I pawed at the boxes of cannoli and Italian pastries sitting on the kitchen table in irresistible pink bakery boxes.

"OK, one, just one for now. They're for dessert!" my mother said. After she put on her oven mitts and carried a tray of lasagna out to one of the folding metal card tables set up outside, I piled four pastries on a paper plate and scrambled into the upstairs bathroom where I ate them behind the safety of a locked door.

Italian pastries weren't my favorites because they weren't loaded with chocolate, but the cannoli and the zeppole gushed with so much sugary cream that they did the trick. I barely tasted them going down as I sat on the bathroom floor with my back propped against the tub, knees up. After I licked my fingers clean, I washed my sugar powdered face and hands, just in case I ran into anyone on my way back down to the party. At the time I didn't know about the chemical reaction, the dopamine surge that was occurring in my brain thanks to the giant hit of sugar. All I knew is that for a little while I felt relief.

While the bocce parties were mostly about the food and the games, the soirées my parents threw on occasional Saturday nights were mostly about the cocktails. On one such wintry afternoon I helped my father set up the folding metal card table in the den next to the brick fireplace. We threw a red-and-white checkered plastic tablecloth over it to smooth a surface for the bar.

In a show of heartfelt hospitality, we laid out a full assortment of bottles and garnishes. I was in charge of arranging the booze and mixers, always excited to impress our guests with my bar table arrangements which usually consisted of alphabetized alcohol on one side and alphabetized mixers on the other. And of course I thoughtfully lined up cocktail napkins, toothpicks, sliced and twisted lemons and limes, olives, maraschino cherries, and "good" plastic cups, the clear kind that look frosted.

Lou and I would peek through the curtains that covered the glass pane on our big wooden front door so that when guests arrived we'd be ready to announce them with great pageantry. One by one and two by two they'd cross the threshold as we bellowed their names in voices and accents befitting a Renaissance festival. Schoolteachers, construction contractors, politicians, housewives, real estate developers, lawyers, and judges all paraded in as my brother and I took their coats with the dramatic flair of a maitre'd at a fine restaurant. There were screeches of recognition to other guests across the room, hair tousles for me, and fake boxing moves for my brother. The air was electric and I jumped up and down as if I were on a pogo stick.

The women wore hip-hugging, bell-bottom pants or maxi skirts that touched the floor, and as they strolled through the party crowd, they left scent trails of L'Air du Temps and Charlie perfume in their wakes. Several women piled their hair high and accented their flamboyant updos with faux flowers, headbands, or barrettes. Their hairstyles contrasted starkly with those of their husbands and boyfriends who sported "high and tight regular boys' haircuts" as my dad referred to the military style that he himself preferred. Always swirling over the entire party was a cloud of smoke, courtesy of Virginia Slims and Winston.

My dad, the evening's bartender, stood behind the card table offering miniature pigs in a blanket with spicy mustard while his friends decided what to drink. He wore his bartender's uniform, a special crushed navy velvet vest. It was a custom-made piece with his nickname, "Smitty," etched into the left side in gold piping. I loved how the nickname seemed to hover right over his heart. The gold piping detail continued around the armholes and outer seams of the vest and made it suitable for duty at even the swankiest hotel bar. Whether he was in pajamas eating a bowl of cereal, in a flowing robe while deciding the fates of law breakers, or in a gold-trimmed vest shaking cocktails, I thought my father was the most elegant man in the world.

Alcohol deserved ceremony. My dad took his role seriously and crafted each cocktail carefully, holding every drink up for inspection with the eye of a jeweler assessing the quality of a diamond. I mimicked him from my position next to the card table, not knowing what I was looking for, but thrilled by the happy ritual of it all.

I was always curious about how the drinks were made and why they were so important to the drinkers. Why were some of them garnished with a wedge of lime instead of a lemon rind or perhaps three olives speared on a toothpick? Maybe the drinks with the olives were more substantial and called for some actual food as a garnish to help them go down. I wondered if the brown liquors tasted like Coke or root beer and the clear ones like 7-Up. I guessed that the brown drinks, the ones that smelled strong and were sipped slowly, were more appropriate for those in a downcast mood. Even the brown-booze bottles seemed more serious, and the liquid was generally served in smaller doses, either straight up or just over some ice. I preferred when someone ordered a more upbeat drink, like a sparkling, filled-to-the-brim gin and tonic with a floating wedge of lime in the shape of a smile. All of the adults I knew drank—at parties, at dinners, watching sports, during evenings while sitting on summer lawns—and there was nothing forbidden about it. The bottles at home weren't locked up or stored out of my reach, and there was always beer and wine in the refrigerator.

By the age of eight, I was sneaking sips from people's left-behind glasses at parties, mostly just getting my lips wet to see what the drinks tasted like. And they almost always tasted like bitter nastiness, but I still liked the covert feeling of getting away with it.

By ten, I was catching buzzes from the sips I stole. An unhappy ten-year-old's booze buzz looks like this: sincere smiles, carefree laughs with no concern about what others think, and cartwheels turned without fear of looking foolish. I equated alcohol with feeling happy, relaxed, and something I had never before been: uninhibited.

By twelve I knew exactly what I was doing when I drank—trying to silence the trash-talking mosquito in my head by gradually numbing my body and brain. I drank full cans of Budweiser and smoked cigarettes with my older cousins when I could, which wasn't often enough for me. The boy-girl parties started at school and booze was a regular feature, whether stolen from parents or procured through an older brother or sister. Drinking not only shut the mosquito up, it helped me survive not being one of the girls picked to pair off somewhere with a boy. If it wasn't "liquid courage," at least it was "liquid indifference."

By thirteen I hung around almost exclusively with drinking kids. At my Bat Mitzvah luncheon on a frigid Saturday in February 1979, a few of the boys in their Sunday best suits heisted a bottle of Jack Daniels from behind the bar and drank it in the temple parking lot. Along with a few other girls, I joined them whenever I could sneak out for a few minutes. Then we tried to disguise our breath with spearmint Tic Tacs. Most Friday nights that year involved pilfering beers from our parents' refrigerators and drinking them in the woods behind the middle school.

By fifteen, my friends and I binge drank on weekends, usually sucking down 24-packs of Budweiser while listening to Zeppelin in smoky, wood-paneled basements. We scored pot and cocaine from dealers that all the local high schoolers knew, and we passed the drugs around on mirrors and album covers. The drugs were fun, but alcohol was my first love. I would gladly trade a mirror full of coke for an oversized jug of Riunite Chablis. Coke did make me feel like Wonder Woman—wide awake in the moment as I yammered on about nothing—but with alcohol, my brain became peaceful, quiet. Nothing ever seemed urgent. It was the closest I could come to disappearing. And the trick to maintaining this inebriated social life as a teenager? Never miss a curfew and never argue with parents.

By eighteen, I was a straight-A student, editor of the high school yearbook, and accepted early to Northwestern University. I was also a blackout drunk.

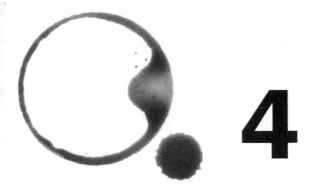

I entered my freshman year at Northwestern assuming that by accepting me the school had somehow made a mistake. I didn't expect to make it through my first semester because clearly I wasn't as capable as all the other kids who spilled out of station wagons loaded with clothes, bedspreads, and albums in milk crates. But behold! Alcohol was available every day and every night in this thrilling new society called the Big Ten. Northwestern was far from a "party" school, but that just meant looking a little harder to find a drinking buddy during finals. There was always somebody happy to close a book and jump into a bottle of vodka, a 12-pack of Old Style, or some other cheap swill. After-study drinking was often followed by early morning pizza—and in between, there was always plenty of junk food to stuff in our faces. From cookie-heavy care packages loaded with brownies, hunks of cheese "product," and smoked sausage, to the classic in-room stash of Doritos, sour cream and onion Pringles, and Pop Tarts, we were stocked and ready to feed our munchies at any hour. But there was no such commitment to exercise.

Northwestern's campus is sprawling, and I considered an eight-minute walk to class a workout, even though I smoked a cigarette along the way. My waistline grew at the speed of Miller Lite, and my breasts seemed to be in a race to grow even faster. After hitting a peak of 183 pounds on my five-foot-five frame, I decided that the answer to all of my problems was a breast reduction.

My mother dutifully found me the best surgeon in our area. Dr. Martha MacGuffie, a little slip of a woman with short, gray hair, oversized glasses, and a personality that entered a room before she did.

"I'm going to do a little drawing on you now," Dr. MacGuffie said, holding my gown open and staring at my giant bare breasts. She spoke directly to me, as if my mother weren't sitting in the corner of the exam room. "This is what the operation would look like." She drew on each breast with a black magic marker, showing where the incisions would be. She circled my nipple, which she explained would need to be nearly removed, drew a line from the bottom of my nipple to my ribcage, and then drew a smile-shaped curve around the lower half of my breast.

"There will be a good amount of scarring, you know, Lisa. Are you going to be OK with that?" she asked.

"Absolutely. I don't care." I said.

"OK. You're a good candidate for surgery, but I won't schedule you until you lose at least thirty pounds." She waited for me to react.

I stammered, "Of course ... yes—of course ..."

"Lisa, your new breasts are going on the body you're going to want to keep, not the body you have now. It's much better to lose the weight first." Her bluntness was jolting at first, but in short time I felt good about it. Being talked to so directly by a woman so accomplished made me feel adult. My poor mother looked jolted as well. She could never have spoken so boldly to me about my weight.

Thirty pounds? *At least* thirty pounds. Fuck. How do you lose thirty pounds? And how do you do it without giving up booze? How was I supposed to skip the nightly cocktail hours and the feeding frenzies that followed?

I looked at my mother. "Sounds fair," she said.

"Excellent," Dr. MacGuffie said. "You lose the weight and get healthy and I'll give you a pair of beautiful, firm breasts." *Yes, fairy godmother.*

My mom and I looked at each other in the car. "Guess we're not going to Dairy Queen on the way home," she said.

"I have to go on a fucking diet, like today," I said staring out the window.

"Only if you want new boobs," she answered with a smirk. I wanted a drink and a cigarette, badly. Immediately I started thinking about which drinks contained the fewest calories. No more margaritas, no more cosmos, no beer, no wine. Maybe I should just do shots.

When I got back to campus I ate salads for lunch and dinner. Joining a gym for the first time, I discovered that running could make me feel good, not unlike a thick slab of chocolate cake. The process of physically exerting myself was far less enjoyable than lying on a couch and sucking down a milkshake, but as I watched those one-tenth of a mile markers add up on the treadmill, I felt something close to high. On top of the endorphin rush, there was the satisfaction of setting a goal and reaching it. It gave me control. I became obsessive and went to the gym six times a week.

Despite continuing to get drunk regularly, I lost thirty pounds in five months. So in the summer of 1987, just before I entered my senior year in college, Dr. MacGuffie gave me a pair of beautiful, firm breasts.

The weight loss thinned my face which seemed to crank me up a couple of notches in attractiveness, at least judging by the looks I started getting in bars. Was this what it was like to be kind of cute? Even hot? I let my curly brown hair grow long and streaked it with blonde highlights. And I started wearing clothes to show my body rather than hide it. Maybe I was becoming someone the hot guys would want to sleep with when they were sober.

When I returned to Northwestern that fall, evidence of my transformation exploded all around me. I was getting looks, whistles, and even compliments right to my face. One night, my roommates and I went to a party at an off-campus apartment where we drank keg beer out of giant red cups and yelled at each other over the blare of R.E.M. I wore tight jeans and a low cut V-neck shirt that showed plenty of cleavage, which looked good for the first time in my life. All night my friends and I held up shot glasses full of Jack Daniels and made toasts to my new chest.

Then from behind me, I heard a familiar voice. "Wow. Lisa. Is that you? Wow." Oh God. It was Rob Johnson, a notorious slut who was once the object of my obsession. He was the ultimate example of my penchant for skinny, androgynous guys who could pull off a nice application of eyeliner. Rob had mile-high cheekbones, bright blue eyes, full red lips, and carefully sculpted hair. A friend had set us up for one of my sorority formals a couple of years earlier.

"Yeah, of course it's me. What's up?" I tried to sound casual, even though my heart was trying to pound its way out of my body. I let my long curls dance on one side of my face, while I pushed the hair on the other side behind my ear.

The last time Rob and I had spoken was after that formal. Rob had cried in my bed during sex. I was at my fattest back then, and I knew that my best chance of getting anywhere with him that night would be through steady, massive infusions of alcohol—into both of us. We started at the pre-party in the downtown Chicago hotel that was hosting the formal, tossing back only a few mixed drinks that I poured less aggressively than my usual. But once we got to the massive ballroom filled with big hair, big music, and big energy, it was time to really start drinking. Double mixed drinks, shots of tequila, more double mixed drinks, more shots of tequila—I made sure it kept coming. My ability to hold my liquor was astonishing, and I could outdrink every guy I knew. Rob couldn't have weighed more than 140 wet, so he was no match.

We were both smashed by the time we fell into my bed late that night. I couldn't believe my luck. I had played the cool girl all night and managed to get the cool guy home. I needed to take full advantage of this one-time opportunity.

In my room at the sorority house, I didn't even turn on a light because I couldn't bear to have him see me naked. I knew that if he got one unobstructed look at my bare body, it would be over before we started. Kissing, groping, dropping clothes to the floor, I wanted us stripped and under the sheets as quickly as possible. And it worked. We were having sex. *Rob Johnson and Me!*

Everything seemed great until I heard a strange kind of whimpering. Was he *crying*?

"Are you OK?" I asked, splayed on my back, trying to find the least unattractive position for my giant naked breasts. "What is it?"

"I don't want to talk about it," he said, still inside me.

"Talk about what?" I wasn't sure I wanted to hear the answer. Was I so unattractive that I had literally brought him to tears?

"It's just—" *Oh God, he's actually going to tell me,* I thought. I had been so excited just to get him home. Why did he have to ruin it? I wished I could pull on a sweatshirt, a t-shirt, his dress shirt—anything to feel un-naked.

63

"It's just that, I know I'm such an asshole, and I didn't think I was going to like you so much. You know, actually like you." Wait, *what*? He didn't think he could like a fat girl? Or he didn't have sex on the first date with people he liked? "It's . . . I know I'm going to blow you off and it's not you. I do it all the time. I don't know what's wrong with me."

He was already giving me the old "It's not you, it's me," and we were still joined between our legs! Couldn't he just reject me *after* sex like a normal person?

I eased him off me and rolled to the side of the bed. I almost told him that fat girls like me didn't have expectations with guys like him but instead said, "It's your choice to be an asshole or not. I'm not going to tell you it's cool to be a dick, if that's what you're looking for."

He had no reply, but at least he stopped whimpering. Then, realizing that I wasn't going to give him my blessing to be a dismissive prick, he put his clothes on and left, looking like an idiot in his rumpled tuxedo with the bright red bowtie sticking out of the jacket pocket. I rolled over into the fetal position.

• • •

The memory of that debacle somehow disappeared as Rob stood in front of me, trying to strike up a conversation. "You . . . you really look great," he said. "It's amazing." Articulate as ever, I thought, and just as insulting. "You know, about that night—" I couldn't believe he was bringing it up. "I just—I made a really big mistake."

"It was a long time ago," I said, surprised by how calm I sounded.

"What are you up to later?" *Oh my God,* I thought. *Oh my God! Rob Johnson is trying to take another run at me.*

64

With exquisite timing, my roommate Kellie appeared out of nowhere, handed me a drink, and grabbed me by my upper arm. "She has plans!" She snorted at him as she led me across the party. *Yeah!* I thought. *Sorry, Rob Johnson, but I have plans. Dismissive prick.*

• • •

Guys everywhere started paying attention to me and I soaked it in. Before I became a serial monogamist, I was a happily single party girl, and pursuing guys became like a game. I'd get drunk and try to go home with whichever guy my Jagermeister-impaired vision had honed in on that night. It was never romantic or heartfelt. It wasn't even safe.

One summer Saturday night before my first year of law school, I was out with friends at a cheesy bar in Paramus, New Jersey, and spotted a dirty-sexy looking guy standing alone. He had shoulder-length, messy brown curls and looked as if he hadn't slept in days. His expression was bored, as if he'd mistakenly landed in Yuppie Town but decided to stay for a drink anyway.

"Check out that guy," I said to Randi, my best friend from high school. "He looks like Michael Hutchence. Hotness." I was pointing my chin toward him, hoping he could see I was talking about him.

"Oh, great. Here we go. See you later," she said, waving as she headed back to the dance floor to join our friends who were jumping around and snarling to Billy Idol's "White Wedding."

As soon as Randi was gone, my latest target slinked right up to me, all business. "Hey, I'm Kevin. What's your name?" He stared into my eyes with a shifty squint. Kevin reminded me of all the sexy bad boys who used to ignore me while I watched them hit on my cute friends.

"Lisa," I said.

There was something overtly sexual and a little aggressive about the way he leaned right in close to me next to the bar, his hip lightly touching mine. "You live around here?" he asked.

"Yeah, not far." I tried to be vague. No way I was going to unsexy the moment by telling him I'd moved back in with my parents for the summer. "Another shot?" I asked. If this was going to happen, I needed more booze.

"Sure," he said, signaling two more shots to the bartender. "And two more beers," flipping his credit card onto the bar. We clinked and downed the shots. Then I guzzled most of the beer and felt the click in my brain that signaled the end of good judgment.

"And you?" I asked. "What brings you to a random club on Route 17 on a Saturday night?" I was wearing a low cut, silky, green button down shirt I'd never returned to one of my college roommates. Kevin focused on the black lacy bra that peeked out from behind the green.

"I'm local," he said. "I do real estate development around here. I have a place in Fort Lee." A little shady, I thought. Maybe mafia? Whatever. This wasn't husband hunting, this was getting bombed and going home with the hot guy. Because I could.

Two more tequila shots later, Kevin put a hand on my hip and pulled me toward him, rubbing my jeans, as if we were dancing. "Do you want to go to my place?" He asked, one eyebrow raised. His lips were full and pink and I pictured kissing him hard. I was sure he'd have liquor at home.

"Yeah, definitely," I answered without hesitating.

When we got to Kevin's building, he waved hello to his doorman who smirked from underneath his straight-browed cap. We rode up several floors, and when Kevin opened his door the lights of Manhattan glittered for miles beyond his floor-to-ceiling windows. "This is it," he said as we stepped onto the balcony and stared into the sparkling lights. *Wow. This place makes him even sexier, if that's possible.*

"You want a beer?" he asked.

"Sure, great." He returned with two Heinekens and pulled me by the hand toward the dark bedroom. I chugged as much as I could during the stumble to the bed.

He clicked a very dim lamp on his bedside table. His furniture was dark wood with dark bedding that gave the room a cave-like feeling. There were framed black and white photographs on the walls, and the smell of the room matched the musky smell I'd picked up while standing close to him in the bar.

He turned to me and dug a hand deep into my hair while pulling my head back and then started roughly kissing my neck. He suddenly stopped and took a step back, looking me up and down. "Take off your shirt," he ordered. Without breaking eye contact I did as I was told, feeling a rush of cold air from the air conditioner on my bare abdomen. "Come here," he said. I took one step forward and he jerked me against him.

With one flip he unhooked my bra and both of his hands were on my breasts. Then he pushed me down onto the bed on my back, and I could feel his hard-on through both of our jeans. His hair was mixing with mine around the sides of my face.

He kissed me deeply for a while, grinding himself against me and getting harder. His breathing became more and more urgent, and he bit my lower lip a few times as we kissed.

"Put your arms over your head," he commanded into my hair while he unzipped my jeans and slid one hand between my legs. He held my wrists together with the other hand. I moaned and arched my back, feeling like I was about to come when he pressed his wet mouth to my ear and said, "I could fuck you right now." *Please!* I thought. "Or I could kill you." *Wait, what*? He said it with the cool of a movie murderer. If I needed to, there was no way I could escape him. But I was drunk enough for my fear to take a back seat to my audacity.

Without blinking I said, "Why don't you fuck me then?"

For a few seconds he stared back with no expression. Then he laughed and started moving his hand in my pants again. Almost immediately I came hard for the first time that night.

I woke up in the middle of the night. Kevin had rolled over and I studied his muscular back and wide shoulders. If he had decided to kill me instead of fuck me, I might have already been dumped in the Hudson River. What would my parents do as the crew dragged my bloated body ashore? I pictured my mother weeping into my father's chest while my friends gathered around, wondering if they should tell Mom and Dad about the drunken party tramp their daughter had become.

Still naked, I slipped out of the bed and over to the dresser where I grabbed my beer and chugged the rest of it along with what was left in Kevin's bottle. Then I climbed back into bed and passed back out.

5

"*What was our first mistake?*" my friend Jane asked me one day at work after we'd both pulled all-nighters on separate projects. "*Getting good grades?*" We laughed the laughs of women digesting an unpleasant reality on too little sleep. I laid my head on my desk.

"You know what they say," I answered. "If we don't want these jobs, there's a whole line of law school grads out there happy to take them."

It was 1991, and I was twenty-five years old, straight out of Rutgers Law School. It never occurred to me to shoot for anything less than the best grades, a coveted spot on the *Rutgers Law Review*, and a job with a New York City megafirm. To be offered a well-paying job by one of the big-name firms was the ultimate stamp of approval for a law school grad. And there was nothing more consistent in my life than my need for other people's approval. Wouldn't I love for those little camp fuckers to see me now.

Big law firms were partnerships, and becoming a partner meant everything. To get there, an attorney had to begin as I did, as a "junior" associate, the lowest life form on the lawyer food chain. Those who lasted beyond three years became "mid-level" associates, and if they made it to their seventh year, they became "senior" associates, eligible for partnership consideration. Some who didn't become partners but were exceptional lawyers stayed with the firm as "counsel," often for the rest of their careers.

I was in the Environmental Group, and our offices were on a midlevel floor of a skyscraper on the east side of Midtown Manhattan. The firm had about eight hundred lawyers, five hundred of them in New York and about half of those in our building. The firm's elite corporate teams were in a building directly across East 53rd Street, in newer, nicer offices.

Several people in my starting "class" of about ninety lawyers, with the ink still drying on their law school diplomas, became hyper-competitive in their quest for the most prestigious work for the highest-ranking partners. Inevitably, at around seven o'clock each night, one of these masochists would stroll into my shared office waving the giant binder full of menus for restaurants that delivered. "Well, it looks like I'll be here until at least midnight," he or she would say with a fake eye roll. "Who else is in for ordering dinner? It's going to be a late one."

"Not me," I'd answer with optimism. "I'm going to plow through and hopefully get out of here in the next two hours." If I was lucky, I'd be able to have a few drinks with some of my friends who worked normal hours. If not, I'd go straight home and pound a couple of beers in front of the open refrigerator. Beer was the only thing guaranteed to be in my refrigerator, and I found the choice easy to justify. First, I really did need to be able to fall asleep quickly so I could get up and exercise. Exercise was nonnegotiable. Second, any normal person would have had a couple of beers or glasses of wine over dinner, so this was no different. And third, fuck you, I've had a long day and I want beer.

My work friend Jessica and I bonded quickly. She was a University of Chicago Law graduate and a year ahead of me; both facts made her infinitely wiser in my eyes. When I was at Northwestern, I had seen the intensity of the University of Chicago and its students. They spent Saturday nights solving complex math problems and making scientific discoveries while my friends and I played Trivial Pursuit for shots before bouncing between frat parties. I imagined the University of Chicago's Law School to be equally intimidating. I never would have made it out of there. Or in, for that matter. My law degree from Rutgers felt embarrassingly inferior, but if Jessica shared this opinion she never let on. She and I laughed at the same jokes, liked the same people, had similar taste in clothes, and even sounded so alike that her father confused me for her when I answered her phone.

While Jessica didn't drink the way I did, she and her husband Russell liked to go out and run around New York City on weekend nights. Neither of them judged me when I got drunk and did stupid things, like leave my wallet in a cab or wave my arms and knock over a full round of martinis. Still, I was somewhat aware that the "STOP, you've had enough" mechanism in my brain was faulty because not even after extraordinary amounts of drinking did I ever tell a waitress, "No more, thanks, just water for me." I wanted another, I needed another, and I was always going to have another. As a result, there was no place in my life for anyone who criticized or even questioned my drinking. If someone dared to speak their concern, I simply changed the subject and then cut them from my life. My universe shrank as a result, but I didn't mind. During my nonworking hours, all I wanted to do was relax, and for me relaxing meant drinking as much as I wanted as often as I could.

One Friday afternoon late in the winter of my first year as an associate, I sat in Jessica's office making plans for the night. "So, I brought my play clothes. I'll change here. We can take off around seven for your place, right?" I asked, fidgeting with the fake gold buttons on my Ann Taylor jacket.

"Yeah, I spoke to Russell. He's going to be late, so you and I can stop at Food Emporium and pick up a munch. We have cocktail stuff at home." Russell, also a Chicago Law graduate, was slogging it out at another major firm in their Corporate Finance group. All I knew about Corporate Finance was that it was stock market stuff and that associates in those groups worked harder than anyone else in a law firm.

Jessica's phone rang and she sat up rail straight. She looked at the caller ID and we both saw that it was Doug, the head partner in our group. She cleared her throat and picked up the phone, suddenly sounding cheery. "Hi Doug. Yes, of course, I'll be right there." She hung up.

"Doug wants to see me. Why does he always come up with new assignments at five o'clock on Friday?" she said, reaching into her desk drawer for her purse. She pulled out a small lipstick case for a quick reapplication. "Do I look OK? Anything in my teeth?" she asked, baring her teeth at me.

I squinted close to examine her mouth. "Nope, you're good." She straightened her funky, square glasses and smoothed her pin-straight blonde bob. As she got up, she grabbed a legal pad and a Cross pen.

"Let me know what's up when you get back. I'll be in my office," I said getting up with her as she left, resenting the fact that this call could jeopardize my weekend.

All week I had been looking forward to my Friday night drinking, but since about ten o'clock that morning I'd been obsessing over it. How many more hours? Where would we go first? What should my first drink be? Should I go wine or booze? Should I stick with one alcohol? Where should we end up? Doug's call threatened all of that. Now I might get pulled in on whatever project was about to appear. Selfish friend that I was, I thought that if Jessica got hit up with work and I didn't, I could still meet other friends and salvage the night.

"Lisa, oh my God." It was about fifteen minutes later when Jessica appeared in my doorway. "You're not going to believe this." She dropped into a chair in front of my desk.

"What?" I asked, assuming that she'd been fired and I was next. I felt faint.

"They're moving us. They're moving us to Corporate Finance," she said, stunned.

"What are you talking about?"

"For real," she said. "Starting Monday, this coming Monday, you and I are going to the Corporate Finance group. They're going to tell you any minute."

"What? No way! I don't even know what Corporate Finance lawyers do!"

Mike, my officemate and a badly overworked antitrust lawyer, stopped pretending he wasn't listening. "They do securities offerings, mostly representing underwriters. You know, Merrill Lynch, Morgan Stanley, Goldman Sachs," he said. "Those guys work like animals! You're screwed. I'm so sorry." Coming from a guy who hadn't had a full weekend off since joining the firm six months ago, this was particularly brutal.

"Thanks, Mike. That's helpful," I said, sounding meaner than I intended.

I turned back to Jessica. "They're not even in our building. I don't want to go over to the corporate side!" In that second,

I shifted from anticipating after-work drinks to needing booze immediately. Could I leave right now and go drinking? Pretend I had already left the building?

My phone rang just then and Doug's number came up. "Motherfucker," I said before straightening up and taking a breath. "Hi Doug," I chirped. "Sure, I can come by. I'll be right there."

"It might not be so bad," Jessica offered as I gathered up a pen and pad. What was wrong with her? This was horrible news. Only getting fired would be worse. "Russell will help us. He knows everything," she said.

My everyday drizzle of fear about being discovered as a fraud who knew nothing took on the intensity of a summer downpour when I considered life across the street. I had no corporate law training at all, having avoided those classes like infectious diseases. I couldn't even balance my own checkbook, let alone understand a corporate balance sheet. And the corporate lawyers were just obnoxious, all hair gel, Italian leather loafers, and summer-share houses in the Hamptons.

As I neared Doug's office, I put my hand to my forehead like a headache sufferer on an aspirin commercial. As a first-year associate, I knew I was trapped if a final decision had been made about my transfer. No other firm would hire me for an environmental group with less than a year of experience. My plan had been to spend two years at the firm getting serious environmental law experience from the point of view of the big-money corporations. Then I would defect, hopefully to a non-profit, pro-conservation organization that would find me an invaluable weapon against big companies. If I had to transfer now to Corporate Finance, my whole strategy would be blown. The sweat beaded around my hairline as I got to the door of Doug's office. A drink. A drink. I really needed a drink.

Doug was in his early forties with a slight build, a thick head of black hair, and black-rimmed Elvis Costello glasses. He had an engaging smile that put people at ease. His spacious corner office was strewn with expensive area rugs and other mementos from trips around the world.

Partners seemed to believe that the more exotica they had on display, the more sophisticated they appeared to be. "Wow, that's a really interesting mask," I had remarked once to a partner as I examined a deep-red clay piece on his credenza.

"Do you know where that's from?" he asked blankly.

"No, I'm sorry, actually I don't," I answered. Apologies were expected when you didn't have an answer to a partner's question. And it didn't matter what kind of question; I would have apologized just as quickly if he'd asked me if I knew his mother's maiden name.

"Well, you should know about that mask," he said, as he arched his back and puffed his chest. "Top Brazilian government officials presented me with that rare Amazon tribal mask when we completed the debt-for-nature swap transaction. As I'm sure you *do* know, that was a major deal for the firm."

After that, I learned not to comment on partners' office decor. In Doug's office, I knew about his wife and two kids only because of their silver-framed snapshots from clambakes on the beach and ski trips in the mountains.

In one of the two sturdy leather wingback chairs opposite his desk, sat Penny, the other partner in our group and the one for whom I did most of my work. Penny was about forty years old, a human firecracker with lots of red-brown hair and the body of a Rockette. She had worked her way up the ladder in a decidedly male-dominated field, and I wondered if that's why she had such a toughness to her personality or whether she had brought it with her. Penny was always clear about what she wanted which was a relief from the senior attorneys who regularly expected juniors to be mind readers. To add to our all-day stress, we young lawyers feared both getting it wrong and looking stupid by asking the senior lawyers for clarification.

Seeing Penny sitting there that afternoon, smiling with Doug, I felt as if I'd been punched in the windpipe. Don't cry, I told myself. Keep a straight face, keep a straight face. Just get through this and then you can drink. . . . and drink and drink.

Doug spoke first. "So, you probably think we called you here on a Friday evening to fire you." He looked at Penny and they both laughed, her head rocking back a little. *Ha ha. Fucking hilarious.*

"No, of course that's not it," Penny said quickly. "Quite the opposite. We have a great opportunity for you, and we hope that you're going to be as excited about it as we are." She sounded like a parent about to tell her delinquent teenager just how great life was going to be at that work camp four hundred miles away. "Please, sit down," she said gesturing to the empty wingback chair next to her.

"OK," I said, parking myself across from Doug. I sat up telephone pole straight in an attempt to mimic Penny's good posture. It felt like I'd been plugged into a socket flowing with anger and fear, mostly fear. Only an immediate infusion of straight vodka might have calmed me down.

"We're sure you've noticed that our group just isn't as busy as usual right now," Doug said. He let Penny finish their rehearsed speech.

"Now, I'm sure you know that our friends in the Corporate Finance group are very busy," she said, "with all the technology deals, IPOs, and Latin American financings going on. They can use all the help they can get and, well, we've agreed that for the next year, you and Jessica will move over there to work with them." There was a pause while they waited for me to say something. I was silent, busy making a mental note to find out whatever the hell an IPO was.

Penny looked intently at me, as if thinking that I was slower than she'd guessed. "We know this is a lot to swallow right away. But know that we're doing this because you two are very bright and can have great futures here at the firm—with the right experience. This is a truly fantastic opportunity for you."

Unbelievable. I'm "bright" with a "great future" and my reward is a one-way ticket to a Siberian work camp. My God, people on the corporate side worked so hard that they probably devolved into nondrinkers. They were the ones always going back to the office after the firm's happy hours, regularly working until midnight, and pulling more all-nighters than anyone else. I *can't* go to the corporate side, I thought. I won't be able to drink the way I need to drink: martini-soaked weekend nights, Bloody Mary brunches, and wine on weeknights. Sure, I could still pound beers in front of my refrigerator, but my social life would be dead.

Both Doug and Penny were quiet, indicating that it was time for me to respond. "Well, thank you. I really appreciate the vote of confidence and the opportunity to go over to the corporate side, but I want you both to know that I'm very happy here in the Environmental Group. It's what I've always wanted to do. I don't have any interest in corporate law or the Corporate Finance group. If it's at all possible not to make this move, I'd like to stay here. Very much, I'd like to stay here." It wasn't perfect, but at least I took a shot.

The air in the room thickened as Doug and Penny forced smiles that quickly disappeared. I felt like the punk in a gangster movie with two guys in fedoras telling me that we could do this the easy way or the hard way. They looked at each other and then looked back at me.

"Listen, Lisa. I'll be straight," Penny said. "This is the best move for you. We can't keep you busy right now. They can. If you aren't willing to go over to that group, I'm not sure what your options will be. We can revisit this in a year, but we both strongly advise you to take the firm up on this opportunity." She had shifted from mildly sympathetic colleague to mother forcing peas on her screaming toddler.

I remembered that the litigators were having their traditional Friday evening happy hour in a conference room down the hall. I wished that I could make a quick break for it and at least slam a couple of Heinekens before swallowing my peas.

The adding machine in my head started doing the math on the full-year lease I had signed on my apartment and the Club Med vacation I had just charged on my American Express. Then I had a vision of all the people I knew from law school who were unemployed. "OK. I'll do it. What happens next?"

At that point nobody pretended to be enthused. The decision was made and now it was all a matter of details and execution. I felt like a hooker in training who's told, "Buck up, Trixie. At least you don't have to kiss on the mouth." It was time to grab Jessica, and get as drunk as possible.

"Your new office will be set up for you by first thing Monday morning," Doug said.

"*This* Monday?" I gasped, even though Jessica had warned me about how quickly this was to happen. "The next time I come to work, I go across the street?"

"Yes. You have all weekend to get your office here packed up. The building people will move it across the street whenever you're ready," he said.

I mumbled some grossly insincere thanks to Doug and Penny as I left, too numb to cry. I wasn't going to be able to cut it over there. The firm's Corporate Finance group was the elite.

They were the top students from Ivy League law schools who got off by reading about their deals on the front page of *The Wall Street Journal*. That wasn't me.

Walking back down the hall to Jessica's office after leaving Doug and Penny, I thought of the obese wife of a tax partner who had tried to make small talk with me at a cocktail party when I was a summer associate at the firm. We were standing in the living room of the firm's senior partner's palatial apartment in Midtown. I was on my third glass of wine, but it hadn't been enough to make me feel comfortable in this uniformed-elevator-man-and-precious-objects setting with the Central Park backyard. I couldn't wait for the party to be over. The harder-drinking associates had promised to take us to an Irish bar across town afterward, where the real evening could begin.

"And what law school are you from?" the tax partner's wife asked, with her Phyllis Diller hair, Minnie Pearl floral dress, and a fleck of spinach between her teeth. My back was pressed against a wall and I hoped I wasn't dislodging a priceless landscape painting from its supports.

"I go to Rutgers," I said. "I'm from New Jersey." I always felt compelled to add this qualifier, which I intended people to hear as, "I could've gone to a better law school, but I decided to stay in state for the tuition break."

Confusion flashed across her face, followed by what can only be described as her literally looking down her nose. "Oh," she said, clearing her throat. "I see. Well, I think it's noble of the firm to take a student from Rutgers."

Thanks only in part to my growing buzz, my mouth dropped open. She stood there for an extraordinarily awkward moment during which neither of us said a word, and then she walked away.

"Screw her." My friend Ed, a midlevel associate at the firm had overheard the exchange. "Next time, you should ask her what law school she went to. I'll go grab you another glass of wine," he said.

Though I tried to shrug it off at the time, I knew that I'd never feel that I was as good as the rest of the lawyers at the firm. It was my default setting, just as when I was a little kid, then in junior high, in high school, during undergrad, into law school, and now at a swanky New York cocktail party. I always compared myself to others and always came up short.

• • •

After I left Doug's office, I did the death march back to my desk, my head swirling all the way. Now I was really in trouble. I had just been knocked into an open manhole with no idea how far down it was to the bottom. The Corporate Finance people weren't the types to train, nurture, or be even slightly sympathetic. All I knew in that moment was that I needed drinks, several of them. I needed to drink and drink and drink—all weekend—so I could take my mind off of what was going to happen to me Monday morning.

6

"**How are you feeling?**" Jessica asked. She was the first person I spoke to late on Sunday morning.

"Like my liver is smoking a cigarette and wondering why I hate it so much," I answered into the phone, still buried deep under my covers and nauseated from the taste of stale tobacco and residual booze in my mouth. When had I come home the night before? Had I brushed my teeth? A sour alcohol stench enveloped my bed.

"Yeah, it was a long night. Russell is already in the office. Poor guy."

"I don't know how he does it. You married an airplane's black box. Indestructible. Where did we end up last night? Tenth Street Lounge? Did you put me in a cab?"

Blackouts from drinking weren't uncommon for me. And blackouts didn't freak me out the way they scared other people. Sometimes I blamed them on my friends for "forcing" me to do shots. Sometimes I blamed drinking on an empty stomach. Or, as in the case of the weekend after the meeting with Doug and Penny, I blamed the unfair circumstances of my life. That weekend I *had* to drink until my memory shut off. Who wouldn't in my position?

Of course I knew how risky it was to run around New York City in the early morning hours, blackout drunk. I could have experienced any number of disasters. I could have stumbled in front of an oncoming subway train, I could have died of alcohol poisoning, or I could have picked up the wrong guy who, unlike Kevin, could have made the choice to kill me instead of choosing to fuck me. I knew I should stop, but I couldn't. Every time I swore *this night will be different*, that night was almost exactly the same.

Jessica filled me in on the end of the previous night. "Tenth Street Lounge? No, we went to High Life after, so we just walked you home." High Life was a bar only a block from my apartment, which made it one of my favorites, especially at the end of a late night.

"So, are you going to be okay for tomorrow?" she asked. "You've been railing about it all weekend." I let out a whiny half moan, half grunt in response.

Snippets of the night before began to come back to me. I remembered pontificating about the injustice of it all to friends and strangers in a string of bars. Instead of admitting to being an extremely well-compensated kid just out of law school, I painted myself as a poor victim who'd been yanked from my humanitarian work and forced to serve as an evil oppressor bent on screwing the public. And I certainly didn't say out loud the real reasons for my self-righteous rantings: dread of having to work harder than I already did, aversion to having my drinking clipped, and, of course, fear of complete failure and humiliation.

Jessica, on the other hand, seemed fine. She had not only made peace with our transfer; Russell had convinced her that it was a great opportunity.

"You heard Russell," she tried again. "He's going to help us. Get some rest. I've got to go. See you in the morning." Great. Now even Jessica was sick of me.

That day was a turning point. In the past, for Sunday drinking, I'd call Jerry or one of my other go-to buddies and set up a boozing brunch. If it was sunny, maybe Caliente Cab in the West Village for margaritas, and if the air was cold, maybe Carmine's on the Upper West Side for red wine and fried calamari. We'd end up doing a bar crawl all afternoon and into the night. Other people were involved, so I considered it social drinking well within the lines. I would never sit home drinking by myself in the middle of the day. That was something an alcoholic would do. On this Sunday, the thought of entering the corporate building the next morning killed any desire to be social. But it escalated my desire to drink, and drink immediately, even though I had a blazing headache and shaky limbs from the night before.

Still in my t-shirt and panties, I groaned my way out of bed. I had no recollection of getting out of the clothes that were scattered across the floor. Without stopping to slide my cold feet into warm slippers, I padded straight for the little wooden wine rack I had bought at a vineyard in Santa Barbara. I crouched down and examined my choices. Quickly settling on a cheap cabernet, I poured a glass with a generous hand. Just seeing the wine exit the bottle and get one step closer to my mouth gave me immediate relief.

The clock read noon, so what was wrong with a drink? I pictured waitresses all around the city delivering trays of bubbly mimosas and Bloody Marys with giant celery sticks to thousands of hungover people. I was no different from them—I was just cutting out the middleman. While standing alone in a kitchen in my panties.

The deep, almost wooden smell of the wine sent a wave of sick dizziness through me, and I instinctively turned my face away from the glass. My breath was heavy and dank, and my teeth felt as if they were wrapped in burlap, which made the smell of the wine even more disgusting, but adversarial senses had to be ignored. The point was simply to get the alcohol down my throat and into my blood. If battery acid worked better to get me buzzed, I would have sucked it down. With one gulp of the warm ruby liquid, I felt my fists unclench and my neck relax. I could even track the movement of the fluid down my throat as the warm fingers of the alcohol massaged my brain.

I wandered into the bathroom and started running a bubble bath. Then I leaned against the sink and looked up. *Dear God, who is that Alice Cooper ghoul in my mirror?* I smelled like last night's cigarettes and my hair hung in knotty clumps. I said to my reflection, "You look like you crawled out of a lagoon." I knew I'd be unemployed by Labor Day.

I decided to have my Sunday check-in with my parents before the wine kicked in. Chugging a glass of cold water helped smooth the abuse another pack of cigarettes had wreaked on my vocal chords.

"Lisa!" my father said when he picked up. "How are we doing? Ready for the big move tomorrow?" I could see him sitting in his recliner with the remote control to his right and the Sunday *Times* splayed across the TV tray table to his left.

"Yeah, I guess," I said with the enthusiasm of someone on crutches looking up a flight of subway stairs.

"Well, we make the best of it," he said. "A lot of those kids out there don't have jobs. It's a great firm you're with. Just hang tough and keep showing up. You can do it." If only I were still five years old and could believe him.

"You're right. I'll be fine," I said.

Dad wasn't much for phone chat. "Your mother is out power walking. Want me to have her call you back?"

"No need. I'm going out for brunch with friends and then maybe a movie," I lied. "I'll just talk to her tomorrow." I held the wine glass to my lips and tipped my head back, letting every drop slide into my mouth.

"OK, but don't stay out too late. Big day tomorrow! Let us know how it goes," he said.

By the time I sank into the bath, I had poured my second glass of wine. By the time I ordered sushi for dinner, I had opened my second bottle. I passed out watching *60 Minutes* with an empty glass in my hand.

• • •

Despite all my magical thinking, Monday morning showed up right on schedule. Puffy, bitter, and exquisitely hungover, I managed to make it to my new office just before nine o'clock.

"Hey, Lisa, welcome to Corporate Finance! Good to meet you!" Alberto, my bright-eyed officemate said, getting up from behind his desk to shake my hand.

Alberto had thin black hair, thick-lensed eyeglasses, and the lean frame of a guy who fed on intellectual challenges rather than burgers and fries. I guessed he was the kind of guy who never cursed at the television while watching a Jets game or shot pool in a dive bar on a Sunday afternoon.

"I know this must be hard for you. I'm happy to help any way I can," he said. My knees went limp with relief as I realized he was secure enough to be an ally.

"Thank you sooo much!" I said. "It's really good to meet you, too." I tried to match the firmness of his handshake and hoped that my breath and skin didn't reek of the weekend.

Just in case, that morning I'd gone heavy on the Christalle perfume.

I took off my coat and hung it on the back of the door. When I turned back around, Alberto was already fully re-engaged in whatever document he was reviewing. I wanted to pelt him with questions, starting with "Where's the ladies' room?" but I decided not to interrupt him for as long as possible. For the moment, I could still pretend that I wasn't a Corporate Finance dummy.

On my new desk sat an envelope and two documents. The envelope was from the firm's in-house travel department. My stomach sank and churned simultaneously. The cover of one of the documents read "United States Securities and Exchange Commission," and had the title, "Form S-1 Registration Statement Under the Securities Act of 1933." *It's already started*, I thought. *I'm already staffed on a deal.* How long had this been in the works? I hated Doug and Penny.

I held up one of the documents. "Hey, Alberto," I half-whispered, half-pleaded. "I'm really sorry to bother you. I know how busy you are. I'm sure you know what this is, but I have no clue."

"You're kidding, right?" His right eyebrow rose over the frame of his glasses. He didn't look amused; he looked alarmed.

"No, I'm serious. I don't know anything about corporate law," I said, fighting back the tears I had hoped wouldn't flow until lunchtime.

"Wow. OK. It's a registration statement. It's the document a company files with the SEC when it wants to go public. This is an IPO. An initial public offering?"

I almost blurted, "Of course I know what 'IPO' means!" but Alberto kept going.

"The company owns a chain of drugstores. They want to sell shares of their stock on the New York Stock Exchange and they have to get SEC approval to do it. We're representing the underwriters," he said, pointing to the name of our client, a huge investment bank, on the document's cover. I needed to find out what underwriters did and fast.

Alberto glanced at the registration statement. "So that's a plane ticket to Orlando?" he asked. I shook my head and shrugged as if he'd just spoken Mandarin.

"See? The company is in Orlando," he said, pointing to the document as if he were giving directions to a tourist. "You're probably being sent down there to do due diligence."

"Due diligence?" I asked as I opened the envelope and examined the ticket. "Oh my God. This ticket is for today? I'm leaving tonight?" Alberto's phone rang.

"I'm sorry," he said. "I've got to grab this. Check out the working group list and figure out who the midlevel associate here is. They'll be able to fill you in." He picked up the phone and his voice became serious as he talked about pricing amendments and red herrings. I felt young and ridiculous. All I wanted was my bathtub and a glass of wine.

A fifth-year associate named Steve was on the deal team. With Alberto deep in his own work, I was forced to present my utter ignorance to this guy who could either take pity on me or put a quick end to my career in Corporate Finance.

"Steve Kingston," a busy-sounding, confident voice answered on the second ring. Using one's full name when picking up the phone was standard practice. A lot of assholes did it even when they knew who was on the other end of the line.

"Hi, Steve, yeah, this is Lisa Smith. I just came over from the Environmental Group, and it looks like I'm on your deal."

"Yep," then silence.

"Um, I found some documents and a plane ticket to Orlando on my chair?" I was so unsure of myself that I reverted to Valley Girl upspeak, making statements as if they were questions. Not the way to be taken seriously in a law firm. "Would it be ok for me to come by and see you today? My flight leaves at eight o'clock tonight." I examined the plane ticket. At least it's First Class, I thought. That meant free drinks for the entire flight. *There should be free drinks in this stinking law firm. How can you crank people up like this without helping to calm them down? What would be my first drink on the plane? Vodka, definitely vodka.*

"Yeah, OK. Come by my office at two o'clock. I might have ten minutes." He hung up. Oh great. And in ten minutes I *might* learn enough to not embarrass both of us.

My phone rang. Jessica popped up on the caller ID. Thank God. "Hey!" I said.

"Hey!" she said. "Wanna meet for lunch?"

"Yeah, definitely," I said. "Dining room at twelve-thirty?"

"Perfect. See you there."

With its twenty-foot ceiling and huge windows, the firm's formal dining room made young lawyers feel that they had truly arrived. Male attorneys were required to wear jackets because lawyers often took clients to lunch there. Jessica and I had already been regulars, whenever we could get away from our desks long enough to run across the street and eat. And because the firm heavily subsidized what we paid for the fancy, all-you-can-eat lunch, the dining room was packed daily with associates.

"There's the Dining Room Hottie!" I said to Jessica as soon as I sat down. For months, I'd been watching a yummy guy with wavy black hair, a white-toothed smile, and tailored suits. I imagined that he'd been the star of a tennis team at some high school in Westchester—a Pied Piper of beautiful preppy girls as he swaggered around in tennis whites. He and I had first checked each other out across the buffet table months before, salad tongs in hand, filling our plates. Intra-office dating was as common at the firm as working past five o'clock, so I was hopeful.

"Let's go up! Let's get food before he sits down!" Jessica said.

"No! I look like garbage. You go first. My head's not in the game today."

"Your head is *always* in the game!" She threw her white linen napkin on the table.

I rubbed my temples. My throat burned. "I can't handle any of this," I moaned.

"Hey, c'mon," Jessica said. "You're going to be fine. At least you're going to Florida. I heard some deal just started up in *North Dakota*. Just pack your bathing suit and hope for the best."

Instead of skipping dessert as usual, I consoled myself with three chocolate chip cookies. I knew I'd punish myself for it later at the gym.

At two o'clock, I wasn't any closer to understanding what I'd be doing in Florida, but I headed to Steve's office carrying the documents, a pad, and a pen. There was a professional hush around these offices that hadn't existed across the street; even the secretaries seemed more elegant on this side of the street, not engaging in gossip or spilling their personal business all over the hallways.

I got to Steve's door and gasped. He was the Dining Room Hottie! He was on the phone with his back toward me, but there was no mistaking that hair, those shoulders, that suit. What kind of sick joke was the universe pulling? Right there, about to turn around, was the sexy guy I'd been silently seducing for months, and our first conversation was going to begin with,

"Hi, I'm Lisa. I don't know shit about fuck." I thought I was going to lose my three cookies.

Steve hadn't noticed me standing there, so when he hung up the phone I knocked on his door. He turned around nonchalantly and then flinched with recognition. After that, he acted as if he'd never seen me before. Fuck, what I would have given for a flask full of Ketel One.

"Steve Kingston, good to meet you," he said standing up from behind his desk and shaking my hand.

"Lisa Smith." He motioned for me to sit down. On his desk was a silver-framed picture of his wife and baby. Douche bag. Well, at least my incompetence wouldn't be the reason I wasn't going to see this guy naked.

"OK. You've worked on deals before, right?" he asked.

"Um, no, not really. I've done environmental due diligence and worked on environmental representations and warranties, but that's all." I heard my voice crack. Steve's face was tough to read, but at least he didn't shake his head or breathe any heavy sighs.

"OK, OK. Read what you can of the registration statement. Try to get familiar with the company." He eyed the red voice-mail light now blinking on his phone, and added quickly, "I'll see you at the airport and we can talk more on the way down,"

"Wait, you're going to Orlando, too?"

"Well, yeah. You didn't think we'd send you down there alone? Some other associate, James, is going down, too. I think he's a second year. I'll stay down for a day, get you guys started."

"OK, great. See you at the airport," I said standing up.

● ● ●

Steve sat next to me in the first-class cabin. Shortly after takeoff, he pulled out *Forbes*. I reached past the *Rolling Stone* in my bag and pulled out a securities law handbook. How fast could I reverse the fact that I was embarrassingly uneducated in the business I was being flown a thousand miles to execute?

"*What* are you doing?" he asked as if I were trying to clean my ear canal with a fork.

I tried to sound defiant, "I'm trying to learn about what we're going to do in Florida?" The Valley Girl had reappeared.

Steve let out a sigh. "Put that away." He paused for a second and asked, "Do you drink martinis?"

Halle-fuckin-lujah. Not only did he speak my language, we were about to start drinking. "Of course," I answered.

"Excuse me, ma'am?" he held up his index finger toward the first-class cabin flight attendant. Did he have a manicure? "Can we please have two vodka martinis? If you have Absolut, that would be great."

That would have been my order exactly. Why did this guy have to be married? It doesn't matter, I thought. Vodka is on its way.

"Of course, sir," she answered and promptly returned with the drinks.

"OK," he said to me, holding up his glass to clink. "You don't need that book. Here's what you need to know about working on this side of the street ... "

By the time we finished our first martinis, I had learned that in Florida we'd be painstakingly reviewing thousands of documents, looking for "red flags," that our investment bank client would want to know about. By the time we finished our second martinis, Steve had taken off his tie and I had kicked off my high heels. I had also learned the important facts about the Corporate Finance group, as in, who was good to work with, who couldn't be trusted, and who was incompetent. I longed to reach for my legal pad to take notes, maybe even create a diagram, but I resisted. Steve would have shut that down right along with my handbook.

After the three-martini flight, we reconvened with James at baggage claim and headed to the hotel. With a bloodstream full of alcohol, I was able to fall right to sleep. It was the first night since Friday that I hadn't cried before passing out.

Catering to type A business travelers, the hotel gym opened at 5:00 a.m., and on Tuesday morning I was the first person to climb aboard an elliptical machine. I was obsessive about exercise, and there was no moderation in sight. Forty-five minutes of cardio followed by thirty minutes of weights was my version of slacking, which I did only if I got to the gym late. And Gina, my personal trainer-by-day, stripper-by-night, had told me once that toxins from drinking would "sweat right out of my body" if I pushed hard enough, so I pushed hard.

Afterward, I met Steve and James in the lobby. James was a standard-issue corporate junior associate with his sharp suit, slick hair, and the nervous excitement of a spaniel. Briefcases in hand and looking as serious as CIA agents carrying state secrets, we set off.

At 8:30, we arrived at the client's offices, which were housed in a little white box of a building off a busy highway. Two lawyers from the company's firm in New York were already waiting. Beth was an unkempt woman with stringy blonde hair and Daniel was a guy about my age with curly red hair and a straight-backed formality. She seemed to be the older of the two, likely Steve's counterpart.

After introductions, we went inside the bleak structure that appeared to have been designed to thwart all evidence of the bright light and fresh air just outside its walls. A square-jawed woman with a permed, brown mullet and floral pants set us up. She smelled like cigarette smoke, and I was sure she went somewhere dark at lunch for strong cocktails and a game of darts. I wished I could grab her for lunch as soon as possible, but she soon disappeared and I was relegated to the document room.

Steve left late on the first afternoon while the rest of us worked long days all week. At around 9:00 p.m., Perky Beth would say, "Let's just see if we can get through these four boxes before we call it a night." She sounded like a second grade teacher trying to excite her class about clean up time. *Let's not*, I thought. Those four boxes were keeping me from the strong drink I needed badly. Then James would add, "That sounds great! We can grab a late dinner after!" *Jesus. I'd rather down a six of Miller Lite and two Slim Jims at the mini-mart than spend two hours in a Bennigans.*

"I think I'll skip dinner," I'd say, visions of my room's minibar sloshing through my mind. Maybe I could call ahead and have housekeeping swap out the gins for extra vodka. "I have an early wakeup call for the gym." At least that wasn't a lie.

Document review complete, the others left on Saturday morning, but the hotel had a rooftop pool with a bar, so I changed my return flight to Sunday morning and yanked my bikini out of the suitcase. The setting was about as sexy as a strip mall Starbucks, but a full day of poolside drinking in front of me meant relief.

From behind my sunglasses, I watched the other hotel guests come and go. Families, couples, and single people—they all seemed relaxed and content, just drinking sodas and iced teas. It made no sense. There was a bar ten yards away—why wouldn't they choose to work on a buzz in the afternoon sunshine? In my striped bikini, sipping from icy cold bottles topped with limes, I felt sexy and sophisticated by comparison.

Except for the fact that I was alone, mission drinking at two o'clock on a roof in corporate Florida.

At 5:00 p.m. I was sunburned, woozy, and ready to go back to my room, so I packed up my unopened book, my suntan oil, and an almost empty pack of cigarettes. "Can I close out my tab?" I asked the bartender, who seemed to have gotten better looking over the course of the day.

"You sure you don't want to tell me once more about your miserable week reviewing documents?" he sniffed, tallying up the damage.

Shut up, buddy and just give me the bill. "Ha, no, that's ok," I said. I opened the leatherette billfold and did a double take. Twelve Corona Lights and a Caesar salad. *Holy shit. Did he pad this?* I would have guessed, say seven, maybe eight at most. "Um, let's not put this on the room," I said, handing him my American Express card. I'd happily stick the firm with the room-service bill for the dinner and wine I planned to order that night, but I didn't want to set off any alarms with an all-day bar bill. People could be so judgmental.

● ● ●

After the Florida trip, I began drinking every day and went far beyond slamming just two beers at night in front of my refrigerator. I might start with the beers, but those were followed by wine and more wine. I always preferred getting together with a friend or two to provide the cover of "social drinking," but that wasn't always possible.

My cocktail hours at home were nothing like those of my parents when I was growing up. There were two of them, so that took care of any need to drink alone. Also, there was ritual attached to their drinking. The state courts closed at four o'clock, but after my father got off the bench he usually played tennis with friends, spent extra time in his chambers, or stopped after work for a drink with the other judges before getting home around six or six-thirty each night.

After my brother and I attacked him at the door, Dad headed straight upstairs to change out of his suit, and this was Mom's cue to prepare cocktails. No matter where she had been in the house, she would soon appear at the bottom of the stairs and call up, "Harv! What are you drinking?" Most of the time his answer was, "Scotch!" Then she'd retrieve the huge green jug of J&B from the liquor cabinet. The booze cabinet was home not only to the frequently tapped standards, J&B scotch and Smirnoff vodka, but also to obscure libations like Galliano, the yellow liqueur in its long-necked bottle. Galliano was a key ingredient in one of my father's specialty cocktails, the Harvey Wallbanger. I knew this by the time I could read because there was a full-size poster hanging in our garage that included the recipe for the drink below a cartoon version of its namesake descending to Earth in a parachute that read, "HARVEY WALLBANGER IS THE NAME AND I CAN BE MADE."

To accompany the weekday cocktails, my mom would pull out a heavy orange dinner plate with a dark brown ring around its rim. She would carefully arrange Triscuit crackers in a semicircle around a slab of perspiring, yellow Jarlsberg cheese, and she'd finish the arrangement with two cheese knives pointing at each other like fencing épées. I often volunteered to fill two heavy rocks glasses with ice for my parents. Still in my single-digit years, I wasn't allowed to pour the scotch or cut the lemon for the twist.

Once my dad reappeared downstairs in either belted dad jeans or sweatpants with a t-shirt tucked in, my parents would give each other a "welcome home" kiss and clink glasses with a "Good health!" toast that felt like a brief but serious prayer.

Their ritual complete, my parents would then sit at the kitchen table in their respective chairs and rehash the day over one drink, maybe two. Sometimes I would stick around and listen to them talk, but usually after the official toast I was back in front of the TV watching reruns of *The Monkees*. The entire family was together at that time of day and I felt safe.

• • •

There was nothing ritualistic or comforting about the private cocktail hours in my New York apartment. The most they had in common with my parents' was that they were nightly. I struggled to stick to no more than two glasses of wine because that sounded like what a reasonable person might drink. But soon the "have another glass" devil on one shoulder began brawling with the "stop after two" angel on the other. That little angel never stood a chance. After three glasses, there wasn't much left in the bottle, so why not finish it? After that, there was another bottle waiting to be opened.

I hit different liquor stores in the neighborhood so that no single proprietor would recognize me as a nightly visitor. One Monday evening I was in a liquor store on First Avenue, considering the display on a shelf of cheap cabernets and hesitating, as if I knew a difference among the vineyards. It would have been tacky to stroll in, grab the first bottle of red wine under $10, and head for the register, so I lingered, acting as if I hadn't been obsessing about drinking all day. I was thinking there should be wine stores for drunks—no bother with labeling anything about vintages or varietals—just list the alcohol percentage. "Wine–12.5%" or "Wine–14%," that's all we need. Eventually, I stopped buying by the bottle, stopped going to liquor stores altogether, and started having cases delivered to my apartment. So I'm an alcoholic, I admitted to myself. But so are a lot of people; our culture practically encourages it. So maybe I could figure out how to just be a really good alcoholic and not end up in the gutter. It's not as if I were a drug addict.

"Coming out" clean to myself—and definitely only to myself—gave me a kind of relief. My condition had a name, and saying it out loud meant that I understood what was going on with me. And I knew that alcoholism would probably mean an early death, but that was a hell of a lot better than life without booze. *That* would be an early death.

No one close to me could learn my secret or they'd try to force me to change. So the secret helped me to develop even more skills. I became so good at sneaking and lying that it should have scared me, but I reminded myself that I was just doing what had to be done. One of the things that had to be done was to navigate the daily internal dialogues that began the second I woke up every day. Six o'clock, the alarm blasts.

Fuck! I don't want to get up. I want to call in sick. *You called in sick the other day. Get up.*

My head hurts. I'm tired. I don't want to go to the gym. *Go to the gym. You're gaining weight. You're fat.*

I hate this. I hate my job. I hate my life. *People would kill for your job and your life. Shut up and go to work.*

I can't. *Yes, you can. Then you can come home to a nice bottle of wine and make it all go away.*

OK. But why do I have to think about drinking just to get out of bed? *You're a High-Functioning Alcoholic. Emphasis on the "High."*

Maybe I'd be happier if I quit drinking. *That's hilarious.*

● ● ●

The dialogues continued and so did I. I worked hard and got great performance reviews. I went to the gym regularly and stayed in terrific shape. I took fancy vacations with my friends to places like Paris and the Caribbean where I danced and drank in the best clubs and sunbathed and drank on the best beaches. I dated other lawyers, investment bankers, and even a couple of artsy types, and almost every date involved getting nicely drunk. On weekends, I partied with my friends and made lots of happy faces for my family.

I was a vision of young adult success and joy. If I were the topic of a biopic, my friends and colleagues would tell the interviewer: "She's living the dream!" "That girl has it all!"

But I was starting to spend more and more nights home alone, drinking and then crying myself unconscious.

7

It is **2:00 a.m.** on a Saturday night in August 1994. Devon, Jessica, and I are on the dance floor at the Kismet Inn, our favorite bar on Fire Island. We've gone in on a summer rental, an A-frame beach house just steps from the ocean. With all of us working big city jobs, the house stands empty all week and overflows by Friday when we're ready to shoot the lights out.

Tonight the band is the Blue Scoobies, a local rock group we love. We're in top summer form, deeply tanned in baby doll dresses and Keds, loaded up on Lemon Drop shots and Absolut vodka with a splash of club soda. We dance like crazy as the Scoobies play "Kodachrome." The bar is packed with raucous people who have been drinking since noon. With no cars on Fire Island, the worst accident usually involves somebody riding a bicycle shitfaced and veering off into a bush. Our house is close enough to the bar to walk.

I have a serious crush on the lead singer, and I'm trying to get his attention, as usual. He calls me "Carly Simon" and makes friendly small talk, but otherwise he doesn't bite. I hear he has

a girlfriend, which makes me want him even more. Dammit—
I want the rock star boyfriend who stays loyal even though girls
try to paw him! Our housemate Danny knows the Scoobies and
hops onstage to sing "The Breeze." Everybody knows Danny
and the crowd goes wild.

Russell, Jerry, and a bunch of other guys we know aren't
into dancing, so they hang around the long wooden bar. They
wear jeans or long shorts and polos or t-shirts. Some sit on
stools and some just lean, all with their backs to the bar so
they can watch the revved up girls who shake their hips on
the dance floor. The band takes a break, and we join the guys,
some of us still dancing as we make our way to the bar. "Lisa!
Shots!" my friend James calls out. We order a long line of
tequila shots for the crew, lick salt off our hands, clink shot
glasses, throw back the booze, and then suck limes and wince.
Some of us let out a screech and slam the shot glass down on
the bar. My eyes burn and I gag a little, but I feel great. We
light cigarettes and laugh.

This is what I live for.

During the next five years at the firm, I worked my way
into a subgroup of the Corporate Finance team, working for
one counsel, a senior lawyer named Charles. He represented
international investment banks starting up their U.S. affiliates.
It was still Corporate Finance, but at least I was no longer dis-
secting technical clauses in underwriting agreements.

Charles had a wicked sense of humor and a head-back,
cackling laugh. And after twenty years with the firm, he knew
the intense pressures of our office. Like many of us, he had a
reverence for the firm's prestige and enjoyed being part of the
huge deals that crossed our threshold. But despite the heady
environment, Charles was warm and humble.

Every night when Charles left to go home to his family in New Jersey, he'd stand in my office doorway, button up his trench coat, adjust his wireframe glasses, and say, "I've had enough of this chicken-shit operation for one day. See you in the morning." Then with a laugh, he would give me a salute and walk out.

I think that what kept Charles going was the challenge and importance of the work. What kept me going was Charles. For years, he was the reason I showed up and threw every perfectionist impulse I had into the job. By the time I entered my fifth year of practice, my starting class of ninety junior associates firm-wide had dwindled to ten. Without Charles, it would have been nine. Still, as closely as we worked together, he had no idea of the wine soaked truths I hid. If he had seen me on a stumbling Saturday night, I would have collapsed with shame.

As much as I adored Charles, I knew I couldn't keep up the pace in his department given the amount that I was drinking. I was always on the lookout for a possible change. Then in 1996, opportunity knocked. The firm wanted an associate to switch out of practice and into its newly formed Marketing Department. I jumped. The job promised better hours and less demanding work, so just like that, I stopped practicing law. But I rationalized the move by telling myself that with less stress, I might even slow down my drinking.

Devon called during my first week in the new department. "Hey! How's it going over there?"

"Good!" I said. "It's low key and damned easy on the brain. And check it out: the other lawyers in the department insist that I leave at 5:30 p.m. like them. Isn't it still light at five thirty in the evening?!"

Fewer hours at work meant more hours to drink. I loved leaving the office and heading straight into the city's happy hour crowd. After a couple hours of energetic drinking in a bar, I'd sometimes meet a pal in a restaurant for dinner and more drinks. Then, on many nights, I'd go home and drink. So as it went, the post-work schedule included bar drinks followed by dinner with drinks followed by drinks at home. Or just bar drinks followed by drinks at home. My routine was nicely simple. It wasn't the effect I had hoped the job change would have on me, but it was workable.

One night, a little over a year into my new job, I had dinner plans with some of my old friends from the legal side. With people having babies and commuting to the suburbs, these dinners were rare. The emails had bubbled around all day: "Is it still looking OK?" "Is your daughter feeling better?" "Only three more hours until seven. I'm so excited to see you guys!" Everyone seemed to want to reinforce the likelihood that the date would actually happen.

I left the office at 5:30 p.m. and met Jerry for a drink before dinner. We met at the original Rosa Mexicano on First Avenue, home of the famous frozen pomegranate margarita.

"Fernando! How are you?" I asked the bartender as I stretched across the Mexican-tiled bar to kiss him.

"Hey!" Jerry said. "I ordered guacamole." I hopped on a stool next to him, and within minutes a waiter showed up carrying a bowl made to look like an avocado skin. It was full of chunks of fresh avocado, and the waiter put on a show of adding lime, onions, and crushed tomatoes, and then he sprinkled in mysterious Mexican seasonings and mashed it all up with a pestle. Fernando presented two frothy, pink margaritas that looked more like icy kids' treats than ridiculously potent alcoholic concoctions.

"Chin, chin!" Jerry said, raising his glass.

"Salud!" I answered.

Our second round came with a tequila sidecar, courtesy of Fernando. When we were about to order our third round, I looked at my watch. It was almost seven o'clock. I had a stomach full of tequila and guacamole, and I no longer felt like having dinner with my girlfriends. Jerry was more than happy to have me stick around.

"You're full. Catch them for dinner some other time."

"I can't," I told him. "I have to go. I can't blow this off."

"Okay, so stay for one more and then I'll cross town with you. Just tell them you'll be a little late."

I left a couple of voicemails for the girls and ordered the third round, which again came with shots on the side.

● ● ●

When I woke up the next morning, I was still in my clothes, and my mouth tasted like the bottom of an ashtray in a Mexican saloon. *When did I come home? Oh shit, did I not make it to dinner?*

My friend Wendy had left multiple messages, each one more pissed off than the one before:

"Hey, Lisa, got your message that you're running late, but it's almost seven-thirty. We need to order." *Beep.*

"Hey, it's eight. We ordered. Are you coming? Should we be worried?" *Beep.*

"Alright, last message. No idea what happened to you. Not cool that you blew us off." *Beep.*

I climbed back into bed, pulled the covers over my head, and called in sick. Physically I was a wreck. Mentally I was worse. Depressed and ashamed, I was the loser who trades a table of girlfriends for a pink margarita. Shorter workdays and less stress didn't lead me anywhere near a life of diminished drinking. All they did was make it easier to start drinking early.

103

8

It could be any Friday evening in the mid-
1990s, it's 6:30, and I'm sitting with my friend Karen at J.D.'s
Pub in Midtown. She's also an associate, and the occasion is a
farewell party for yet another departing colleague.

We peel the moist labels off our Amstel Light bottles, trying
to remove them in one piece without tearing. We talk about how
another one of us is "escaping over the fence." J.D.'s main room
is long and dimly lit. We are unwinding, putting the week behind
us. Still wrapped tightly in our suit skirts, we sit on dark wood
chairs with our jackets hung over the backs.

Along with paying for a fancy party sendoff, the firm tries
to help the departing associate land a job with one of the firm's
clients. The higher-ups hope that the associate will then turn
around and hire the firm, so these goodbye parties are always
crawling with partners.

This group likes to drink, so the open bar is a big draw.
No one pays much attention to the table lined with the sterno-
warmed buffet trays full of mini egg rolls, chicken fingers, and
fried mozzarella sticks. The untouched cubes of cheese on a
plate sweat little beads of moisture.

By seven the room is full of smart, overworked, young lawyers. In packs, they lean against the bar, stand in the room's open

space, and, like Karen and me, sit at wooden tables covered in red-and-white checkered tablecloths. People stop by our table to chat, mostly about how exhausted they are, how awful their week has been, and how we need to get together for lunch in the Lawyers' Dining Room. We all swap work stories, and in each tale the storyteller is the most oppressed of all the firm's associates.

By eight only the hardcore are left; the people who will close the firm's tab and move the party on to the next bar, usually a hipper place downtown. We throw back final shots of tequila to fortify us for the journey onward. Unless Karen and I have to return the office, we are a few beers and a couple of shots in, ready to go along with the others.

Most of the time, I end up able to remember at least a few fuzzy memories of the night out with work friends. But sometimes I wake up the next morning still in my suit with no recollection of where I went or with whom. No idea of what I did. Nothing but a big black screen where all my visual memories should have been projected. Then I shudder my way through the next work day, looking for judgment in the eyes of colleagues, fearing the wrong kind of phone call, hoping that I didn't do something so unredeemable that it will cost me my career.

● ● ●

One day I received an email invitation to a party the firm was holding for its alumni. Attached to it was a list of people who had accepted the invitation. Having been at the firm for more than seven years, I knew a lot of them. My eyes rested on one name.

Alan and I had dated off and on several years earlier, and we ended it because each time it seemed that neither of us wanted a commitment at the same time. He was from Pennsylvania and we met when he was a first-year, new to New York, and I was a summer associate. He was a great looking former college baseball player with deep green eyes and thick blond hair that he kept short. About three years later, Alan returned to Pennsylvania where he'd been named a partner in a firm based in Pittsburgh. He was very close with his family, loved dark humor, and his brain always moved faster than mine, so I lost our intellectual debates.

Despite not having seen him in years, I emailed Alan to see if he wanted to meet for dinner after the party. He did, so I skipped the party and went straight home to primp and drink.

I put a little extra swing in my walk when I entered the Greenwich Village restaurant where Alan was waiting for me, sitting casually on a barstool. His emerald eyes had the same sparkle that I'd remembered. "It's *really* great to see you," he said as he stood to greet me with a kiss on the cheek and a hand pressed against my arm.

Alan had always liked to try new places in the city. We had spent many nights checking out the latest restaurants written up in the *New York Times*, and I was pretty sure that when we were together, he drank more than his usual. We often started the night with martinis, split a couple bottles of wine, and then finished with B&B. The mornings after those dates, I barely remembered what I ate.

Alan and I sat down and took a long, smiling look at each other. He looked a little older, but it only made him more handsome. With a mischievous smirk he said, "You look great."

I wore a pair of tight black pants, a black camisole, and a sheer mesh purple shirt with flowers splayed all over it. It was my favorite outfit.

Our table was available right away, and Alan carried his martini with him. I ordered one as soon as we sat down. Soon afterward we ordered a bottle of wine.

"So, how was that party?" I asked.

He gave me the rundown on the people we both knew, adding enthusiastic, occasionally biting commentary on their current situations. He'd already had a couple of cocktails, which brought out the comedian in him. As always, I was happy to listen to his hilarious takedowns of obscenely successful people. Seeing the dark side of this otherwise squeaky man endeared him to me. And of course it freed me to dish right back without fearing judgment.

We finished the first bottle of wine in record time. As Alan held the bottle and let its last drops fall into my glass, I asked, "Should we order another?"

"Sure, why not?" he said. And the evening breezed by as we told each other our stories in the rhythm and glow of one of those delicious nights—when you're both at ease, you're both available, and you both know that you're going to end up naked.

Three hours later and waiting for the check, we were solidly drunk, so the offer tumbled easily from my lips, "Do you want to stay at my place?"

We climbed all over each other in the cab, sliding around the faux leather back seat. He had me pressed against the wall of the elevator all the way up to my apartment and then we went straight for the bedroom. The booze did a wonderful job of rinsing away all inhibition, but the attraction was real.

Later that night, obsessive thoughts began to rumble around in my mind. What were we doing? What was he thinking? What was *I* thinking? This wasn't just a romp, that was clear. Safe. I felt safe and protected when I was with him. It was an enormous change from what I had recently felt on my own.

The next morning, I stood in my bathroom wearing a silky robe and examining the pink puffiness around my half-shut, bloodshot eyes. I kept pressing and pulling at them, as if that would make the swelling go down. Good grief, I didn't want him to open his eyes and flinch with regret. But when I shuffled out of the bathroom, he was already sitting in my big club chair lacing his dress shoes and smiling.

"I'd like us to see each other again," he said "You know it would be great if you came out to visit Pittsburgh."

"Absolutely," I said. "That would be ... um ... great."

• • •

That weekend, my friends and I gathered at Jessica and Russell's giant, ground floor duplex on the Upper East Side. By then, they had a year-old son, Nathaniel, so it was easier for us to gather at their place than for all of us to go out. Jerry, Devon, and our friend David, a partner at a major law firm, were all there. We drank expensive wine out of fancy goblets and nibbled from a spread of cheese, crackers, olives, and pâté.

I blurted it. "I had dinner with Alan the other night and I'm going to go out to Pittsburgh to visit him." Every head in the room spun in my direction.

"Oh boy, here we go again," Jerry said, laughing. "I thought you were done recycling men."

He was right. I had recently sworn off backstepping, but when you spend a significant amount of your time shitfaced, the things you "swear" don't always add up to much of a covenant in the light of day. Still, I'd spent the previous 24 hours wrestling my way through the facts. Alan had settled down in Pittsburgh, surrounded by married friends with kids. He was one of the only people I knew who owned a house. He was an Irish Catholic Republican and I was a Jewish Democrat. When we were dating, those differences had kept things feisty, but as the years passed, would feisty become fiery and would fiery eventually become vicious? If we got back together at this point in our lives, it would be serious. Suburbs? Marriage? Kids? Did

I want all that? And would it help me to stop drinking so much? It would, wouldn't it?

"We really reconnected," I told Jerry. "I think we're both at the same place in our lives for the first time. I wouldn't get back together with him if I didn't think he could be the one."

"Are you *serious? The one?*" Devon croaked. "I mean, Alan's great, but *are you batshit crazy?*" She poured more wine all around. "You can't move to Pennsylvania. And what the hell, you haven't mentioned his name in four hundred years, and now after one dinner you're back together?"

She was right. But neither she nor my other friends knew how miserable I was, drinking alone every night, looking down the road and seeing nothing but long hours in an office followed by long hours of drinking followed by long hours of headaches and nausea *in an office*. That was my future. But a fresh start with a great guy, leaving my current life far behind in the cloud of dust my Range Rover would kick up as I rumbled up the gravel driveway of my country house. What was wrong with *that* picture?

"No!" David said. "You can't do that! You're the New York-est person I know!" David was from a small town in Maryland, and to him New York was still the city of daydreams and magic. He was doing great at the firm, and when he wasn't working his tail off he actually did the things that most New Yorkers only say they're going to do, like watch improv in forty-seat theaters and spend afternoons walking around Battery Park instead of dashing straight through it.

"And what about us? And your family?" Jessica added. She bounced Nat on her knee and he giggled. *Would my kid giggle like that? What if my kid turned out to be the same kind of nervous wreck I'd been? Could I be a mother? Wasn't having kids the next grown-up thing to do? I must want kids, right? I bet I'll want kids when I get my drinking under control.*

Russell walked into the kitchen to open another bottle of wine. "You're not going anywhere," he said. The bass in his voice signaled that this crazy conversation was over.

I went outside to smoke. The duplex had an outside garden space with a picnic table, and after Jessica became pregnant the garden became our smoking section. Devon and Jerry got up, grabbed their drinks, and followed me out. We sat down on the benches and our three lighters lit up the outside space as we inhaled and then exhaled simultaneously, smoke streaming over our heads. It looked like a choreographed move, and all three of us laughed at the synchronization of it. Then we laughed even harder about the synchronized laughs. Deep, head-back laughter that died down with a smiling sigh. And then they both looked at me with so much love in their eyes that I had to look away.

• • •

Six weeks later, Alan and I decided that we would live together in Pittsburgh. On a visit to New Jersey a short time later I told my family about our plans. Boyfriends came and went in my life, so they hadn't given my recent trips to Pennsylvania much thought. Neither my dad nor my brother seemed upset when I brought up the move. They both expressed some version of, "If it's what you want, I'm happy." They'd both always been like airtight PR agents to the stars: never uttering a word about my private life unless the topic had been approved. My professional life, however, was a free zone.

"You're leaving a lot behind with that job," Dad said.

"It's OK, Dad. I can work at Alan's firm. He showed the Managing Partner my résumé, and the guy said I'd be a fit in their marketing department. So, I've already got a job. It's a fantastic firm."

My dad laughed. "See? All the time you were unhappy at work? Now that job is letting you write your own ticket. That's great."

As always, my mother had more to say on the subject. "I really don't like that you're going to be in Pennsylvania. We barely see you as it is." We were sitting in the kitchen, just as we had done for serious talks when I was a kid. But now I kept my hands underneath the table so she wouldn't see them shake. She was wearing one of her track suits, the kind that adorned countless older women in Atlantic City casinos, and she accessorized with a full face of makeup and gold bracelets that swung from her wrist. She had just come from her weekly manicure and hair appointment.

"Mom, think of it this way," I said, "People just don't work as hard out there. That means I can come home a lot. And when I do, I can stay for a few days or even a week instead of having to race back to Manhattan."

"Don't try to lawyer me out of this. It's too far. And what about kids? Alan's Catholic and he takes it seriously. You're going to raise Catholic kids?" she asked.

"I told you already, we're going to raise them with both religions. We'll celebrate both sets of holidays. Lots of people do it." I tried to give a casual shrug, but I felt my lip twitch.

"So tell me this," she said, "when you have a boy, are you going to have a christening or a bris? Thought about that one?"

Sweat began to dampen the back of my neck. What time was it? Four o'clock. Absolutely close enough to five, especially on a Saturday. There was no navigating that conversation without alcohol.

"Do you want some wine?" I asked as I pulled one of their white wine glasses out of the cabinet. I knew how she'd answer, but offering tempered the creepiness of drinking "alone," right next to my mother.

"No, not yet," she said. "I want to know what it will be—a christening or a bris."

I opened the refrigerator and poured a very full glass of cold, white wine, taking a long drink while my back was still turned to her. What I felt like saying was, "Mom, I'm a goddamned alcoholic! I'm drowning in a fucked-up life! I'm drowning in cheap cabernet. I'm drowning in tequila. I'm drowning in vodka. When people aren't looking, I take an extra swig. I drink the second I get home from work. I drink in the bathtub. I drink after the party's over. Mother, I'm drowning and Alan is throwing me a line!"

But what I said was, "I don't know, Mom. We'll cross that bridge when we get there."

"Well, I'm not happy with that," she said.

"I know you're not."

When she went upstairs to change, I poured another full glass of wine. My parents kept their cases of wine in the basement, so I scrambled down there and pulled out two more bottles to chill in the refrigerator. My parents didn't pay attention to their wine inventory until it got low, and that had always worked to my advantage.

• • •

The wedding weekend arrived in June 2000, less than two years after Alan and I had reconnected, and guests from all over the country descended on New York City. Many of them stayed at the Gramercy Park Hotel, just across the park from The National Arts Club where my parents had been longtime members. It was always assumed that I would be married there.

One of the things that connected Alan and me was that we both preferred casual events. We planned a rehearsal dinner at John's Pizza in Times Square on the Friday night before the wedding. No formalities, no speeches—just a big buffet of pizza, garlic knots, salads, and fried calamari. And of course, an open bar.

"Do you care if your father and I don't come into the city on that Friday night?" my mom had asked a few weeks earlier. "The dinner is really for you and your friends, and I'm going to have a house full of people."

"That's fine, I guess," I said. But I wondered, wouldn't people think it odd that my parents had skipped my rehearsal dinner? Maybe even odder was that I was more concerned about public opinion than the glaring fact that my parents wanted to skip my rehearsal dinner.

Alan was clearer. "I'm really disappointed," he said. I was worried that he'd taken it personally. But not worried enough to do anything about it.

The day of the wedding was stifling, the hottest of the year with sweltering humidity. I wore a cream colored Badgley Mischka gown with a skin-tight bodice and flouncy raw silk skirt that I'd found at the Saks sample sale. I spent the afternoon getting ready with my bridesmaids in an upstairs room at the club, having our hair and makeup done while we threw back bottles of champagne and ate chocolate-covered strawberries.

My dad proudly walked me down the aisle and both a priest and a rabbi married us as two hundred friends and family members watched and fanned themselves, thanks to a failed air conditioning system at the club. I nearly fainted under the chuppah, but I blamed it on the heat, not fear or the full bottle of champagne I had already consumed by myself.

Within minutes of wading into the crowd during the cocktail hour, Alan and I separated. Our reception area comprised several of the club's rooms, and he and I spent most of the cocktail hour apart. The party was a swarming ant farm of energy and activity, and we connected with our guests independently.

Through the evening, I drank only champagne and was grateful that I had gotten a good amount into me before the ceremony. It was hard to get a drink, especially when everyone wanted to talk to me, and I could feel my buzz starting to die. My stomach was too tight to grab any of the shrimp, mini quesadillas, pigs in a blanket, or other standard wedding appetizers that the formally attired waitstaff offered around.

"Here, you have to eat something," Devon said, shoving a plate of mixed pasta toward me. Her blonde hair was swept up and she wore smoky eye makeup and bright pink lipstick. Bent on avoiding every possible tradition trap, I had I let my bridesmaids wear any black dress they wanted.

"No thanks, sweetie. I'm good for food," I said. "But who do you have to fuck to get a drink around here?"

Devon laughed and said, "I can't believe you're married!"

"Me neither," I said. Oh my God. Married. It certainly didn't feel different. But why didn't it feel more blissful? Would that happen after the wedding? Would marriage make me normal?

Through the crowd I could see Jerry and David rushing frantically toward me. "Hurry up!" David blurted. "The band called you for the first dance!"

"Seriously? The cocktail hour is over? Can somebody get me some champagne, please?"

"Yes, but let's go!" They tried to cut a path through the crowd, but people kept stopping us to grab a minute with the bride. When we finally made it to the parquet dance floor, I gasped, "Where's Alan?" as my head darted around like a neurotic bird.

They both shrugged. "He's *your* husband," Jerry said.

"What should I do?" I begged David as the eight-piece band began to play "our" song. Perspiration broke out on my back and chest under the gaze of dozens of guests who stood in a half circle, murmuring and bobbing up and down as they craned their necks to look for the groom. The air conditioning had been fixed by then, but that didn't keep me from sweating.

"Let's dance!" David gallantly held out his arm like an awkward prom date trying to hide his discomfort behind theatrics. I grabbed the hand he raised high in the air and rested my other hand on his shoulder, and we started slow dancing. I tried not to meet anyone's eye, imagining my mother trying to fake a smile as she watched this unfold.

Midway into the second verse, Alan came crashing through the crowd as if he were trying to make it through the doors of the A train before they slammed shut.

"I'll take it from here," he said, as he cut in on David and flashed a broad smile. David dipped forward in a dramatic bow and scurried off.

"Sorry, dear," Alan said into my hair. "The guys had me at the bar. I'm really sorry."

"It's OK, it's all right," I said, nodding to people with exaggerated smiles as we circled the floor. I caught my mother's eye and couldn't tell if the tight look on her face was sadness or worry.

• • •

"How are you doing, honey? Are you OK?" my mom asked three months later as we did the *New York Times* crossword puzzle together over the phone. "We miss you so much."

Alan was out for a long Saturday run with one of his buddies. Because he didn't drink the way I did, he was still able to train for marathons and stay in great shape. I, on the other hand, had all but stopped exercising for the first time since college. But I hadn't stopped drinking. I'd gained seven pounds since the wedding.

"Yeah, I'm good," I answered. The wine swirled around in my oversized glass as I fought back tears.

By the end of summer I had deemed noon on Saturday the official start time of the weekend cocktail hour. This didn't make me feel guilty at all, especially if I'd had a particularly productive morning of shopping, laundry, and miscellaneous errands. Once the car was officially settled back in the driveway, it was safe to start opening bottles.

My chronic unhappiness had gotten worse since the wedding, but I was determined to fight through it and make this thing work. Although I knew it wasn't helping, I couldn't put the bottle down. Alcoholism was the monster I had planned to leave in New York, but it had followed me to Pittsburgh where it cast a long shadow across my shiny new life.

How easy it is to keep drinking to excess despite living under the same roof with a normal person. Even though Alan and I had gotten drunk together many times, it was almost always at my instigation. And as was the practice with most normal people, as he had gotten older he drank less. I had hoped that our life together would show me what that felt like, but instead I just found places to hide the bottles.

At my wedding shower, someone had given me cookbooks, and I'd managed to learn to prepare three dishes: bowtie pasta with shrimp, filet mignon with walnut oil dressing, and linguini with chicken and peppers. One night after work as I stood in the small, charming kitchen of our small, charming house, I was making the linguini dish and drinking wine.

"Do you want a glass of wine?" I called out to Alan.

"Sure," he said from the den where he was watching the evening news in front of a roaring fire and flipping through the *New York Times*.

I was already a couple of drinks ahead of him. I'd learned quickly that making dinner offered the perfect way to knock back wine unobserved. And there was a great hiding place for extra bottles behind the cleaning products in the panty. Alan never cleaned.

While the pasta cooked, I carried a platter of cheese and crackers into the living room, lit candles, and admired the perfect scene. Cocktail hour with my husband, just as my parents had done it. Then I went back into the kitchen and slugged down another enormous glass of wine while I put dinner together.

"Mmm, this is great, thank you," he said, as we dug into dinner in front of the television. Against all trendy advice about How to Bond, How to Live the Old-Fashioned Way, How to Make the Most of Your Marriage, and How to Create Intimacy, we usually dined seated on the couch and facing the screen. I curled up next to him with my bowl of pasta on my lap. Alan rubbed my shoulder and kissed my head. My work was done and my buzz was fully formed. Be happy, I thought. Look at how lucky you are. Think about how many women would happily cut the brakes in your car to have this guy, this house, this life. Ungrateful bitch.

As we watched a repeat of *Law & Order*, I kept losing the storyline. My head was bobbing, and when my eyes closed the room began to spin. I was dangerously close to slurring, so I stood up and said, "I'm wiped out. I'm going to do the dishes and then go read in bed."

"OK, I'll be up a little later," said Alan, kissing me sweetly. I carried the bowls into the kitchen and filled my glass with cabernet before I started the dishes.

Alan was a night owl and I usually passed out early, so most nights ended with our finding the way to bed separately. In the mornings, Alan usually sprang from bed with energy that trumpeted, "Behold! Another day is upon us! A glorious chance to do glorious things!" For me, morning usually meant nausea, headaches, light-headedness, and waiting until Alan left for work before I soaked a pillow with tears. On the morning after the linguini dish, the tears wouldn't wait.

"Babe, what *is* it?" he asked me. Showered, dressed, and ready to leave for work, he sat on the side of the bed. I curled around him in a fetal position and cried and cried and cried. He stroked my hair and pleaded, "Has something happened?"

"I don't know," I gasped the words through my sobs. "I'm just so miserable all the time. I don't know why. I'm just so sad."

"Tell me how I can help. Whatever you need," he said, which made me cry harder.

The words were right there—*I can't stop drinking.* They were simple and clear and would have offered a bright red signpost to the road out. But I wouldn't say them. If I said them, people would try to get me to stop drinking. I was drinking every day and increasing my intake with every passing week. I knew that this pace meant that I was probably going to lose my job. It meant that I would probably devastate my family. It meant that I'd probably die young. But to let anyone try to take away my alcohol? Nothing was more terrifying.

● ● ●

Alan and I agreed that I would start seeing a psychologist for my depression. Stacey wasn't much older than I, and she seemed to want to overshadow her youth with seriousness. On Thursday evenings in her waiting room, I'd watch the little rock formation water fountain and try to relax. But the minute I walked into her office, warm tears would begin streaming down my cheeks. Embarrassed by the depth of my grief, I would put my hand to my face and sob as quietly as I could, but there appeared to be no bottom to the reservoir. Stacey would wait silently as I wept. Soon she prescribed an antidepressant, and I took it religiously.

When I didn't feel any better after a couple of months, she asked me, "How much do you drink?" Shit. I knew that alcohol and antidepressants were a bad combination.

I feigned surprise. "Not much," I lied. She must have asked me this when I first saw her and I must have lied then, just as I did when asked the same question by any medical professional. "A glass or two of wine a night," I lied again.

She saw through me and I knew it. Hadn't I hidden my shaking hands? Could she read my thoughts? Did she know that in every session I conducted a silent countdown until the moment I could get home and drink?

"Mmm. I don't think the wine is helping you. Do you think you could cut it back to maybe a glass or two a week?"

"Sure, yeah." *Absurd.*

"You know, if you can't there's help for that. Twelve-step groups and others." She waited until she realized that I wasn't going to respond and then said, "Just give it a little thought." *Uh-huh. That's exactly how much thought I'll give it.*

I vowed never to utter a remotely honest word to her or anyone else about my drinking.

• • •

Barely a year after our wedding, I chose to end my marriage in the parking lot of a mall. Alan and I were walking to our car after another miserable lunch during which I cried into multiple glasses of chardonnay and moaned about my chronic unhappiness. "I can't do this anymore," I finally blurted. "I'm going back to New York."

"You're giving up?" Alan said. "I know you're having a hard time, but we'll change whatever we need to. We're a team and I want to help you."

My heart was breaking. He was genuinely good and I was genuinely awful. And he had no idea how utterly desperate I was for another drink.

• • •

I moved back to New York a few days after September 11, 2001, right in the middle of the chaos, horror, and grief. People all over the city clung to the people they loved, and I was grateful to be once again surrounded by my closest friends.

In Russell and Jessica's apartment, Jerry and David told me their stories. Jerry had been in his office just a few blocks from the Towers. "It was a fucking horror show. Everyone just hauled ass out when the second plane hit and got as far away as they could. I was covered in the dust and shit. Some dude and I just kept walking uptown—then the Towers came down. People were screaming and crying. Some of them were running toward the buildings. They must have had people they knew in there." Devon had sprinted out of her downtown office as well. Russell had been on a business trip in London and David had been in Midtown.

The city was enveloped in fear. There was fear of anthrax, fear of war, and fear that something else unexpected and devastating was coming just around the corner. Almost everyone I knew had a connection to someone who had died. A cousin's husband, a former colleague, a friend from high school—it seemed that no one was unscathed. We lost two friends from

Fire Island, Luke and Martin. Luke was at Cantor Fitzgerald, and Martin just happened to be at Windows on the World for a breakfast that day. I read that a group at Windows had gotten onto the roof and were calling loved ones, waiting for help. I pictured Martin in that crowd, calling his wife and two young kids. Every time I thought of it my stomach surged. When I read that some people at Cantor had died instantly with the first plane's impact, I hoped that Luke was among them.

Everyone we knew was drinking harder, as if the end was near. The bars were overflowing with people talking and talking about that day and the fallout. Many people couldn't work in their offices, so it was easier than ever to drink around the clock. Suddenly my drinking didn't look so shocking.

Despite the circumstances, I luckily found a job in legal marketing at another big firm in New York. I had subleased my apartment when I moved to Pittsburgh because Alan and I had heard rumors that it was going to go co-op. If that happened, we wanted to buy the apartment and flip it for a profit. But it didn't happen, so when the subtenant's lease expired I moved back in.

Walking back into my apartment, I felt a renewed sense of doom. It was as if all my alcoholic ghosts had remained, lurking in the eaves. And oh how happy they were to see me home again. "Welcome back, my lady. May I pour?"

The first call I made was to Stuyvesant Square Liquors on Second Avenue. All they needed was updated credit card information, and soon a case of double bottles of cheap Yellow Tail cabernet would appear at my door. Finishing the transaction sent a warm sense of comfort through my body. Then, as we were about to hang up, the clerk said, "Good to have you back." I thought I might barf.

9

Just yards from my apartment, there was a great bar with hamburgers as thick as drugstore paperbacks. Kenny's Place was dark and cool inside, with a deep brown wood bar and red-and-white checkered tablecloths. It was a favorite hang for my friends and me, thanks to the bartenders who knew our names and more than forty Rolling Stones songs in the jukebox. Before long, I found myself at Kenny's every night, even if I went alone. The most consistent regulars were the retired schoolteachers and firefighters who lived in the nearby Stuyvesant Town apartment complex.

In the later hours, Kenny's attracted a seedy crowd. I struck up friendships with these dusky people—the kinds of friendships that left out basic facts like professions, last names, and just about everything we did beyond the pub walls. The most significant relationship that came out of that bar was the one I formed with cocaine.

The first time I tried cocaine, I was fifteen years old. It was at a high school party in a friend's basement, and one of the guys had pilfered some coke from his older brother. People kept going in and out of a small bathroom where there were lines laid out on a mirror. It felt cool to be open to trying drugs, to hold a cut-off

123

straw in my hand, to sniff and then squeeze my nose as I'd seen people do in movies. That first hit was like fireworks going off in my brain, fireworks that wrote across my face, "I'M FUCKING HAPPY!" But it made me shaky and the buzz wore off quickly.

In the years that followed, coke was often slinking around the periphery of parties; it was there, but people never waved it around like tequila shots. I didn't crave it or even ask around for it, but I never minded bumping into it. Cocaine was like a fling from my young years: I remembered him fondly, didn't mind seeing him at parties, maybe even helped set him up with a new chick. But he couldn't turn my head because my boyfriend was booze. Then came the nights at Kenny's, where my fling and I were reunited. And this time we clicked. This time it was love.

One night, one of my first-name-only bar buddies pulled out a small glass vial with a tiny spoon attached to the cap and slipped it into my hand under the bar. I thanked him and headed into the bathroom where a teeny spoonful in each nostril felt so magnificent, the moment could have been punctuated by its own Led Zeppelin intro.

Being scorched by the pressure of my competitive New York law firm, I was ripe for the return of cocaine. Coke made everything flash brighter, faster, clearer. I could work with intense focus for hours. I could work through a night and into the sunrise without yawning, and I'd churn out the work of three unaltered people. And the best part of all: coke made it easy to keep drinking.

Coke and alcohol got along beautifully! If I'd drunk so much that I was getting slurry and slushy, coke snapped me up crisp and straight. If too much coke had me wound up and toe tapping, booze would mellow me back down. Each drug helped me hide the other. They were like two illicit lovers who together could fulfill all my needs, and neither one minded sharing me. I knew then how viciously addictive cocaine is, but I didn't care.

I believed I could control it or stop using it at any time. For some reason, I thought it would be different for me than alcohol, which by then I knew I couldn't control.

By mid-2003, my phone held the numbers for three drug dealers, and I called them as often as I called my mother. Having drugs delivered to an apartment in New York City is as easy as ordering a pizza or a hooker. Somehow the simplicity of the transaction made it feel less illegal. Of course, I understood that as a legal professional, my new activities meant that I was dabbling in disaster. A drug bust, an arrest—those would bring more than shame, more than a record or even jail time. They would mean the end of my law career. But my life was like that joke about the guy who can't be persuaded to give up cigarettes. His wife begs, "*Why* don't you believe that smoking can kill you?" He says, "Hasn't killed me yet."

Each time I bought coke, I hated myself a little more. I knew that I was spewing more poison into an already toxic swamp of dysfunction, but I needed to keep drinking, so I invited coke to find a cozy spot at the edge of the swamp. Not long after rediscovering the happy white powder, I was fully hooked. I no longer worried about the consequences. I just needed the drugs.

Henry was my primary dealer. He was a good-looking half-Greek, half-Cuban kid in his early twenties with wavy black hair, full red lips, and scruffy stubble. A part-time business student and a full-time drug dealer, Henry was a smart kid just stupid enough to convince himself that dealing was a good way to pay for school. He usually showed up at my door with the *New York Post* in hand, complaining about Mayor Bloomberg's administration.

"Hey, Lisa, what's going on?" Henry brushed past me into the apartment one evening when I was working on a client proposal. His visit was critical, as I needed coke to support the all-night drinking I had planned. He instinctively craned his neck all around to make sure I was the only one home, and I stood back to let him perform his routine inspection.

"Not much," I replied. "You busy today?" It's the rhetorical question people ask each other in law firm elevators.

"Always busy, always busy," he mumbled as he made himself comfortable on the couch and unzipped his backpack. He looked like any other student on the street, but instead of asking him about how his classes were going, I cared only about his drugs.

"Want a Heineken?" I asked him as I fished in my giant handbag for my wallet.

"Yeah, sounds good. What do you need today?"

"Can I get an eight ball?" I asked. I handed him a beer and yanked together the large, heavy navy curtains in the living room window. Someone had told me that if you could see the Empire State Building from your apartment, the government could spy on you.

"Sure, sure. No problem," he said, pulling out seven miniature plastic Baggies that each held about a half gram of cocaine, some of it already crushed into a powder. I put $250 on the coffee table and he counted it.

By the time we finished the transaction, Henry's cell phone was buzzing with his next call. After he left, I triple-locked the door and rubbed my hands together in excitement.

When I finally closed the laptop at around three o'clock in the morning, I had written a strong proposal and emailed it to the partners. Receiving work product at that hour isn't unusual in a law firm, so it didn't raise red flags. Frequently, it garnered points for effort and commitment. I often wondered if the partners would mind at all if they knew that any of us were doing coke. I wondered if any of them were doing it themselves.

There was a new problem, though. Sleep. At this point, I was more likely to get Brad Pitt in my bed than a restful seven hours. I was probably averaging four hours a night, and it showed on my pale face. That morning, my body shook all over and my stomach was sick from the combination of wine, coke, enough cigarettes to plug a porthole, and no dinner. It's no coincidence that coke had long been the fashion industry's drug of choice. No appetite means "no food" which means "no fat." I was sick as hell and the kind of skinny I'd always dreamed of.

The hangover was immediate. I could feel it the minute I closed the laptop. I lay in bed naked wishing I were just straight booze crashing, which by comparison felt like a cup of warm chamomile tea. But anytime I did coke, I drank more wine than I would have without it, and the combination of the two was like a baseball-bat concussion.

In addition to all the physical symptoms, the come down from coke and wine meant a crushing, black-hearted depression. Tears streamed from my eyes and the chorus of self-hatred raised its voice. It told me that life had no meaning, I was a fraud, I'd never have real love, nothing was ever going to get better. The mind fuck went on for hours as I thrashed my way through broken sleep.

Somehow I managed to get to work the following days, swallowing potentially toxic levels of Advil and industrial-sized cups of coffee. I considered drinking booze to kill the pain, but I stopped myself. Morning drinking was only for serious alcoholics, not high-functioning partiers like me.

Then one night I had a blind date, a guy somehow connected to my cousin Robbie. All I knew was that he was a "nice, good-looking, Jewish lawyer named Jeff," and that was enough for me.

At Jeff's suggestion, we arranged to meet for a drink at the P&G Bar on the Upper West Side at eight o'clock on a Thursday night. The P&G was a dearly loved dive bar that everybody had a good story about. Great pick, I thought. I'm going to like this guy. But there was one big problem: I'd already be drunk by 8:00 p.m. In those days my drinking started the second work ended. I couldn't remember the last time I would have been sober enough for a blind date starting even as early as 6:30 p.m. The situation called for a plan.

I ducked out of work early, and by five I was home getting ready. I poured myself a glass, more like a goblet, of cold chardonnay and brought it into the bathroom while I showered. The glass gathered condensation beads as the heat of the room took the chill off the wine. I reached for it and took a gulp as I toweled off. OK! I thought, feeling the first threads of relief. Blind date. No more than two glasses first. Jeff can't think I'm some kind of drunk.

I stood naked with my hands on my hips in front of my closet, staring at my wardrobe. Separate from my work suits hung about ten different pairs of black pants. They were indistinguishable on the hanger, but they were in a variety of materials, some fit tighter than others, some had lower waists, and some had flared legs instead of straight. Some made me feel sexy, some sophisticated, some young. Some of the pants hung next to duplicates I'd bought while shopping drunk. I stood there and debated which would more likely lead to a successful date with Jeff, the Jewish lawyer. On most nights out, I would pair these pants with a black or white camisole, topped by a sheer shirt, usually a tight one. Some of the shirts had buttons and some were pullovers. Some of the shirts were silky and some felt like netting. I had several colors and styles, but they could all be called "dark." I chose a pair of tight pants that made me feel sexy and finished the outfit with a pair of high black leather boots. It was a standard uniform for the New York City alcoholic too lazy to put outfits together.

As I dressed, I continued drinking, only gradually, and stopped frequently for cigarette breaks in the living room. Then I put on makeup and finished my outfit with giant silver hoop earrings and a diamond necklace. When I went to refill my wine glass before doing my hair, I realized that I had made a terrible error. I was at the end of the bottle. I had *finished the whole thing off.* It was just after 6:30 p.m., and there was still almost an hour before I had to leave. This was a treacherous moment. One wrong move and I would slip into an inescapable pit of getting too drunk and destroying the night. Three options came to mind, none of which were guaranteed to get me to the P&G in a date-suitable state.

First, I could just stop drinking until I got to the bar—maybe have a coffee until then. Hilarious. Second, I could open another bottle of wine and just sip over the next hour. That would make me tired. Orrrr . . . I could do some coke to straighten out and feel like a supermodel by the time I got to the P&G. Not exactly a dilemma.

Out came the drugs, the mirror, the spoon, the blade, and the straw. The brilliance of my decision was confirmed by the spectacular rush that went along with the ritual: sprinkling the coke on the mirror, crushing it down with the back of a spoon, carving just thick enough lines . . . That first prickly blast into my nostrils followed by the chemical drip down my throat told me that it was going to be a fantastic night.

Time flies when coke is on the mirror. The next thing I knew it was 7:30 p.m., time to go. I put away the coke paraphernalia, guzzled another glass of wine, and went into the bathroom to brush my teeth and gargle hard.

Shit, I thought, suddenly staring into the mirror. A five-year-old could see that I was flying. It was only seven thirty on a Thursday evening, but I was already wearing my Saturday midnight face. There was nothing I could do about it.

I hoped that Jeff had been out with people after work and might be riding some kind of buzz of his own. Please, Jeff, please be a boozer. Please be a cokehead.

129

Walking into the P&G, I recognized him immediately. The rumors about him had been true: he was hot. He had light brown curly hair, blue eyes, and long eyelashes. He wasn't tall but he was fit. His handshake was firm and his smile was big. *But wait, jeans and a leather jacket? Shit, those aren't work clothes. Damnit, he went home after work. He might be completely sober.*

We parked ourselves on stools near the back of the bar and the bartender came over quickly. "What can I get you two?" he asked.

"Absolut Citron and soda on the rocks," I answered, trying to give Jeff a sexy smile with my side glance.

"I'll have a Diet Coke," Jeff said.

WAIT, WHAT? Apparently I gave him a look as if he'd just killed our first baby. "Um, I'm not a big drinker," he must have felt compelled to explain. "I might have a couple of beers on the weekend, but I don't really drink during the week." *Holy fuck. I'm a bottle and a half of wine and a quarter gram of blow into this thing.*

"Oh yeah, that's cool," I lied. "I don't go out much during the week either." Two beers in a week—*might* have two beers in seven days? That meant he also might not. He was one of *those* people. "So what else do you do besides work? Since you're not getting wasted in bars and all." It was meant to be funny. He didn't find it funny.

"I'm training for the marathon," he said. *Of course you are.* "I had to run before we met. That's why I said eight." Suddenly, I felt annoyed, as if I had been lured on this date under false pretenses. Who suggests meeting at the P&G at eight on a Thursday night without any intention of drinking? Freak.

We didn't have a lot to talk about, so I managed to find common ground: the Yankees game on the bar television. Spending so much time in bars, I had become proficient in pretending to care about the Yankees. And sometimes I'd even pretend that a Yankee game was my reason for being in a bar.

Not having brought any coke to counter the alcohol and keep me from getting sloppy, I was doomed. I tossed back two Citron and sodas, and as the coke wore off so did the illusion of my sobriety. By the time the bartender poured my third drink, I was flat out, drunk-ass wasted. By now the bar was packed, but neither a rocking party atmosphere nor even a sense of chivalry compelled Jeff to order so much as a light beer.

What happened next can never be undone. It can't even be forgotten, although the details have never been any more than fuzzy.

Seeing me a little wobbly on my barstool, Jeff reached out for my arm to steady me. My drunken brain mistook this as a gesture of affection. Clearly, he was already falling in love with me! As he held my arm, I leaned in toward him, grabbed him by the neck, and pulled him toward me with my eyes closed, going in for the kiss. That was more movement than my sloshed body could handle, and as I lunged forward I slid off my barstool and crashed to the floor, my shoulder and hip hitting first followed by the rest of me in a thundering heap.

I didn't want to look up, and the first thing I heard was the "Whoa!" of the crowd that had just witnessed my tumbling display of jackassery. To make it worse, nobody moved. For what felt like at least ten seconds, the shock of the crash froze all the gawkers. They just stared as if they were waiting for a director to yell, "Cut!" Eventually my date slid off his barstool and tried to lift the mess that was me. Clearly repulsed, Jeff rushed me out into the street and hurled me like a shovel of shit into the first cab he could find.

When I woke up at 7:20 a.m. the next morning, I saw a second bottle of wine, empty, on my kitchen counter. I was throwing up by 7:30 a.m., but I had to be in the office for a ten o'clock meeting. *I can't do it*, I thought.

But I couldn't miss the meeting. My boss was in town from Portland, an unusual circumstance. His being based on the West Coast had made it simple for me to work from home whenever I liked, which helped to keep my drinking and drugging undetected. If I kept my wine and coke use in balance, I produced good work without a problem.

That morning, though, I had to be in the office and not appear completely wrecked. Tremors shook my entire body. How was I going to get my act together in an hour?

There was only one sure way I knew of that would calm me down and give me some semblance of equilibrium. Ironically, it was drinking. Booze would mellow my headache and stop my shaking. Many times I had promised myself that I would never drink in the morning, but this was no time to quibble over empty promises.

In the kitchen, I pulled the bottle of Citron out of the freezer. Then I opened the refrigerator door and found no orange juice or other mixer. It would have to be straight. I took out a shot glass and threw back two quick belts. My whole body shuddered as if it was just waking up from a bad dream, but the vodka was settling me down.

Who drinks in the morning? What kind of person wakes up after a night of boozing feeling shaky and nauseated and weak and then tips back a bottle of vodka? How was I going to rationalize this fucked-up development to myself? After a night of getting blasted, normal people wake up feeling shitty, moan their way to a bottle of Advil, go back to sleep, and then, once they can bear the idea of food, chow a greasy cheeseburger and fries and vow never to drink again. What did it say that *my* answer to near alcohol poisoning was more alcohol?

In fact, I found it all fairly easy to rationalize. My slide into round-the-clock drinking was something I was entitled to. It made me ashamed and it made me despise myself, but it also made me feel better because it was a crucial weapon in the fight against being me. I felt entitled to do whatever it took to win the battle against the unfair circumstances of my life, this life in which I played by all the right rules and still ended up miserable and lonely and riddled with self-hatred.

I learned to master the art of keeping things separate. There was my real life with all its alcohol-soaked secrets and there was the role I portrayed in the stage play of my life. In the play, the protagonist was healthy, strong, and the successful envy of ambitious career women around the world. But every day at 5:30 p.m., she took her bow and the curtain closed. Then the actress sat in front of the vanity mirror framed in bright round bulbs and slowly wiped off her stage makeup with cotton balls . . . while knocking back highball glasses of Grey Goose.

It wasn't as if I'd worn myself weary of living some super-woman life I'd carved and now, exhausted, I'd turned to a bottle to escape. That wasn't it. The crazy thing is I had *never* been the person I pretended to be, and the cracks in the façade were spreading. And into the cracks began to flow more and more booze.

• • •

On days when I had to go to the office, I could survive a dry morning by counting the hours until I'd be able to drink at lunch. One of my favorite drinking spots was Kaju, a sushi restaurant not far from my office but not close enough for my co-workers to frequent. It was small and family-run with a long sushi bar. The rolls, sashimi, and sushi under the glass always looked fresh and tempting, but the real draw was the machine at the end of the sushi bar that heated up the sake. It looked like a polished, metal soft-serve ice cream machine.

One morning in the office, just after eleven, it became clear to me that I couldn't hold out until twelve-thirty to drink. I couldn't concentrate on anything on my computer screen. My hands shook too much to keep a pen steady and my legs were bouncing up and down like a punk band drummer's. A thin layer of sweat covered my neck and chest.

Screw it. "Marie, I have an early lunch. I'll be on my phone if you need me," I said to my assistant. I slung my coat and purse over my arm and swished past her, not meeting her eye.

I sneaked out the back of the building and jumped into a cab. My knees bounced during the entire ride and I buried my head in my hands. Let's *go*.

"Hello!" the owner's wife said with a big wave as I walked into Kaju at 11:30 a.m. Her hair was up in a tight bun and she wore an apron with what appeared to be the restaurant's name spelled out in Japanese letters.

"Hi!" I said, utterly relieved to be in the dark restaurant with the magic sake machine.

"The sake is not hot yet. Very sorry," she said. She switched on the machine and it whirred into action. I should have been embarrassed that at eleven thirty in the morning she felt compelled to apologize for not having my booze ready. Instead, I sat at a table for four and stared at the machine, watching for a sign that it was time.

Relief finally came in the form of the three hot sakes that accompanied my California roll. With my body calmed down, I went to the restaurant's bathroom and pulled out the toothbrush and toothpaste I always carried. Three brushings and three sticks of gum later, I headed back to the office. It was almost 1:00 p.m. Now I would count the hours until five o'clock.

10

Not long after the morning drinking
started, cocaine also found its way onto the breakfast menu.
Amped up on coke, I never felt drunk, and I never looked
drunk. I looked happy. "You're always smiling!" colleagues often
chirped at me.

"It's the coke!" I wanted to say. "And I'm putting on an act!
I'm a complete fraud! I'm actually an addict who can't get out of
bed without wine and a line!" But, I didn't say that. I'd say things
like, "Life is good!"

Addiction seemed to be playing a game with me, upping
the stakes and waiting to see if I'd fold. I needed to drink a bottle of wine to get the buzz that used to come from one glass. I
had to become quicker and cleverer with my lies. *How* did I get
this bruise on my arm? An honest answer would have been "I
have no idea. I probably fell out of a cab." But like lightning I
could launch, "Stupid subway door was closing just as I was getting out." *Why* didn't I show up at your wedding shower? "I was
just going to call you! You won't believe this. I got food poisoning—ended up in the freaking ER."

Then there were the "out of sight" transgressions. Nobody knew that I had stopped contributing to my 401(k) because I fully expected to be dead by forty. No one would have guessed that I never got manicures anymore because no matter how much I drank I couldn't keep my hands from shaking. And I had to work harder to convince myself that the paranoia didn't mean I was going crazy. I lived in constant fear of being found out, and that made me more and more reclusive. The less time spent with people, the less chance of being discovered. But snorting cocaine alone on my couch also made me feel like a degenerate. Thanks to addiction I was desperate to be alone and I dreaded being alone.

• • •

My brother's first child was born on a rainy Wednesday in July 2003. When my mother called at 3:00 p.m., I was at home working on a proposal and doing lines of cocaine off of my favorite mirror. I switched the call to speaker and picked at what I hoped was just ground-in cigarette ash on the navy blue cotton slipcover. Then I opened a new pack of cigarettes.

"Wait, you're not making sense," my mom said. "If you're not in the office, why can't you just get in a car now and leave for the hospital before rush hour? The bridge is going to be murder after four o'clock." I was silent, distracted by the stain on the slipcover. "For chrissake, Lisa, your brother had a baby! What are you doing that could be more important?" *You really don't want to know what I'm doing,* I thought. I picked up the razor and scraped perfect little white powder rows on the glass.

I took a deep breath. "I told you, I'm working! I stayed home so I could concentrate on this pitch without the phone ringing all day. I'll get in a car as soon as I get this out. I promise." The part about the pitch was true. The implication that it needed to be done that day was a lie.

"All right, do what you want," she said. "I'll see you whenever you get here." I pictured her shaking her head while trying to figure out how to end a call on the cell phone. I made sure the call had disconnected and then screamed, "Get a clue! I don't give a shit!"

My family had already been at the hospital for hours—all of them right there since my sister-in-law Andrea had gone into labor. Why was I dragging? Was I jealous of my brother's happy marriage and new kid? Was I upset to be pushing forty without any love prospects? The real answer was that because I didn't have to show up in the office, all I wanted to do was be alone, drink, and do coke. Nothing was more important, not even the birth of my niece. That was how my brain now worked. It wasn't my brother's happiness that I resented. It was being lured away from drugs.

It stinks in here, I suddenly thought, sniffing under my bare arm. *Did I shower yesterday? Probably not.* I'd been alternating between cold shaking and sweating for the past forty-eight hours so I was gamey. *Where did I put those scented candles?*

I grabbed the straw to do another line. OK, two. But I had to be careful, I was running low. Sitting back, I watched my right knee bounce up and down uncontrollably and felt my pulse thunder. I didn't dare check my heart rate. A loud buzzing sound thrummed through my head. *Why do they even care if I'm there? It's not like the baby is going anywhere.*

The phone rang again. I jumped. It was my brother. I coughed, took a deep breath, and sat up straight before answering. "Yo, Big Daddy! How's it going?"

"Good," he answered. "When are you getting out here?" Great. Mom had put him up to calling. I'd become a family project.

"Soon, soon. I'm just finishing up here. I'm about to call the car service. I can't wait to see you guys!"

There was no way to put off seeing the baby. Then I'd be the sister who didn't care. Any normal woman would be excited to become an aunt for the first time. She'd be speeding to the hospital, already having ordered a monogrammed silver bracelet and a handmade baby blanket. Not Auntie Lisa. I sat right there on the couch wondering if any small baggies of coke might have fallen behind my dresser.

My entire body was trembling, a low-grade, insistent rumbling as if someone had dropped a quarter into a vibrating couch. Henry hadn't called me back yet about when he could get here with more coke, so I resorted to calling his cell phone and leaving a message. This direct contact was a breach of the drug service's protocol, so I violated it only in emergencies. I would have called him directly more often if it wouldn't have gotten Henry in trouble, or worse, gotten me blacklisted from my best drug connection.

The thought of going without booze while crashing from a two-day bender was terrifying. I pictured myself huddled in some hospital corner drenched in sweat and catching vomit in my open hands. Maybe the hospital cafeteria sold wine? If they did, I could say I was having a drink to celebrate. "Anyone else want one?" I could ask. Or even better, I could pick up a bottle of champagne on my way out of the city to celebrate. Excellent idea! But then I'd have to share it with all those people and I'd get barely a full glass. *Bring two bottles? Three?*

I padded barefoot into the kitchen and emptied the last of the double bottle of Yellow Tail cabernet into my juice glass. In a ritual held over from college, I hummed "Taps," as the glass bottle clanked among its fellow dead soldiers in a plastic bucket at the bottom of my kitchen pantry. I had to be careful about throwing them away. Recycling items in my building were to be left next to the elevators on Mondays and Thursdays. That meant that everyone on the floor could see what was being tossed, so I dumped my empties on different floors each week.

Damn, it's so much easier to stay stocked up with wine than coke, I thought as I willed Henry to call me. The guys at Stuyvesant Square Liquors loved me. They were always right there with a case of double bottles shortly after I called, and in return I tipped the delivery people well. I also tried to tidy myself up before they arrived. I'd wipe off smeared makeup and pull my unkempt hair into a ponytail. There was usually no time to do much about my outfits, so I'd just try to find a clean t-shirt and boxer shorts. Maybe they'd think I'd been busy cleaning. I'd throw strewn clothes into my bedroom and clear away evidence of smoking or drinking from the view of someone standing at the front door. Then I'd take a deep breath and plaster a fake smile before opening the door. But around that time I had developed a weird, sporadic twitch in my right eye. The delivery guy might have thought I was winking at him. God knows who else thought I was flirting. It was just another reason not to leave my apartment.

Back on the couch, I lit another cigarette. I pictured my brother about to let me hold his newborn, and I realized that my extended hands looked as if they belonged to someone who had just witnessed a murder. There was just no stopping the tremors. He'd be appalled, wouldn't he?

Wait, why didn't I tell my family that I have a cold? They never would have let me near the newborn. I used a work excuse—rookie mistake. I was slipping, losing my ability to stay one step ahead. A year or even a few months ago, I would have answered the phone coughing.

Shit, I thought. *I have to do this.* I crawled onto my bed and called the office car service, giving myself an hour. Standing up to go to the bathroom gave me a massive head rush, so I braced myself against the door frame. The fluorescent light reflected the yellow bathroom walls, increasing the pallor of my already hideous yellowing skin. *Jesus, my face looks like an old religious scroll. Do I have jaundice?* My eyes were bloodshot and my eyelids puffy enough to be popped.

As I stretched back out on the bed, my slow-motion brain assessed the bruises scattered across my legs. They were yellow, green, and purple. I poked at them, noting which ones appeared to be healing, which were new, and which ones could be linked to a memory. A few had come from banging my legs against the glass coffee table, which I did regularly getting up and down from the couch. Sliding the coffee table farther away would have solved the problem, but then it would have been more difficult for me to lean over for coke, so I just kept adding bruises. I had read that alcoholics bruise easily because their livers don't function properly. Huh. Interesting. Where did I leave that wine glass?

While for most people showering was relaxing, for me the shower was a place of discomfort and even lurking danger. The spray felt like piercing pellets of sleet against my skin. And I had to be careful to never let my eyes close for long because I could easily lose balance and fall over. And the rhythm of the falling water, the smell of soap, the texture of shampoo—everything seemed to be trying to nauseate me. I tilted the spray straight down and crouched into the tub, grabbing the sides to steady my way down to sit. The water sprayed my head and ran down my face and back. I scrunched myself as far forward as I could, put my head between my knees, and readied myself for what often came next—the heaving followed by vomiting liquid followed by more heaving. *God, I'm so sick,* I thought.

Post-shower, my hands and feet always swelled up, red and throbbing. I made a mental note to research whether that was also an alcoholic thing. After another huge glass of wine, my heart rate seemed to slow down. I grabbed a few Tums from the giant plastic bottle I kept on the dresser, trying to pick through for the cherry ones. They were the least disgusting.

What did I need to wear? Something nice? No, everyone would be exhausted and casual. Jeans and a sweater would be fine, but they couldn't be in bad shape. Even though this was going to be all about the baby, my mother would inspect me anyway.

I never opened my bedroom curtains, even on beautiful days, so I always dressed in semidarkness. Sometimes the result was that midway through the day, I'd realize that my shirt was stained or my sweater had a few bad pulls in it. It didn't really matter to me, but I worried that people at work would notice. "Why can't she keep her clothes clean or replace that worn out sweater?" I imagined them asking each other. "She makes money. It's called a dry cleaner, for God's sake." My mother, however, would happily comment on my clothes. "What is that? A ketchup stain? Lovey, I know that's one of your favorite sweaters, but it's time for it to go. Really. Don't even give it to Goodwill. It's too late." I took a pair of dark jeans and a black sweater into the light of the living room for inspection. *What a pain in my ass.*

I pulled my hair into a ponytail, and before attempting to put on makeup, I wrapped a couple ice cubes in paper towels and pressed them to my eyelids as I lay across my bed. My heart beat hard every time I stopped moving. Was this going to be the day I fell over from a massive cocaine-induced heart attack? That would ruin my niece's birthday.

Heavy makeup seemed like a good idea for the trip to New Jersey. By the time I was through painting over the battered landscape of my bare face, I thought I looked decent, definitely not my best but better than most of the people I saw getting arrested on *Cops*, so that was something. At this point in my life, my standards had shifted. Just an hour earlier I looked like the kind of drug hag the Feds drag from the door of a trailer as she screams that she doesn't know anything about the meth lab inside.

By the time I got myself dressed and made up, it was about four twenty. I had ten minutes before the car would be downstairs. Before I put away all my drug gear, I used a razor blade to load what remained of the coke into a brown glass bullet, a small container that could hold up to a gram. Unfortunately, there was nowhere near that much in it when I twisted the cap shut. My bag, I needed to sort out my bag. It was an oversized burgundy leather piece that I carried everywhere. It had multiple compartments that could be zipped, concealing their contents from prying eyes. Holding it between my knees, I sifted through it to make sure that nothing incriminating was visible. I loaded one side pouch with my cigarettes and the coke bullet, took a deep breath, and stood up to leave. On the way out, I looked at myself in the mirror by the front door. "I hate you," I said to my reflection. It was a sure sign that I was starting to crash when my usual, "fuck you," degenerated to "I hate you."

The Lincoln Town Car sat waiting, engine running, with a white plastic sign in the window that read the car number and my name. The driver flipped open the locks and I climbed into the back seat. I always loved the feeling of sliding across those Town Car leather seats and breathing in the myriad of scents—cherry-pine car freshener, stale cigarette smoke, lingering perfume, and whatever deli sandwich the driver had just eaten.

We would cross the George Washington Bridge and could be at Hackensack Hospital in half an hour. The driver was heavyset, and under his black blazer he wore a white shirt that pulled at the buttons and exposed his undershirt. His head was huge and was topped with a swarm of Albert Einstein hair. "You have voucher or gold card?" he asked in a thick Russian accent. He had turned his head to face me from the front seat, but his thick, sausage fingers still gripped the steering wheel.

"Gold card," I answered. My nose had started to run, so I pulled out a tissue to blot my upper lip as I handed him the card.

"OK. Thank you. Traffic very bad. Rain, accidents. Traffic very bad," he warned.

The crash from my binge started hitting hard, and I slid down into the back seat, suddenly exhausted. Could I do a bump of coke from the bullet if I sunk down low enough back here? No, I can't do that. This is the office's car service. I can't be that stupid. These drivers are like cabbies, they see everything.

Fifteen seconds later I didn't care. I needed a bump. Once we got onto the FDR Drive, the highway noise would be louder. I dropped my bag to the floor where the driver couldn't see. Then I blew my nose to clear it and to accustom the driver to hearing my nasal sounds. Fishing the bullet out of the side pocket, I set it up, sticking my head halfway into my bag to take the hit. No impact. So I took another. Shit, I was really running out of blow.

The driver wasn't kidding about the traffic. Before we even approached the 63rd Street exit, we were all but stopped. I slouched on the passenger side with my head resting in the corner of the back seat, tissue held under my nose. I watched the raindrops form patterns on the window. They would pool and pull each other down in streaks, slowing as they joined each other and then speeding up as they approached the next drop. I felt like tracing their paths with my finger, but I couldn't be bothered to lift my hand. There was something comforting about the way the drops settled at the bottom of that downward path. Rest, I thought, they got to rest at the end.

The cars were packed tightly enough for me to stare out the window at the driver of the silver luxury car in the lane to our right. He looked like a businessman on his nightly commute home, wearing a zombie-like expression as he stared ahead. What was on his mind? Had he been drinking today? Probably. He must have had a chance during lunch at least. If someone had an opportunity to drink, why wouldn't they?

The tiny gusts of coke hadn't really helped, and the post-binge crash seemed to be pulling my blood down my body and into my swollen feet. Was I going to puke again? Riding in the back of cars always made me a little sick, but the stop-and-go of the traffic that afternoon brought the nausea on in record time. Why did these drivers always have to hit the gas and then slam on the brakes? Moving around might help, I thought, so I pulled my compact mirror out of my bag to check my nose, just for something to do. It was running pretty steadily, but it had also become red from my aggressive wiping. I really looked as if I had a cold, and I chastised myself again for not thinking of the illness excuse fast enough. Even worse, thanks to the extreme dehydration of a long binge that had turned me into a sponge, my foundation and blush were soaking into my skin. My pores looked like mini manhole covers and the carsickness had turned me ghost-light green.

I suddenly realized that this plan was ridiculous. Only another drug addict would think I looked passable. What would happen when I arrived at the hospital? A nurse or security guard would see me shuffling up to the front desk and immediately announce, "The emergency room entrance is around the corner." "No, no," I'd say, with fake enthusiasm and a smile, trying to open my half-shut eyes. "I'm here to visit the maternity ward!

My brother's wife just had a baby!" The joy in my voice would so excite the person at reception that they'd overlook the fact that I was the color of an unripe banana with a dripping red nose.

Just distract yourself, I thought. *You have to show up for this baby thing.* Traffic continued to slog, and my brain became crowded with visions of drug and alcohol offenses that I had committed against my family. I thought of Saturday mornings when I would drink vodka sodas at the dive bar in the Port Authority Bus Terminal before catching the 8:10 ShortLine bus to visit my parents. The bartender was great, mostly because he made no eye contact. It was the same with the bar patrons at that hour. We had a mutual understanding that only true alcoholics would be in a skeevy bar before eight in the morning. There also were the times I did lines of coke off the top of the guest bathroom toilet at my parents' house. They never picked up on it, but why would I expect them to? They had no children smarmy enough to do such a thing.

What if I dashed into the hospital and quickly said that I was exhausted and was probably coming down with something? That might earn me a quick in and out—and points for the effort. The car driver seemed cool; maybe he would even wait and run me back into the city if I could get my family to kick me out of the room fast enough.

My head was throbbing with the chatter of ten thoughts bashing into three imagined conversations, and then it happened. A buzz coming from the floor of the car sent me lunging for my bag. *Please, please, please, God. Let it be Henry!* Grabbing the phone as if grasping for a life preserver, I read the number on the screen. "YES, YES, YES!" I shouted. The driver gave me a quick glance over his shoulder and then turned back to the snarled traffic, unfazed.

"YO!" I yelled into the phone as I answered.

"Yo," Henry said. "You home? I'm not far. I can make a quick stop by."

"Yes!" I barked. "I'm not there right now, but I can be back in about fifteen minutes. Wait give me twenty," I said, adding time for an ATM stop.

"OK. No more than that, though. I'll need to roll. I'm the only one out right now."

"No problem! I'll see you soon."

We were just about to the 63rd Street exit. "Excuse me, sir," I leaned forward. "This traffic is too crazy. I'm not going to be able to make it to the hospital in time. Can you please turn around?"

"You pay fare either way," he said.

"Yeah, that's no problem. Just turn around. Here, can you make this exit?" I directed, desperate to not waste more time crawling all the way uptown before turning around.

"It's OK. I can make it." *God bless his focus. God bless Russia.*

"So, I really need to get to the corner of 23rd Street and First Avenue right away. Can you please make it as fast as possible?" "Yes, lady. Going fast as I can. I drop you, I get new fare. We want same thing."

Sitting back I thought, *I really just did this. I turned the car around.* Now I had to tell my family that I wasn't showing up. I was seriously not going to show up to meet my only brother's first child. *Well, screw them if they end up pissed off at me. I'm six months behind on my own problems. I'm a fucking drug addict and I need to meet my dealer. Can't this fucking Russian drive any faster?*

As we started back south on the FDR, I took a deep breath and dialed my brother's cell number while I was still feeling self-righteous enough to call him. This was the flogging I

146

had coming to me. The self-flagellation would come later. *Stay focused*, I thought. In twenty minutes, I'd be back in my safe house and Henry would sell me a handful of happiness. Just dial. The phone rang five times before my brother's voicemail picked up. Did he see that it was me calling? *Did my brother just ignore my call?* He knew why I was calling, didn't he? I'll bet he tossed the phone on the bed in disgust.

Thank God he didn't pick up. I left a pathetic message. "Oh my God, I'm in the car and I've never seen such dead-stopped traffic. It's a total rainstorm and there are accidents everywhere. I'm so, so sorry, but it would take me like two hours to get out there and then visiting hours will be ending. I feel terrible about this, but I promise I'll get out there this weekend." At that point, it probably didn't matter to either of us what kind of bullshit seeped from my mouth. It probably surprised neither of us that it would be two weeks before I'd find my way to New Jersey and first hold the baby.

11

In the fall of 2003, I started going to work under the influence. I could no longer wait until lunch to infuse my bloodstream with more alcohol, so I would drink even before leaving my apartment. One morning before a monthly meeting with a team of partners I downed an oversized screwdriver; when I was the one mixing, that was a tall glass of vodka with some orange juice for color. Then I did a few fat lines of coke.

Paranoia haunted me whenever I was in a public place that wasn't a bar. I was sure that people could smell the alcohol. In the elevator of my office building I pictured people sniffing the air to figure out where the smell was coming from. Straight-faced behind my sunglasses, I would lower my head and exhale into my hand to check for booze breath. Sometimes I'd even imagine that I'd failed to notice a cop and his drug-sniffing dog at the back of the elevator. Those dogs scared the shit out of me, and it wasn't rare for me to walk an extra seventeen blocks to avoid running into one in the subway. Even with not a wisp of coke on me, I was sure they'd know. Paranoia turned me into Pig-Pen, walking around the city followed by a little drug cloud.

Swiping my key card, I walked past the glass security doors onto the twenty-third floor. My office was large, with a wall of windows looking out on the tourist chaos of Times Square below—probably middle-aged men with cameras around their necks, Europeans wearing telltale sandals with socks, and t-shirt vendors hawking their wares from behind carts. I gazed down and wondered how many of them had already had a drink.

I flopped into my ergonomically correct chair and wheeled myself to my desk, dropping my head in my hands. Breathe, breathe. I was wearing one of my better black suits with a baby blue Ann Taylor button-down shirt and black Ferragamo heels. With my head still in my hands, I sat up straight and rubbed the heels of my hands against my temples. Get your shit together, girl. It's showtime.

The phone on my desk rang and Jerry's office number flashed. "Hey!" I answered on the second ring.

"DOG! You made it in on time!" He was probably cleaning his oval eyeglasses with the tail of his dress shirt and then squirting Visine into his bloodshot eyes.

What? I bristled in self-defense. "Of course I made it in on time. I have a meeting this morning."

"Settle, settle. I'm just giving you a hard time. You sounded a little banged up last night. I'm double-checking."

"I wasn't bad last night!" I wanted to end the call and get back to focusing.

"If you say so," he said.

"I have to go. Meet up for a pop after work?" I asked.

"Done! Just let me know where and when. Later." He always hung up first.

He'd rattled me. I hadn't been that bad the night before (had I?). The coke was put away by ten o'clock, and the combination of Tylenol PM and red wine put me down before midnight. When I'd gotten out of bed at six fifteen that morning, I felt as close as I ever did to refreshed. *Just get that first drink down and all will be OK.*

I stopped in the ladies room to check my lipstick and inspect my nose for blood. *Should I do a couple of quick bumps out of the bullet in my bag, just for a little extra energy? No, just hold off,* I thought. *Don't risk your nose running all over the meeting.*

In the conference room, I flipped on the lights and placed the necessary documents around the heavy, oval mahogany table and tucked all the rolling leather chairs neatly in their places, and then I examined my handiwork. Perfect. Nothing wrong with that picture. I spat my gum into the trash can before anyone arrived. I assumed that anyone chewing gum before eleven in the morning had been drinking, so I believed others assumed the same.

"Lisa! Good morning. How are you?" Greg, a senior finance partner, breezed into the conference room. Like many old-school partners, he wore suspenders, wireframe glasses, and the furrowed brow of someone who spent his mornings poring over *The Wall Street Journal* on commuter trains. My head was buzzing, but it was just the right buzz. I'd gotten good at teeing up for these meetings, not too loopy, not too jacked. When the balance was just right, the energy in my head felt like the calm hum of a window air conditioner set on low. It created a pleasant purring that didn't call attention to itself.

"All's good!" I answered with a big smile. If the partners liked having you in the room, that was a big deal. It was almost as important for your career as producing creative, well-executed work.

"No sesame bagels this morning, huh?" he asked, bending over the platter.

"Hmm, that's unusual. Should I ask catering?" I asked.

"No, no. That's OK," he answered, looking deflated. *Shit. One demerit. Can he tell I'm drunk? Will he keep a closer eye on me now because of the bagels?*

About a half dozen more partners filed in and exchanged greetings, the scents of their colognes and aftershaves circulating with the smell of coffee and bagel yeast. It was what morning smelled like in Normal World. I'd become more accustomed to the scent of cigarette smoke and the chemicals Henry's supplier used to cut drugs.

Technically, office attire was "business casual," but everyone wore suits. Alanis, the only woman, stood out despite being dressed as conservatively as the men. Women had become the hottest accessory in business development. Every client wanted a female on their team, so partners like Alanis—smart, accomplished, and personable—were in high demand.

"Hey, Alanis," I said, taking a seat across from her.

"Hi Lisa. How are you doing?" She glanced at my plate. "Hungry this morning, huh? You probably worked out already."

Trying to look like anything other than a drug addict, I had grabbed a bagel with cream cheese, grapes, and two mini-muffins.

"Yeah, I guess I am," I answered with my best smile.

Maybe it was just standard food commentary. She couldn't smell booze, could she? She hadn't noticed any of my sniffling, right? Women always checked out what other women were eating, didn't they?

The group settled in around the table, and Rob, the lead partner, started the meeting. "OK. Good morning. Can you all put down your phones?" Instead of engaging in small talk, everyone around the table had been reading from their devices while waiting for the meeting to begin. All of the bowed heads made it look like a prayer circle. There was a pause and shuffling.

"Lisa, I think you have a number of items to report on," Rob said, looking at me expectantly.

I snapped myself back into the meeting. "Yes, yes I do," I said. "OK!" It was as if the director on a movie set had yelled, "Action!" My work brain fully kicked in, and for the next several minutes I focused on delivering my report with the authority of Walter Cronkite.

"On the project finance front, we had a nice uptick in our work last month and brought in three new matters, two in Latin America and one in Asia." I rolled on through my full report, careful to keep my voice steady and make occasional eye contact.

"Perfect," Rob said when I was done. "Nice work. Now let's just go around the table." Just like that, I was done. The weight of the meeting slid off my shoulders as easily as a negligee off a hooker.

It was time for my favorite part of the meeting, trying to decide who else in the room had been drinking and/or doing drugs this morning. According to statistics, up to 20 percent of lawyers had a substance abuse problem.

But "a problem," what exactly did that mean? Getting a DUI? Throwing up at the office Christmas party? Sleeping through an important court date after an all-night bender? Or to have a "problem," did you have to be like me, by 8:00 a.m. have a bloodstream dancing with cocaine and enough booze to blow over the legal limit?

It was hard to concentrate on the rest of the meeting, but I was good at faking it with an occasional nod or scrunching of my eyebrows to show acknowledgment.

Then a jolt of fear shot straight through me. *Holy shit, did I leave my open pack of cigarettes next to my computer? Fuck!*

There's a tiny baggy loaded with coke in that pack! What if someone walks into my office and picks it up? I might as well walk out to security and present my wrists to be handcuffed.

Fuck. I have to get out of this room right now. But I can't leave. Sweat started to form on the back of my neck, and saliva filled my mouth as if vomit was going to rise. My perfect buzz was crushed, and I was back to being just a paranoid cokehead verging on hyperventilation. Everything in the room started to swirl.

Heather. Allison. Rick. Any of them might have cruised into my office to bum a cigarette. They knew that I always had smokes and that I always shared, so if any one of them saw the open pack on my desk, they would feel free to pick it up and reach in. Fuck! I was a wreck. I had to get back to my office. Heather and Rick might be cool but Allison, she was an associate on partner track. She couldn't find coke in the office and not report it. She wouldn't take that risk just for a smoking buddy. And *would* Heather and Rick really be cool about drugs in the office? *Fuck, is one of them walking in there right now? Is my career being covered with lighter fluid as I sit here praying that nobody tosses a match?*

I dug my fingernails into my hands. *Relax,* I told myself. *Breathe. No one's walking into your office. No one's touching your cigarette pack. Remain calm.*

But what if someone is? What if someone is??? My thundering heart rate started to scare me. I took more deep breaths. *Shit, I must be calling attention to myself. Calm down, woman. You don't need a room full of heavy-hitting partners thinking you're practicing for childbirth.*

When the meeting wrapped about forty minutes later, the partners gathered to chat over the buffet and their second cups of coffee. I hurried to the door as fast as I could without running, and once out the door I sprinted past the elevator and ran like an EMT down the stairs.

When I rounded the corner to my office, I saw it. The distinct gold shimmer off the corner of my Marlboro Lights pack. Thank God! It hadn't been touched.

I slammed my door shut and lunged at the pack. *Fuck me. I left a baggie of coke on my office desk!* I fell into my chair and put my head between my knees. Taking deep, slow breaths, I tried to calm down by reminding myself that nothing bad had happened. After several minutes, my heartbeat stopped thumping like a bass drum. But there was no escaping the fact that I had just left cocaine out in the open, on a desk owned by my employer. My employer, the law firm.

12

I woke up one Sunday a couple of weeks
later with a horn section blaring in my head. My mouth tasted
like wallpaper paste. Water, I needed water. As I rustled the
sheets to move, I kicked a leg. *Fuck. What happened last night?*

A mop of near-black curls twisted on the pillow next to
me. A bare, male arm stretched up toward the headboard as if
it were grasping for something. Rolling over to get a look at the
face without waking the guy—whoever the hell he was—I saw
thick dark eyebrows over deep-set eyes and a mole on the left
cheek. *Oh shit! It was the cute guy I'd been seeing around my
building. Shit. Shit. Shit. What did I fucking do?*

His face was definitely younger than mine. *Jesus, how old
is too old for one-night, blackout stands?* He looked peaceful as
he slept, but a tornado of memories began to whirl in my brain.
Images from the night before appeared in snippets, like tiny
pick-up trucks and cows swirling around the storm's eye. The
elevator. We ran into each other in the elevator. *Name, name,
what's his name? Mark! Yes, Mark!* How satisfying it was to
recall the name that quickly. I used to take pride in things like
learning to flip a canoe and re-enter it in record time or finishing

157

the Sunday *New York Times* crossword puzzle in pen. These days all I had to do to earn a mental high-five was remember the name of the half-naked guy in my bed.

I had a flash of us sitting on my bed drinking wine, and I saw two empty glasses on my dresser. Okay, so I'd invited him in for a glass of wine. *But how did we end up in here? Did we at least start in the living room?* My panties were still on. Just my panties. *Okay, we probably didn't have sex.* The rest of my clothes were in a pile on the floor. Not great, but it certainly could be worse. Peeking under the covers, I saw that Mark had underwear on, too. *OK. Breathe, breathe. What the hell else happened here last night?* I dragged my brain like a river that held the missing bodies.

Coke. My nose was numb so it couldn't have been long since I'd used. Did he do it too or did I just sit on the bed like a hardcore drug addict blowing lines in front of a total stranger? My gut told me I'd been doing coke alone.

At least he wasn't a cop. He was always in street clothes when I'd seen him around the building. *But what if he's an undercover cop! No, I'd be arrested by now. Unless he's staking me out to get to my dealer. Is he going to arrest me and threaten a Class C felony drug charge unless I testify against Henry?*

Something told me that these weren't the morning thoughts of most women after a night with a new guy.

I needed a drink. Wearing my red and white Indian print robe, I walked into the kitchen. There were two empty wine bottles on the counter. Not terrible, but then again, I was already in a drunken blackout when I met Mark in the elevator.

I opened the refrigerator door and held onto it for support. What to drink, what to drink—white wine from that open bottle or a couple shots of vodka? I grabbed the wine and drank directly out of the bottle. Speed was important in case Mark wandered into the kitchen. The wine slithered a cold soothing trail down my throat. It also quieted the trumpets in my head, so I took a few more long swigs.

In the living room, I lit a cigarette. As I squinted away from the sun streaming through the window, I turned on the air conditioner to mask the smell of smoke. Had Mark smoked last night? He didn't look like a smoker. He looked like someone I might have known in Hebrew school, one of the over-confident little brats who grew up in the suburbs and then moved to Manhattan to become a big swinging dick.

Despite having just slugged back more wine than most people would drink at a dinner party, I stood there shaking. Strands of hair hung around my face, and even they were shaking. Who has hair that shakes? *I'm a disaster*, I thought. At least it was Sunday.

Feeling like I might be able to fall back to sleep, I brushed my teeth, gargled with Listerine, and tiptoed back to the bedroom. I dropped my robe on top of the clothing pile, pulled on an old US Open t-shirt and a pair of men's boxers, and climbed back into bed, careful not to touch or wake Mark.

A couple of hours later, I regained consciousness and realized that Mark was splayed across me as if he'd fallen from a building. His left arm stretched over my back, and his hand rested near my face like a claw. Ugh. I still didn't want to wake him, but I had to pee. As I slid out from under him, he let out a sleepy moan and rolled over. Like a sewer rat, I scurried into the bathroom before he could fully awaken.

There it was, the mirror. I had two mascara black eyes— Courtney Love by daylight. Soap and water took care of that, but there wasn't much to be done with the rest of me. I had a weird combination of bloat from alcohol, droop from lack of sleep, and gauntness from lack of food; for the latter, I thanked cocaine. There was no way through the knots and frizz in my hair, so I pulled the mess back into a ponytail. More Listerine made sense.

Mark would probably run screaming once he woke up and got a good look at me in the sunshine. That was fine with me. I had a *Law & Order* marathon to watch and wine to drink. No need for him to linger and ruin my Sunday.

"Good morning," he cooed with a big smile when I walked back into the bedroom. My God, his teeth were straight and lightbulb white. He reached his arms over his head, stretched the length of his body, and moaned in a way that seemed awfully comfortable for a guy in a total stranger's bed. Where were confusion, shame, and the signature male impulse to get the hell out? With this guy there was no scrambling for his clothes or fumbling his way to the front door. Instead he looked at me with the cozy face of a man who was perfectly happy right where he was. "How are you?" he purred.

"I'm fine," I answered, still standing in the doorway. *I'm fine.* It was astonishing how many times a day that lie tumbled from my mouth.

Mark pulled the covers away from my side of the bed and patted the mattress. "Come back to bed," he said.

Was he serious? The place smelled like a hotel suite after a bachelor party, and I looked like the hooker who'd forgotten that her shift was over.

"That's OK," I said with a shrug. "I'm kind of awake now." *Should I say I need to run to the drugstore? If I don't come back for a couple of hours, will he take the hint?*

"OK," he said, still smiling. Wow, he was happy in the morning. To my relief, he sat up and started pulling his jeans on. I was dying to ask how old he was and what he did for a living, but he must have told me that the night before. Anything told to me after five o'clock blew from my mind like jet fuel from an F-14.

As he pulled on his navy blue polo shirt, he said, "I could really use some coffee. Do you want to grab breakfast?" He did another big stretch, arms overhead and back bent. He was shorter than I remembered.

"You know what? I'd love to, but I have to work today and I really should get started. It's already nine-thirty!"

"No problem. I'll get going," he said, pulling on his Puma sneakers. "I've got stuff to do for school today, too."

Oh my God. A fucking student? Please let him at least be a PhD candidate who came late to education.

"Oh, what are you working on?" There was a good chance I should have known the answer, but it was more reasonable to forget about a project than the fact that he was a student. Why was I starting a conversation when I needed another drink?

"Just an assignment for one of my finance classes. I'm working with a group, so we're going to meet up later at the Baruch library." *Yes! Now I know where he goes to school. But why is he still in school? Drop it.*

"Sounds good," I said, moving toward the apartment door and hoping he would follow. How weird that he was now going to return to his fourth-floor apartment and not even leave the building to go home. This was a new achievement—creating an embarrassing scene with a guy without even having to step outside.

When we got to the door, he wrapped both arms around me and gave me a bear hug. "I had so much fun with you last night. I'm really glad we met, finally," he said with a little laugh. *Oh shit.* Another memory came trickling in. I'd admitted to calling him "the cute guy from the building." *Somebody please shoot me with a rhino rifle.* He released me from the hug and stood back with his hands still on my arms. "I want to take you out on a real date," he said. "Can we do that this week? What night's good for you?" he asked.

What was *wrong* with the guy? He was cute and nice and way too young for me. What could he possibly want with me?

"Sure," I said. "Tuesday is probably OK." *Just leave*, I thought, already working on my cancellation excuse.

"Great. Give me your number." He followed me into the kitchen where I turned my back to hide my shaking hand as I wrote my number on a pad. "Did you just get back from a trip or something?" he asked.

"No, why?"

"You have a ton of mail on your counter. Looks like a couple of months' worth!" *Thanks, Inspector Clouseau.* I barely opened my mail in those days, instead letting it pile up until I "had time" to go through it. Seeing the pile with fresh eyes, it was ridiculous.

"Oh, that's just accumulated crap," I said. "I pay my bills by phone mostly."

Mark gave me a curious look, and we both stood there until he realized that I wasn't going to offer any further defense of mail mountain. Then he gave me a quick kiss on the lips and headed to the door. "I'll call you about Tuesday. Thanks again for last night!" he said and bounced down the hall.

I triple-locked the door behind him and went straight for a cabernet. Just holding the bottle gave me comfort. Soon it would be open and I'd be able to start forgetting the little bit I could still remember about last night. With a large glass in hand, I lit a cigarette and turned on CNN, wondering how much coke I had left for today.

• • •

Remarkably, Mark didn't go away. He hung around my apartment as often as I'd let him. On those nights, we ordered in Chinese food, sushi, or pizza. We used cheap plates, paper towels for napkins, and my glass coffee table for dining in front of the television.

A sneak look at his driver's license revealed that I was ten years older than he. What was the appeal for this guy, other than the fact that getting to me was as easy as pressing the elevator's "up" button? Sure, I had a great job and a nice apartment, but I was also divorced, smoked like a European, and drank like Ernest Hemingway. Not to mention that while killing a night watching cop shows, I was as likely to blow a line of coke as I was to each a chocolate chip cookie.

Mark drank the way normal people did. On a weeknight, he might have a beer or two. On weekends, maybe a little more, and then he'd cut himself off. And no drugs. Why didn't he ever say anything about the coke?

What I learned was that my apartment had become a kind of refuge for Mark. He had roommates downstairs, an annoying couple who sat around smoking pot all day. Turns out that I looked like a real self-starter just for having a job that didn't require a paper hat.

• • •

"Hurry up!" I screeched at Mark as we stumbled over snow and ice on East 18th, heading to Pete's Tavern for brunch one Sunday morning in December, a couple months after we met. I flailed my arms at him. "Let's go!" It was five minutes after noon, five minutes after restaurants could start serving liquor. "There aren't going to be any booths left!" My heavy work boots and old Levi's were half-covered in snow.

163

The first major storm of the year had just hit New York and the city looked like a postcard. In no time that sparkly white snow would be dirt-brown-and-pee-yellow slush, so running around in it now seemed like an urban responsibility. But I had a goal. Mark, however, seemed happy to be out in the fresh, cold air and in no particular rush.

"I should have brought my camera," he said. "Black and white pictures of this would be so cool." He was hunting the clear spots on the sidewalk to plant his feet, careful not to skid in his sneakers. I stopped ahead of him and stood with my hands on my hips, and he said, "Just go ahead if you're that anxious."

"OK, I'll meet you there," I said. I left him navigating the street like an old lady trying to keep her precious Pradas out of puddles. "It's just that I'm freezing!" I yelled back at him, taking the next two blocks at double speed.

Sunday brunch at Pete's was my favorite, mostly because it was one of those bars that always made you feel respectable for drinking, even if you were the first one to dash through the door and belly up to the bar. The added festivity of the holiday season seemed to make getting tanked an obligatory act.

Pete's, one of the oldest bars in the city, had two large windows facing Irving Place, both of which had "PETE'S" written in an arch of gold letters outlined in black. For the holidays, the windows were framed from within with strands of little white lights. Outside, strands of multicolored lights hung above the front entrance, and two giant wreaths hung above those. That morning seemed particularly festive to me, with little snow piles teetering on the top of the metal gates that surrounded the empty outdoor seating area.

I pushed open the heavy dark wood door, giddy with anticipation of the bustling crowd and the long, dark bar that reflected the bright glow of the red lights that lined the ceiling. But something was off. There couldn't have been more than ten people in the front of the restaurant. It was already ten after twelve! The booze should be flowing. Where was everybody? In the back room? Home having their cocktails in bed? And it got worse. Some of the people weren't even drinking. They were there for the food. I felt like a birthday girl, sure that she's throwing open the door to her surprise party only to find that she's interrupted a Bible study.

The room smelled of spilled beer and the soap they'd tried to clean the floor with. "Just one?" the waitress asked, appearing in front of me with a single menu in her hand. The waiters and waitresses at Pete's were indifferent when a party of one showed up. Every day they must have seen people get hammered on their own. Some of those waiters and waitresses probably did the same thing when they weren't working. The most welcoming places were the ones that employed functional drunks, and functional drunks knew where to find all the most welcoming places.

"Two, actually," I said. "We're going to be two."

"How about this booth right up front?" Like all the furniture, the booths were a heavy, dark wood with lots of scratches, and the tables were covered with red-and-white checkered plastic tablecloths. I had a picture in my office of my dad and me clinking glasses over one of those tablecloths on the day I was admitted to the bar. After the swearing-in ceremony, we'd gone straight to Pete's to celebrate.

"That's perfect," I said, flopping down as if I hadn't sat in hours. The TV over the bar was tuned in to the football pre-game show. I was sure that by kickoff, the place would be standing room only. "Can I get a Bloody Mary, please?" No sign of Mark yet, so I added, "Can you make it a double?"

"Sure thing. Only the one drink comes with brunch, though. I'll have to charge you for the second vodka," the waitress said, taking her pencil out of her hair to start the tab.

"Not a problem."

"I'll grab you another menu." As she walked away, I rubbed my hands together for warmth and in anticipation of that fat cocktail. I was shaking badly because with Mark hanging around·in the morning, I hadn't been able to take more than a couple of quick belts from a vodka bottle while he was in the shower.

Mark appeared. He stood over me and unzipped his puffy, down coat, peeled off his knit hat, and shook his hair. I could feel the cold that hadn't yet melted off of him. "Good thing you risked cracking your head open to get a booth," he said, looking around at the empty bar.

 Without lifting my head, I said. "I told you. I was cold."

The waitress reappeared with my Bloody Mary, served in a pint glass with a grinning lemon on the side and a crisp stalk of celery standing at attention in the middle. She set it in front of me, and I tried not to grab it immediately. "Right, you were cold," Mark said as he sat down.

"What can I get you, hon?" the waitress asked.

"Diet Coke, thanks," he said. *Fuck you*, I thought, rolling my eyes. He couldn't seriously want a Diet Coke at noon on a Sunday. *You're not going to make me feel bad. Tomato juice with vodka is normal on a weekend, Your Honor.*

Mark ordered a bacon cheeseburger, extra bacon. He felt about pork products the way I felt about martinis. There were never enough. I ordered a chicken Cobb salad, no bacon, no blue cheese, dressing on the side.

I picked at my salad and debated how long I'd have to wait before ordering my second drink. Mark was always a slow eater, but he seemed to be taking an inordinate amount of time with his burger.

"So that movie was great last night," Mark said. "It's so much better hanging out at home than running around the city freezing your ass off between bars."

What did we watch? What did we watch? I couldn't recall a thing about the movie, so I changed the subject. "You're twenty-eight years old! You should want to go out and party on a Saturday night!"

"Nah," he said, swirling a long French fry around in ketchup. "It's OK sometimes, but it's different when you don't have a ton of cash. You've never lived in the city on a budget." True.

"I'm meeting Jerry to watch the Jets game downtown after brunch," I said.

"You're not going back to the apartment? I have my stuff there," he said. "You know this would be a lot easier if I had my own keys." He wasn't looking me in the eye.

"To my apartment?" I asked.

"Yes, to your apartment. I sleep there practically every night."

"I don't have a problem opening the door for you."

"But if I had keys, you wouldn't have to. Plus it would be kind of cool for me to work from up there sometimes. You know, without the idiots getting high in the next room all day."

This was a genuine dilemma. Giving him keys to my place was a big deal. There was a lot that went on in my space that was not just private, but illegal. What if he walked in when Henry was delivering drugs? Actually, it was Henry I was worried about. If Mark walked in on a drug deal, Henry would freak out and disappear. And then we'd have a problem.

Mark had a point, though. His roommate situation sucked, and I was in a position to help. And I did love spending time with him. But unfettered access to my apartment was out of the question.

"Well, it's not really a problem, but you know, I like living alone. Even though it's great when you're there. So if I give you a key to use the place during the day, you could come over only if we've actually spoken and it works for me."

"That's fair," he said.

"Alright. We can try it." Right away I felt a stomach surge of worry that I'd made a mistake. "Oh, and also you still have to leave in the morning when I get ready for work."

"Why? What's the problem with mornings? Do you not shower or something?"

"No!" I answered. "I need my space to get ready privately and get my head together for the day. I've told you that. Besides, you're just getting keys. You're not moving in."

He nodded. We had an agreement.

13

I should have known it was too good to last.

"You know, most people don't party like that by themselves on Sundays," Mark said while I was watching CNN one Sunday afternoon. As far as he knew, I was on my second glass of wine. And there was only a small amount of coke on a compact mirror in front of me. It seemed reasonable to me, even restrained for a Sunday.

"How do you know what most people do?" I asked, lighting a cigarette. The air was heavy with smoke and stale wine despite all the odor-eliminating candles I often burned. I was still in my boxer shorts and t-shirt. "It's Sunday. Most people have been sitting in sports bars drinking since noon."

"Are you serious?" He was perched on the edge of the couch looking at me as if I'd just said that the Kennedys were killed by other Kennedys. I slid down the couch, farther away from him. The navy blue slipcovers were filthy.

"Absolutely. Maybe not everyone's drinking right now. I mean, some people have kids, but most people . . ." I said, as I tried to think of another rationale he'd go for. "Especially anyone with a job like mine with huge stress all week. Sunday is when everyone with a real job is staring down the barrel of Monday." Mark's thick eyebrows furrowed like a cartoon villain's. I could hear my tone becoming belligerent. "You're a student at twenty-eight years old. You have no idea what it's like to work a job like mine. If I want to blow off steam on a Sunday, I'll do it however I like."

I didn't need some little college kid telling me what was normal. Isn't normal whatever you're used to? My hands had been shaking for ten years. This was my normal. And I knew how much drinking and using I could handle and still keep my job, so things were under control.

"OK, I'm just saying, most people don't drink so much and don't do coke all the time," he said.

"I don't care about what most people do. Maybe if I were just taking some classes and day trading like you, I'd be different..."

"Have you ever thought of going to rehab?" he asked. *What? Has he not been listening?*

"*EXCUSE* ME? Rehab? No, I have *not* thought of going to rehab." I took a long slug from my wine glass. "And even if I did need it, it's not like I could tell my office, 'I'll be out for a month at a FUCKING REHAB.' I can't believe you just said that." *The balls on this kid.* He didn't really know me anyway.

"OK," he said, sinking his fingers into his hair and dropping his head into his hands. "I'm sorry I brought it up. Don't be mad."

"Don't ever bring that up again. Ever." I said. We sat there quietly for a minute and I felt myself sweating. "I think you should probably go downstairs. I kind of want to be alone now." It was Sunday! I needed to be out of my head for as long as possible before Monday rolled around. And I was about to fill my glass again.

Mark didn't fight me and he left. Too bad I was going to have to get rid of him. He was nice to have around.

Late the next morning, Mark called me at work and acted as if nothing had happened. "Hey, what's up? You want to eat dinner tonight?"

"Not if you're going to give me a hard time," I said.

"No, no. I'm sorry about all that. I was just worried about you."

"Well don't be. I'm fine," I answered. "I'll call you when I'm leaving."

As cool as I thought Mark was about my using, I should have seen it coming. He was around a lot, and even though he saw relatively little, he saw enough to make a healthy person wince. Having him around helped me sharpen my sneak skills; as he sat right there on my couch, I was managing to ingest at least twice what he witnessed. The glass bullet filled with coke was tucked into a lipstick case and sat on a shelf behind my bathroom mirror. Lipstick cases were tailor-made to accommodate the one-gram vials that a coke-addicted woman needed to carry or hide. Who would suspect it to be full of blow? A glass of wine in a tumbler was parked in the cabinet underneath the kitchen sink. During an afternoon of slowly sipping wine in front of Mark, I would steal off to the bathroom or the kitchen to bump up with a couple quick blasts of coke or slugs of wine. I knew it was fucked up, but I was good at it, so it made me feel kind of proud.

One morning I had a nine o'clock appointment for my annual mammogram. Wanting to be as "healthy" as possible for the exam, I managed to lay off the coke that morning and had only a glass or so of red wine before I left. All I needed to do was stay steady until I could get home again and balance myself out with wine and coke for the rest of the day.

Returning home from the appointment, I was in a celebratory mood. But as I unlocked my apartment door, I heard the buzz of television news. *Mark's here? What the fuck?*

He was sitting in the chair at my computer desk and swiveled toward me as if I were an office pal interrupting a dull day on the job. "Hey, what are you doing home?" *Wait, is that accusation in his voice?*

"I told you, I had a doctor's appointment. I had to stop back here for something I need for work," I lied, already feeling the shaking and sweating as the timer ticked away the minutes until I would be desperate for another drink.

He stood up and walked toward me. "You were drinking this morning."

I shut the apartment door and stood there, keys still in my hand. "No, I wasn't. And I told you not to come over today. What are you doing here?"

"There's red wine splashed in the sink. It wasn't there when you passed out last night." He had caught me and I was livid.

"Fuck you," I said, giving him my best angry woman glare. I stomped into the kitchen, slammed my keys on the counter, and threw my bag on the floor. The deep, double-sided kitchen sink was white porcelain. A streak of dried red wine ran down one side like a blood trail and swirled in crimson circles around the drain. Turning on the faucet, I grabbed the spray attachment and went after the wine as if I were hosing a filthy car in a summer driveway.

I walked back over to Mark and said, "There's no wine in the sink and I wasn't drinking this morning. Now get out and leave your keys." I felt lightheaded, but I couldn't tell if it was from anger, the need for a drink, or the awful truth of what I'd just done.

"You're crazy," he answered, not leaving. "I talked to my friend's mother about you. She's been sober for twenty years. She says you're an alcoholic and a drug addict. You're cross-addicted and that's way worse than just being one of those. She says if you don't go to rehab, you're going to die and that if you don't admit it and get help I should get as far away from you as I can."

"Really? Your *friend's* mother?" With my hands planted firmly on my hips, I barked at him like a furious school nun. That is, if the nun has the mouth of a Bronx barmaid on a night the Yankees lose to the Red Sox. "Who the *fuck* do you think you are, talking to people about me? And I've told you that I know what I'm doing. I know my goddamned limits. I don't need fucking rehab. There's nothing to rehab. If you think I'm going to spend the rest of my life never drinking again and going to meetings in shithole church basements to drink bad coffee and crybaby my problems to a bunch of losers you're out of your fucking mind."

"If you won't get help, I'm leaving, for real," he said. His eyes were glassy with tears.

"Fine. Nobody's stopping you." He gathered his school bag and the pillows he'd brought up from his apartment. Then he put on his sneakers, and I held the door open for him.

"My keys," I said, as he was leaving. He dropped them gently into my hand and walked out into the hallway. I said "goodbye," slammed the door, and rushed into the kitchen to pour a double-sized glass of wine. Relief, I just needed some relief, even though I felt numb.

14

A few days after Mark's dramatic exit, I sat on a couch at a small party in the Tribeca apartment of Devon's friend Ethan. He was about my age and a successful physician with a wide circle of friends. He was short and fit with thick brown hair sculpted high on his head. As he greeted guests, he flashed big, genuine smiles and threw his head back with laughter that wiggled his rectangular glasses.

Envy erupted in my stomach as I looked around. The art pieces on the walls were real, the kind made by human hands. The furniture was solid and sophisticated, and it not only was appropriate for the large open space, it complemented the art beautifully. Same with the rugs—neutral colors and patterns that picked up flecks of color from the walls. I slurped an expensive merlot that should have been sipped and felt waves of self-hatred. The difference between this apartment and my own made me feel like a grumpy child.

The sound of a jazz album I couldn't identify wafted through the dimly lit room. Why didn't I know anything about jazz? Because irresponsible children don't know anything about jazz.

Devon, Jessica, Russell, Jerry, and David were all there, and we had gathered toward the end of the living room near the large windows overlooking the sparkling city lights. I was tired. So very tired.

"Hey, did you see those pictures of Whitney Houston all messed up?" Devon asked. She wore all black, a fitted cashmere turtleneck, skinny pants with a fancy gold buckle on her belt, and tall riding boots.

"That chick's a mess!" Jerry said. "She should go to the tank. She can afford to go to any one she wants. I'd go to Clapton's place in Antigua." Jerry wore his weekend gear: expensive jeans, a tailored button down shirt, and brown leather loafers. He ground his half-smoked cigarette into an etched pewter ashtray that looked like an expensive Mexican artifact.

I said, "I think I'm an alcoholic."

All five heads whipped toward me. "What are you talking about?" David said.

"I don't know, maybe not," I wimped out.

"Why would you say something like that?" Jessica asked, spreading hummus on a piece of toasted pita bread. Russell tightened his lips and raised his eyebrows. I could see that he was listening closely.

"I don't know," I said. "I drink a lot, more than I should. I overdo it," I said. "You know that. You guys have all seen it."

"Yeah, but a lot of people sometimes drink too much when they go out," David spoke in his lawyer voice. "If you were an alcoholic, you'd be messing up at work. Didn't you just get a big raise?"

"Yeah," I said.

Jessica tried to reason through it. "Maybe you're a heavy drinker, but that's different from being an alcoholic. I think of an alcoholic as someone who needs to drink to sort of 'maintain,' to get through the day."

Right then I could have offered them completely convincing evidence. Just an honest look at an hour-by-hour breakdown of a regular day in my life would have gotten me carted off to rehab. But I let them talk.

"You shouldn't say things like that," Devon said. "You're not an alcoholic."

"Yeah, I think you have this one wrong," David added.

Jerry just stared at his drink.

Of course they had no idea. With our exhausting work schedules, we didn't have time to get together very often. They weren't around to see those nights after dinner parties when I went home and drank another bottle of wine. They certainly didn't know that I'd become a morning drinker. But I kept my mouth shut and let my friends file the subject away in a folder labeled "Strange and Unfounded Party Outbursts."

"You're probably right," I said. "I'm probably just burned out from pushing it too hard."

The realization that the most important people in my life didn't really know me filled me with loneliness. I was alone in a little boat floating way out on the open water, and the people on the shoreline were getting smaller and smaller.

15

It was 2:00 p.m. on the first Friday of April 2004, shortly after the party at Ethan's, and I needed to place my drug order for the weekend. I shut the door to my office and dove under my desk to find my purse and grope around for my phone.

There were new messages on my work email and voicemail, but they could wait. I popped three Altoids into my mouth, even though I had already chewed three pieces of gum on the way back from Kaju. Henry, I needed Henry.

After punching in the digits for the drug dealer service, I stared at the phone, willing it to ring. Henry was as predictable as New York potholes in the spring, but I couldn't relax until I got that callback.

I kicked my red high heels into the pile of dress shoes under my desk. It looked like the shoe section on the last day of the Barney's Warehouse sale under there, a bunch of expensive pumps, flats, and boots that I kept in the office so they wouldn't be destroyed on bad weather commutes or caught in subway gratings on the street. But I tossed them around as carelessly as someone throwing strings of beads off a Mardi Gras float.

Scanning my email and pretending to concentrate gave me something to do while the seconds ticked along. In under five minutes, my cell rang. Before speaking, I tried to wipe the Christmas Morning! look off my face as if that would help me to sound less desperate. Apparently I was uncomfortable with the idea of being judged when speaking to people who shoveled life-slaughtering drugs into the hands of trembling addicts. "Hi," I answered.

"Hi, who's this?" It was the same woman who usually gave a callback. She sounded young and healthy and a lot like my administrative assistant who sat just outside my closed office door.

"It's Lisa on East 20th Street. How are you?"

"Oh hey, Lisa. I'm good. How are you doing?"

"Great. Glad it's Friday," I said.

"I bet you are. It'll be about an hour or two. That okay, hon?"

"Sure. Great. 441 East 20th Street. Buzzer 192 in the lobby." She would pass my message to Henry and he'd make the trip. He knew the address well, but I had to be sure there was no chance of confusion.

"Got it," she said. "Have a great weekend."

"You, too. Thanks so much!"

As I started gathering the work I'd need to take home for the weekend, I wondered about the woman on the phone. What did she look like? How old was she? *What was her life?* I had no idea how the city's drug trade worked, so every time we spoke I wanted to ask her how she got the job. Was she related to the higher-ups in whatever drug chain this was? Was it a New York mob family or an offshoot of a Colombian cartel? How did they know she wouldn't turn them in? Did they threaten her kid? She didn't sound as if she was under threat. It was probably a pretty good gig. The pay must have been decent, given the risks, and I bet she got all the drugs she could use. Then again, if you got tired of the gig, quitting probably wasn't an option.

With a big proposal for one of the world's largest companies due the following week, I had a good excuse to shut myself in at home all weekend.

"Marie," I said to my assistant. She looked up at me and cocked her head. "I'm going to pack up my work for the weekend and head out. I'll be on my phone if anyone needs me this afternoon."

"OK," she said, spinning back to her work. Why didn't I just say "I'm heading out"? I was going to be neck-deep in work all weekend; why did I feel the need to explain myself to a twenty-three-year-old administrative assistant?

The trip home dragged, and once I was safely in my living room I paced like an expectant father in a 1960s waiting room—except that I carried an enormous glass of red wine in one hand and a cigarette in the other. By four o'clock, Henry knocked on my door, and we zipped through our business in less than five minutes. Then I closed the door behind him and looked at the mirror that hung just to the right of the door frame. I realized what an important item that little mirror was in my life. Half the time it sat on my glass coffee table lined with rails of coke, and the other half it hung from the wall and offered my last important look before I walked out into the world. It was the kind of piece that fellow coke addicts would have acknowledged with a nod and a, "Hey, there's a good mirror."

I crushed a small rock down to a snowy powder pile with the back of a spoon and then formed several lines with my American Express Gold Card. Holding one of several cut-down plastic straws that I kept with my other drug implements—the razors, the small glass vials with tiny spoons attached to the

cap, the rolled up dollar bills for when I was out of straws—
I leaned over the mirror on the coffee table. This was the
moment I'd been focused on since my last hit eight hours ago.
I wanted this bump as much as I'd ever wanted anything. I
wanted it more than a promotion with a raise, a perfect boyfriend, or a winning Mega Millions ticket.

One long inhale on one side of my nose followed by one
long inhale on the other and I felt sharp, happy fireworks go
off in my nasal passages. And then came the crackling and tin-
gling in my bloodstream. My body shuddered. *OH GOD, so
much better.*

Back in balance, the world became a livable place. I took a
long draw of wine, sat back, and lit a cigarette. At that moment
my life was as good as it could get, and the weekend ahead
would offer me the addict's trifecta: justified isolation (I couldn't
be out and about when I had to work), nonstop using (to work
that hard I needed the chemicals), and a legitimate reason for
feigned resentment ("I hate that I have to work all weekend!").

Inside and locked up tight, I remained unshowered in a
pair of men's boxers and an old Northwestern sweatshirt for
most of the weekend, except when I pulled on a pair of jeans
to head out for minor errands. No errand was so short or simple that I didn't first need the fortification of drink and drug. In
time the whole thing became Pavlovian; whenever I began the
routine of leaving the apartment—pull scraggly hair into a careless ponytail, check nose, find purse—my unconscious heard
the ring of the bell and began to twitch for drugs and booze. I
was like people who can stuff themselves to discomfort by eating every bit of a seven-course meal, but something tells them
they still need chocolate.

Despite what many would deem a fall into a slovenly exis-
tence, during these sequestrations I did try to keep my apart-

ment feeling moderately respectable. The reek of cigarette smoke could easily overwhelm my apartment's 850 square feet, so I lit candles, sprayed Lysol, and left windows open whenever possible. If I wanted the windows open, that meant pulling the curtains aside, which invited anyone with a pair of binoculars to see into my apartment, so I shifted the drug set up into the bedroom. That room remained in full darkness with curtains pulled. My big brass bed with the purple floral Donna Karan linens and piles of pillows became home to the ever-present mirror and all of its implements, a kind of mission control.

My bedroom, living room, and kitchen sat side to side, so all weekend I traveled a well-worn path between the three that resembled the McDonald's arches. My living room couch, set up with my laptop, was at the bottom center. An arc to the left led to booze in the kitchen and an arc to the right led to coke in the bedroom. I plodded between the three rooms over and over working, drinking, snorting, barely eating, drinking, working, snorting, sleeping, drinking, working, and snorting as night turned to day turned to night turned to day.

Sometime between two and three that Monday morning, I shut the computer down and headed into the bedroom. I had cut off the coke a couple of hours earlier, hoping I'd get some kind of sleep before heading into the office. Then it hit—the depressing, awful crash of coming down and the dread of the approaching morning, a Monday no less. My heart beat with irregular thuds and my head felt piercing pressure, as if some angry masseuse was jamming her thumbs and fingernails into my temples. That perfect moment of Friday afternoon now felt like months ago.

Then came the birds. They began their incessant high-pitched chirping outside my window at around 4:00 a.m. The sound always made me sick with all its chatter and scramble, all its purposeful busyness. Their miserable racket announced the onset of another awful day, and I hated them for it.

• • •

Nothing unusual happened that weekend. There was no inciting event that led me to pull the alarm on my life. There was no drunken accident, no falling from the kitchen ladder or crashing through a glass tabletop to send me to an emergency room. There was no drugged dialing that left me to later wince in shame, no professional humiliations, no family explosion. No blackout followed by waking up next to a stranger.

So maybe what was unusual about that weekend, what led me to finally launch the white flag is something that will forever remain an unknown to me. Had my unconscious been trying all along to scream, "Stop this! You're going too far! You're killing yourself!"? And on that Monday did one of those screams break through like a champagne cork blasting from the pressure and releasing a torrent behind it? Did some kind of spiritual guardian step in and stop me from pressing that elevator button that day?

I don't know what it was that turned me around to make all those phone calls, to walk through the rehab doors, to sign the documents that locked me in. But on that Monday morning an epiphany burst like an aneurism.

part three.

Your bottom
is where you
stop
digging.

16

After Dr. Landry left my room at Gracie Square, I stared at the ceiling and waited for the nurses to lead me through the pre-Librium drill. The pain of withdrawal was God-awfully worse than anything I'd ever heard about. In movies, junkies often lie on metal cots in stark, cold rooms, sweating and shaking through a swift montage: "addict sweats . . . addict rolls over . . . addict shakes . . . addict thrashes . . . addict moans . . . and then addict peacefully sleeps and wakes up tired but somehow new." But real-world withdrawal takes a lot longer and tortures the body in very specific ways.

My starkest memory of this process was not the physical part, but the mental. Even though my head felt as if it had been slammed onto a bed of tiny nails that shot hundreds of stabbing pricks across my skull and neck, the only thing my mind could focus on was how badly I needed to drink. Pain. Need drink. Pain. Need drink. It was a continuous loop in my brain.

When I moved even slightly, waves of pain spread through my body straight to my toes, popping up at every pit stop along the way. Lifting my arm to massage my head or trying to move my legs to put my feet on the floor led to enormous aches and hot stabs of pain. Once my hand finally reached my head, even the lightest pressure of my fingers into my scalp made me wince.

The nausea was profound. I wouldn't have been surprised to puke up my liver or some other vital organ that had decided, "Fuck this. I'm outta here." After a few rounds of dry heaves over the toilet, I realized that my stomach had nothing left to reject, so from then on I dry heaved in bed where it felt less uncomfortable and disgusting.

For months already I'd been waking up soaked in sweat with full-body tremors, so the constant shakes and sweating were the least surprising aspects of withdrawal. Withdrawal was like my usual thrashing misery, but on steroids. The agony of it all made me cry until I thought I'd run out of tears.

Need drink. Need drink. Pain. Need drink. Need drink. This was the dominant drumbeat. But before long, it became "MAKE IT STOP! GIVE ME THE FUCKING LIBRIUM! MAKE IT STOP! GIVE ME THE FUCKING LIBRIUM!"

All I knew about Librium was what I had read somwhere— that it might have been the "little yellow pill," Mick Jagger sings about in "Mother's Little Helper." What I didn't know was that it was the first benzodiazepine, a class of psychoactive drugs. Had I known that a benzo is a sedative and a kissing cousin of Valium, I might have been more game to take it the previous night. In detox, the Librium was meant to knock me out and downgrade the drama of withdrawal from a knife fight to a screaming match; the process would still suck, but no one was going out in a body bag.

But between me and the Librium stood the staff physician and the blood test I had refused the night before.

While the Asian nurses on the fifth floor were charged with leading me to meals, taking my blood pressure all day long, and keeping my contraband locked away, the detox nurses from the third floor were responsible for all things addiction.

A nurse named Ashley from detox appeared in my room. Younger than the other nurses, she was tall and thin with a head of bad blonde highlights topped by a three-inch, brown yarmulke of root growth.

"Hey, Lisa. You ready to go see the doctor?" she asked, snapping her gum at the end of each sentence. As miserable as I was, I immediately knew that I liked her. I could picture her standing outside the facility, chain-smoking Virginia Slims with other nurses her age and swapping stories of hard-partying weekends and tattooed boyfriends on Long Island. I hoped that she wasn't headed for a spot on one of these beds.

Leaning against both Ashley and the hallway wall, I wobbled slowly to the elevator. I noticed the same two patients I'd seen when I arrived the night before, a woman and a man, both Asian. They wore the same clothes as the night before and separately walked laps around the floor. The woman appeared to be in her mid-twenties and was very thin. She wore brown sweatpants and a white t-shirt with a butterfly embroidered on it. Her flip-flops were the kind that people wear in the shower at the gym—no thong between the toes, just a thick white and blue striped plastic band across the front of the foot. She walked slightly bent over, hands clasped behind her back, head bowed—like a speed skater on Thorazine.

The man was more animated. Older, maybe in his mid-forties, he wore expensive-looking pajamas and sturdy leather sandals. I wondered if his loftier clothing indicated that he was signed on for a longer stay. While the woman took almost catatonic lap after lap without stopping, the man seemed to want to take in every bit of information he could and share his thoughts on all of it. His voice boomed judgmental commentary and commands to no one in particular: "TOWELS SHOULD *NOT* BE ON THE FLOOR!" and "PUT AWAY THAT MOP!" Every time he passed my room I braced myself for some kind of nutty wrath directed at me.

During each lap, he checked the pay phone for change. I wanted to tell him, "no one carries money here," but I didn't think it would stop him, and I also didn't want his undivided attention. I tried to convince myself that he was harmless (why else would the staff let him walk around like that?), but he scared me. Sometimes he would stop to study something on the floor, and in those moments he reminded me of a Scotland Yard detective, maybe conducting an investigation of a strangling.

Outside the nurses' station, there was a large white erasable board that displayed the day's schedule and the nurses' assignments. The pacing man approached the board and called out the list of duties. "Wake up and breakfast. Nurse LIL-LIAN?" He shouted. "Medication and examinations. Nurse EMILY?" He seemed surprised and annoyed by what he read, as if someone had assigned tasks without first consulting him. The first few times he shouted his announcements I found it funny. But then it went on for days and nobody stopped him. It became maddening.

The people who paced, the chatterers, the catatonics, the screamers—this crowd made me feel fixable by comparison. How utterly normal I thought I appeared, just some worn-out corporate raider who needed a recharge. But I knew that if there had been a bottle of vodka anywhere in that building, I would have happily broken all rules to get my hands on it. That was one of the many thoughts I kept to myself.

Eventually, Ashley and I made it to the doctor's office on the detox floor. Time seemed to move slowly when there was no drink in my hand, so the three-minute journey seemed like a long one. The simple act of walking now felt like trying to run on an underwater treadmill, and I couldn't even navigate a straight line without a person and a wall to hold me up. In the doctor's office I began to feel as if I might pass out, but fortunately I was able to fall into a chair before that happened. PAIN, PAIN, PAIN! NEED DRINK, NEED DRINK, NEED DRINK! The loop continued.

Dr. Stanley, the detox unit physician, was young, with dark hair, pale white skin, and shiny red cheeks that looked as if they'd just been pinched. He didn't greet Ashley and he barely looked at me. He had a snotty, petulant affect that, along with his pallid skin, made him seem like an evil Eddie Munster. I figured that his detox doctor friends were taking spa treatments with the celebrity drunks at Promises in Malibu while he'd been exiled here, to some shitty little detox/nuthouse hybrid in the middle of the dirty city.

"OK, let's take a look at you," he grumbled. By then I was slumped like a rag doll in the chair next to his desk. There was no examination table or array of pharmaceutical products, just a lot of sharp, metal objects on a small stand. As he set up the needle to draw my blood, I pulled my arm out of my sleeve like a junkie waiting to be shot up.

"Give me your arm," Dr. Stanley said. He strapped the rubber band around my upper arm and limbered me up by bending me at the elbow a few times. Then he glanced along my arm for a usable vein and settled on one far too soon. With careless roughness, he started jabbing the needle into my arm. After three awful, unsuccessful stabs, I exploded in tears. "Stop it!" I screamed. "You're HURTING me."

"Your veins aren't good. They roll," he said.

"My veins are fine!" I wasn't an intravenous drug user, after all. "I've had blood drawn a million times. Stop it!"

"It's going to have to come out of your hand." *My hand? What the fuck? What kind of sadist draws blood from your hand?* Then he jabbed the needle into the back of my left hand, and I shrieked.

"WHAT THE FUCK!!" I shouted. Did he hit a nerve? Searing pain began at the stab site and radiated out to each fingertip.

"OWWW!" I screamed. And then I started sobbing—really deep, heaving sobbing, and I showed no sign of stopping. It was as if that needle had signaled all my pain to spout at once. The needle had pierced some deep well of agony, and I just let it gush. Dr. Stanley didn't react to my hysterics as he marked the vial and reorganized his implements of torture.

It took me a few minutes to calm down. Ashley waited patiently, and after my heaving subsided, she acted as if nothing out of the ordinary had happened, "Ready to go?" she chirped. Then she gave my back a quick rub as she helped me up from the chair.

"Yeah. I really can't wait for the Librium."

"Oh, not yet," she said. "We have to go downstairs for your chest x-ray first." I let out a long sigh. Under normal circumstances, the prospect of having my lungs examined would have terrified me because when I drank and used, I lit cigarettes like a tag team. If someone asked me if I smoked, I would have said, "Only when I drink." That was the same as saying, "Every waking hour."

But I didn't care about their finding lung cancer at that point. I would have done anything to get Librium into my body. My legs buckled as if I were in a moonwalk at a kid's fair. I held on to Ashley's elbow.

Gracie Square's lower level was also dimly lit and dank smelling. About eight detox patients stood in line for x-rays, men and women of all ages. This morning's crop, I thought. Everyone had been outfitted with the heavy silver aprons. They looked like a team of dueling knights waiting to be called for a match at the Medieval Times restaurant. A team of exhausted, out of shape, and generally wrecked fifth-string knights. Why the hell did the nurses make us all wear hot, heavy aprons while we waited in line? And why did this place own so many lead-proof aprons? Why didn't they use their money for bottled water and anything else that might actually make us feel *good*?

Looking like one of the sandwich board people on the streets of New York, I was overheating underneath my sweater, so I started to cry again. No one reacted to my open weeping. A few of the other patients looked at me, but no one said a word. How is it they all seemed so calm through such an awful process? Drugged? Maybe some of them were repeat visitors, accustomed to the routine. *Shit*, I thought. *I really don't want to get used to this routine.*

After the chest x-ray, I was cleared for dosing. Because I ate with the Asian patients, I would be taking my meds when they took theirs. While I waited, I daydreamed about the idea of having "meds" doled out to me in a rehab. Something about it felt kind of edgy. Keith Richards, Eric Clapton, and me.

When we returned to the fifth floor, Ashley handed me off to nurse Jane, and we approached a small window behind which a tiny Asian woman with thinning black hair and narrow, rectangular glasses sat next to a huge collection of metal drawers, all loaded with medications. "Dr. Landry says you have to take Librium and also Lexapro because you're depressed," Jane said.

"Great," I said. At that point I would have chewed shards of dirty glass if it meant relief. The more drugs, the better.

Because I wasn't drinking, I wondered if this time the antidepressant would have a chance of working. Was depression my real problem? I kept hearing that I was depressed. But this was New York, who wasn't depressed? I was sure as hell going to be depressed when I went home and couldn't drink. But if Lexapro fixed my depression, would that make it easier for me to not drink? I'd never before connected my depression with my drinking; would this place put a stop to both? But then who would I be?

A dose of Librium was a tiny yellow capsule that didn't look like it would deliver much of a punch. I wrinkled my nose while inspecting it, and then tossed the Librium and the round, white Lexapro tablet to the back of my throat and washed them down with water from a Dixie cup.

After I'd been interrogated, stabbed, scanned, and medicated, it was time for lunch. I sat at the emptiest round table I could find, sliding down the curve of the pink plastic chair. Two nurses worked the lunch crowd. One stood next to a metal cart full of covered meal trays and shouted the names written on each one. Patients would raise their hands, and the other nurse would deliver their lunches.

With my elbows on the table and my head in my hands, I heard a nurse call out, "SMITH!" I half raised my hand in what might have looked like a Nazi salute, and the nurse placed a tray in front of me. When I lifted the lid off the plate, I saw something that might have been a piece of turkey. It was April, but that gray slab looked like something left over from Thanksgiving. Next to it sat a pile of mashed potatoes that managed to be both lumpy and runny. A pile of yellow-green string beans bathing in a greasy substance served as the vegetable. No way I'm eating this garbage, I thought. I pictured myself at the Bloomingdale's that was about to open in SoHo. Thanks to rehab, I'd be heading into that fitting room with my arms loaded with pairs of teeny jeans.

Several patients had meals much different from mine. They had a stir-fry with sliced chicken and broccoli over rice that looked like it could have come from a real restaurant. "It's the Mandarin menu," a nurse said. "It's for Asian patients who are happier with familiar food." The higher food quality was lost on the patients. Many wore parts of their meals on their chins, shirts, noses, and cheeks. A few had food in their hair.

My head became fuzzy and I felt myself slouch lower down my chair. It was the Librium! Praise God for Librium! How do I get more Librium?

Afraid I might pass out in my food and suffocate, I waved for a nurse. "I just took Librium," I mumbled. Without a word, she walked me to my room, holding my elbow as if she were helping an old lady across a street. My knees hit the bed first and then the rest of my body flopped onto the mattress in a helpless heap. I had barely slipped under the sheet before I fell into a long, deep sleep. My first alcohol-free sleep in ten years.

17

Where am I? I blinked my heavy eyelids open and saw my brother sitting near me in the wooden chair that usually sat at the foot of the bed. He was hunched forward, reading a book. Years earlier, Lou had worn his brown hair in long beautiful curls, but for several years now he'd kept it law-firm cropped.

A pool of drool had formed on the pillow as I slowly emerged from my stupor. He glanced up.

"Hey!" he said. His brows furrowed as he sat up and pushed his eyeglasses up on the bridge of his nose. "How are you doing?"

"I'm OK," I said quietly. I wanted to be brave and nonchalant for my brother. "Pretty awful around here, huh?"

"It's not so bad," he said. "I couldn't find you. Why are you on this floor? It's not detox."

Holy shit, I hadn't given them a thought—my family. What if they'd shown up to hear, "Sorry, no Lisa Smith in detox. Maybe you have the wrong hospital?"

"I messed up," I said to Lou, closing my eyes. "This probably wasn't the right place to go. The detox floor was really scary, but they put me up here and it's OK."

"Are you sure? You don't have to stay here," he said.

"No, no. I'm already this far." I curled up tight into a ball and fought to keep my eyes open. "I think . . . I thi—" I mumbled and then I fell asleep with my brother still by my side.

When I woke up again, my parents were also in the room. With hazy thoughts, I wondered about what must be going through the minds of the family members who had known me all my life, the people who had watched me learn to walk and ride a bike and graduate from high school. But I quickly turned away from those thoughts. I couldn't handle another sobbing bout.

My mom sat in the chair, her hands clasped in her lap, leaning forward with her mouth slightly open, as if she was trying to unscramble a secret code on my face. I reached toward her, and she took my hand and squeezed it.

My dad stood next to her with his hand on her shoulder. "Are we OK?" he asked. He walked over to the bed, kissed my cheek, and rubbed my hair. I smiled weakly and stayed curled in the fetal position.

"Yeah, we're OK," I said. That did it. The tears started falling, but my body was too tired to sob with any energy, so I whimpered like a little girl trying to be brave as her mother applied bandages after a bike accident. They all sat there in silence and let me cry. Finally, I calmed down and said, "I'm so sorry about all this."

"Hey, it's OK. Last year it was Mom," Dad said, referring to a car accident that had landed her in the hospital with a wrecked ankle. "This year, it's you. We get through it!" Ever the optimist. And ever confident that I could do anything I set my mind to. But quit drinking? He had no idea how bad it had gotten.

"This place is really skuzzy, Lisa," my mom said. In her cotton khakis and matching sweater set, she was the most put-together person I'd seen since check-in. She was looking out the door into the hallway, and I hoped the pacers wouldn't pass by. "Don't you want to go somewhere else? We can get you into a nicer place if you really need this kind of thing. You don't have to stay here."

"No, really. I'm OK. I went through all these tests and then I took that Librium stuff and it really knocked me out. I feel a lot better than I did this morning. I just want to get through this. I don't want to move."

"Shirley, leave her alone. She said she's OK. Let her get some help here. Why crap around to start the whole thing over?" my dad said.

I waved my left hand, bandaged from the stabbing. "I'm this far along. I might as well just do it here. Besides, the food here sucks and I might come out a supermodel." My father and brother laughed. Mom didn't.

"So how long did the doctors say you should be here?" my dad asked.

"I think since I started the Librium today, the earliest I would leave is Friday. Maybe you guys could pick me up on Friday? I can spend the weekend with you. Then I'll go back to work Monday."

"Of course. We'll come get you Friday, whatever time they tell you," my mom said. It felt good to have an exit strategy. My eyes were closing again.

"Alright, let's get out of here and let her rest," my dad said. He rubbed my head again. Lou came over and kissed my forehead, then he hugged Dad while Mom bent down to the cot and hugged me.

"Can you call us every day?" my mom asked. "It doesn't seem like we can call you."

"Yes. I can call. I have a phone card. There's a pay phone."

As they left, I started crying harder, heavy with guilt as I pictured them driving back to New Jersey. Then I was asleep again before the tears could dry on the pillow.

I woke up on Wednesday to Jane and her blood pressure contraption. "Do you feel better yet, Lisa? You have a busy day today. The doctor will check you after breakfast. Then you'll go to the meeting on the third floor," she said.

"Meeting? What are you talking about?" I was trying to sit up straight in the bed without a headboard.

"Twelllve Stepsss!" she sang. "You're still a detox patient. You cried your way up to this floor, but you're still a detox patient. Meeting at ten thirty on the third floor."

"No, no," I shook my head and laughed. "I didn't sign up for any 12-step program. I'm just doing the detox to get clean. I can explain it to the doctor."

Jane tipped her head back and let out a full, heavy laugh. "Ha! That's not how it works. If you come here for detox, you go to meetings on the third floor every day. I don't think you'll get out of *that* one with the doctor."

After breakfast, the doctor on duty confirmed my fear. "Every patient being treated for substance abuse is required to go to 12-step meetings." He spoke respectfully, but I couldn't help but feel he wanted to end his statement with, "Duh!" He added, "This is not negotiable."

"I don't like those programs," I protested. "They seem, I don't know. . . creepy, like some religious thing . . . or you know—culty." Thanks to the Librium, I no longer sounded like a lawyer. I sounded more like a gauzy-headed girl on her third day at Woodstock.

"Come on, Lisa," he said. "Where else are you going today? Take a shower. You'll feel better. Then just go sit there. You don't have to say anything. Just sit and listen. Who knows? You might hear something interesting."

That was tough to argue with. I rolled my eyes. "OK, OK." Jane winked at me and smiled as she led me back to my room. The Librium had made me feel dramatically better than the day before, but I still wished that I'd find a pint of vodka between the mattress and the bedspring, left behind by the last patient in my room. I wanted a drink very badly. How was I supposed to go to a 12-step meeting without drinking?

The doctor had been right about the shower part. I smelled like a high school football player after a summer practice—if he'd then rolled in a dumpster shared by a cheese shop and a chemical plant. I figured it was mass amounts of toxins finally seeping from my long-suffering body. The lack of light in the bathroom was a blessing because I was sure that dark and furry things were growing on the walls. Unfortunately, neither Devon, the most hygienic person I knew, nor I had thought of flip-flops for the shower when packing. We thought we were packing for a spa rehab where Robert Downey Jr. would give me a sponge bath and then Ben Affleck would wrap me in a warm towel.

To make the shower bearable, I pretended I had just seen a janitor scrub the floor, then I took the fastest shower of my life and dried off with a stained and dingy sandpaper towel.

Ashley took me to the meeting in the day room on the detox floor. The Librium had knocked me back to a slow shuffle, so we were a little late. About thirty pink plastic chairs formed a circle and almost every one had a patient already planted in it. I settled into one of the few empty chairs and was grateful not to see the guy who had threatened to fuck me up.

A short Latino man with thick, black hair and a thick, black mustache lectured sternly at the front of the room. Wearing a tan, button-down shirt tucked into jeans, he paced back and forth and waved his arms as he spoke. "Man, you keep this shit up, you ain't gonna be so lucky next time to end up in here. You're gonna end up with your ass in jail or lying dead in the street. That's what's gonna happen to you, man. This shit ain't funny. If you ain't lost 'em already, you're gonna lose your job, your house, your car, your family, and your whole life. This shit ain't funny. Do not laugh. I am serious."

As his words banged around in my head I became scared and mesmerized at the same time. He was passionate, he was firm, and he was right. Holy shit, he was right. If I got lucky enough next time and didn't kill myself or land in jail, I would be right back in rehab. I couldn't stop drinking without help and if I didn't stop drinking, I'd lose my job and alienate everyone I loved. I rocked my head back and rubbed my face with my hands. Dr. Landry was right. This guy was right. If I didn't clean myself up I was fucked.

I surveyed the detox crowd. There were more tattoos than teeth in the room, but almost every one of the guys wore expensive running shoes. The group included people of all ages, sizes, and colors—about twice as many men as women. Some of the people might have been in their teens while others clearly qualified for social security. Stripped down to sweatpants and hospital robes and slouched in their chairs, they looked like a bunch of pissed off delinquents sentenced to detention.

It was obvious that most of these people were not here by choice. I doubted that any of them had awakened one morning in a beautiful apartment and realized that they simply couldn't go to their six-figure jobs that day. The vast majority of them had probably been arrested and thrown in here or dragged in under protest by weary loved ones who prayed that this time it would stick. Maybe some of them had been signed in under threat of being fired.

On the wall directly across from me was the detox unit's equivalent to the white schedule board. Across the top of it, in big, green Magic Marker capital letters, it read: "GET UP. GET DRESSED. GET WITH THE PROGRAM." It looked like the only thing on the board that wasn't erased or updated each day. This was a permanent command.

The Latino lecturer went on, getting louder. "You do not pick up, *no matter what.* That's it. I am serious. It is the one rule. If you pick up, you will lose everything. I was in your chair. I don't ever want to ever sit in it again. That's why I do not pick up no matter what. My life today is real good. When I was using, I had nothing, inside or out. If I pick up, I go right back to what I had before and worse. Believe it. YOU DO NOT PICK UP NO MATTER WHAT."

OK, geez, I thought. *I get the idea: "pick up" means to start using again, and you don't do it "no matter what!"*

What if I gave all this 12-step thinking a shot? This guy was saying—proclaiming, actually—that his life sober was better than ever, not worse. Could that be true? He certainly seemed genuine. And what would be the reason to try to sell us bullshit? *Maybe I should view "Get up, get dressed, and get with the program," as a challenge*, I thought. *I'm nothing if not competitive.* I was already pretty good at the first two out of three.

At the end of the meeting, I started toward the door when everyone began to join hands around the circle. Did I have to join hands? Was the soap in my bathroom antibacterial? The man to my left looked to be about three hundred pounds and wore a pastel, floral housedress. I was too busy staring at him with a slack Librium jaw to notice whoever was on my right. Oh well, what the fuck. We all joined hands and bowed our heads and they chanted some kind of prayer.

• • •

Dr. Landry came by shortly after lunch. I was curled up in bed, half-asleep. He stood in the doorway, folder in hand. He ran a hand through his salt-and-pepper hair and then adjusted his glasses,

"Lisa. How are you feeling today?" His voice jarred the quiet of my room as he sat on the chair at the foot of my bed. Trying to push myself up into a sitting position, I ended up in a slouch with my back against the wall. My hair hung over the side of my face so I felt half hidden from him.

"Better, thanks," I said. "I'm really tired though. The Librium."

"That's OK, that's normal. Do you still feel shaky?"

"Yeah."

"Anything else?"

"Nauseated. And I have a headache. But it's not like yesterday morning." I felt coherent, almost clear headed but for the Librium. That was strange.

"OK, that's good. I want to ask you a question. What brought you here? You told me yesterday that you drink, all day, every day. That you can't stop. What happened to make you come here?"

My face became hot and my eyes filled up. "I don't really know. I just, I got this feeling Monday morning that I couldn't do it anymore."

"Do what?"

"You know, function. Get out of bed. Go to work. Do what I'm supposed to do."

"You mean physically? You physically couldn't do it? Or you mentally couldn't do it?"

I had to think about that. "I don't know. Both. I mean, I was dressed and heading to work, but my body—I felt like I had to do something or I would die soon. I can't get up without drinking. I shake and feel sick all day and I . . ." This was my doctor, no reason to hold back now. "I throw up every day and I shit blood." Dr. Landry didn't react. He just nodded, so I continued. "But I guess in my head, you know . . . I was . . . I *am*, I'm just so tired. I just hate who I am now. I do terrible things." I was grateful that he didn't ask me to describe the terrible things. That must be procedure—don't freak the patient out too soon.

"Can you give me an idea of how much you drink each day?"

"It depends." I knew the answer and it didn't really "depend." I'd run the routine through my mind a hundred times trying to justify it and to count the calories.

"Average, take a guess," he said.

"Two bottles of wine, maybe a little more, or about a liter of vodka. I don't like to finish the whole thing, but sometimes I do. Sometimes it's a mix of wine and vodka. Or whatever else is around. Sometimes I drink less. Sometimes more."

"And how long has that been going on?"

"That much every day? About a year," I said. Wow. I heard myself.

"Have you tried to cut back?"

"Of course!"

"But you haven't been able to," he said.

"No."

"And you use cocaine?"

"Yeah, but not that much," I lied.

"Do you think you could stop that?"

"Yeah, probably." Another lie.

"You're a lawyer, right?" My heart thumped a giant boom.

"Yes." I looked down to the dingy sheets. He didn't need to tell me that cocaine is a controlled substance and that possession could be a felony.

"Have you thought about suicide?" he asked.

I waited a beat, pretending I wasn't sure of my answer, and I tried to sit up a little straighter. I didn't want to end up in a padded cell. But how much worse could that be? I was so tired of lying. "Sure," I admitted. "Who hasn't thought about suicide at some point? Sometimes I'd just rather not be here."

"Have you ever gone further than that? Maybe fantasized about how or when you'd do it? Or gotten something that could help you do it?"

"No. No, I never got that far," I said, which was also true. "I couldn't do that to my mother."

"But you're unhappy with how your life is now, is that right?"

"Yeah."

"Would you say you're depressed?"

"I don't know. I don't know what that means. I don't always feel totally black."

"Are you ever happy?"

What a question. I had to think about it. How do you know what "happy" means if you've never been happy? "Happy" like people in an engagement ring commercial? "Happy" like the prom queen when they rest the crown upon her perfect blonde hair? Or happy like the strange phenomenon I'd heard of, when there's nothing particularly special going on, but life feels wonderful anyway? "Sometimes, I guess, for a while," I said. "But I don't think I could say I'm a happy *person*. I don't wake up happy. I never have."

"Are you ever happy when you're not drinking or taking drugs?"

"No. If I'm not drinking, I'm hungover and trying to figure out when I can drink to feel better. If I'm not drinking, I'm sick and miserable." Dr. Landry waited in case I had more to say. But I just scrunched the sheet between my hands.

"Is that why you drink the way you do? To stem the unhappiness?" He waited for my answer as I scrunched sheets, scrunched my forehead, scrunched my eyebrows . . .

"I don't know. I guess. I think that's why I used to drink—to make myself more comfortable, to relax, to get rid of the anxiety. Now I don't have a choice. I just have to drink."

"Do you know much about the disease of alcoholism and addiction?" he asked.

Oh, God. Here we go. "I've heard people say it's a disease, like a brain thing," I said.

"Yes, it's a disease."

"How can it be a disease if drinking is something you choose?"

He looked up from his clipboard and adjusted his glasses again. "That's a good question, Lisa. Alcoholism is a disease that involves brain chemistry, often tied to an underlying mental disorder, like depression. The drinker *does* choose to drink, but once a line is crossed and the drinker with a genetic predisposition begins to drink alcoholically, it's very difficult to reverse. Eventually, as you've experienced, the alcoholic drinker can no longer just stop after one or two as people who aren't afflicted with the disease can."

"Are you saying that I can never drink like a normal person because I'm an alcoholic? Wait, are you saying that I'm not supposed to *ever* drink again?" Something kicked in my stomach.

"The only effective treatment we've seen is medication to address the brain chemistry issue combined with abstinence from substances supported by a 12-step program. Based on my preliminary evaluation, that is what I would suggest for you."

His finality seemed preposterous. Why couldn't I get better and then work hard at drinking socially, stopping after one or two. Oh, who was I trying to kid? Stopping after two? *That* sounded preposterous. "But you're saying, *never* drink again?"

"That's for you to decide for yourself, but from what I've seen you're a smart woman with a very serious problem. If you don't address it and you keep going, you'll find yourself back here, if you're lucky. People who can drink socially don't generally come in here requiring a medicated detox."

Tears began rolling down my face. I had pulled my knees to my chest and was rocking back and forth. Dr. Landry continued.

"My guess is that all along you've been drinking not to be social but to self-medicate your depression and anxiety. And now it's gone beyond your control. I think you need to embark on a long-term program of recovery."

I knew it. I knew this was what they were going to say. Of course, I knew. FUCK, FUCK, FUCK. Even though I had to acknowledge that they were probably right, it enraged me that these know-it-alls wanted to try to take booze away from me. But why was I so upset at the idea of stopping the very thing that had made my life unbearable? I knew the answer. Because I had no idea what the other side looked like. If life was miserable even when I was numbed out, what would it be like without the numbing?

Then I thought about my friends. FUCK. FUCK! FUC-CCKKK! The happy hours, the parties, the brunches, the toasts, the weekends at the beach. Now I'd be the broken one, the one who needed to be treated differently. Would they feel uncomfortable drinking in front of me? What would that feel like for me? And Jesus, what do non-drinking people do all night? Anyway, my angst wasn't just about the idea of saying goodbye to the social drinking. What about dealing with Monday morning stress? What about getting ready for a blind date? What about getting buzzed *just because it fucking felt good*?

I nodded silently at Dr. Landry. But I wondered if it showed on my face that inside I was screaming, "Bring me a tall, cold vodka *right now* or I'm going rip this room apart!!!"

18

Later on Wednesday, Jerry and Devon
visited. We sat on the hard plastic chairs of the detox day
room. Patients and visitors sat together as hospital staff hovered nearby, looking out for potential exchange of illicit substances or dangerous objects. It made me sad that only a few of
the patients from the morning meeting had visitors. Had they so
badly fucked up their personal lives that nobody could be bothered to support them anymore? Had they had any loved ones to
alienate in the first place? God, I was lucky to have my family
and friends. And I had been such a shithead to them for years—
all the lies, all the neglect, always letting the booze come first. I
shivered at the thought of being truly alone in this place.

Signs hung all over the walls with slogans like "Keep it
Simple," "Let Go and Let God," and "One Day at a Time." Utterly
banal sayings that made me even warier of joining one of these
12-step cults or "groups," as they called them. The morning
speaker had been very compelling, so I was on the fence. And
no one had said anything about God outside of the prayer at
the end, so they didn't seem religious. Just another part of this
whole enterprise that I didn't understand. Devon's Gucci loafers

stood out in stark contrast to all the hospital slippers and running shoes. Both she and Jerry were in suits, which reminded me that I was spending a workday in a mental hospital. Devon clutched her handbag in her lap. "What's all that crap?" she asked, pointing at the wall. "All those signs?"

"Aren't they fabulous? They're 12-step slogans. They're supposed to help you get sober. No one has talked to me about them yet," I said.

"What do you mean 'yet'? You're just here to dry out. You're not going to stop drinking for good, are you?" she asked.

"I don't know what I'm doing," I said. "Right now I'm just trying to get through this."

"I told you I didn't like this place. They're going to try to brainwash you," she said.

Jerry jumped in. "Are you kidding, Devon? This place is priceless!" He sat back in his chair and checked everyone out. "You think they have an outpatient program? You know, show up in the morning, a little counseling, some group therapy? Maybe a vegan lunch, seaweed wrap, and then out in time for happy hour?"

I was too medicated to laugh out loud. All I could do was close my eyes and bob my shoulders up and down. I remembered that I once almost bought Jerry a "Betty Ford Center" t-shirt, thinking it was hilarious.

"Do you ever stop?" Devon asked, heaving a sigh.

I wanted to tell my friends true stories for a change. "So when I got to this floor my first night, it was really bad. Like there were women fighting and some guy threatened to fuck me up." I rested my forearms on my thighs because it was hard to sit up straight.

Devon's eyes bugged. "Are you kidding me? Why didn't you call me? What the fuck? Why are you still here?" She let go of her purse to flail her arms. "I knew this place was a mistake! I should have called Smithers."

"No, no," I said. "I couldn't leave. I signed that 72-hour psych hold thing. They take it seriously. They wouldn't let me leave even though I wanted to call the police."

"Yo, call the police from in here? No way," Jerry said. He let out a laughing snort, running his hand through his gelled hair and rocking back in his plastic chair. On the other side of the experience, Devon seemed to be fighting back tears.

"Yeah, but they kind of made me a deal," I said. "They let me off the detox unit and put me up on the Asian floor, just for sleeping and meals. It's quieter up there. They're still crazy, but it feels safer."

"Asian floor?" Jerry sat up straight. He dated Asian women almost exclusively.

"What are you talking about? You're not in detox?" Devon said.

"No, I *am* in detox. But I'm not staying on the detox floor. This place has an Asian floor. All Asian patients, doctors, and nurses. They're not addicts up there, just regular crazy, all kinds."

Jerry squealed, "Dude! No way! Can you get me in on that, maybe some numbers?" Devon and I rolled our eyes at each other.

"Are you eating?" Devon asked me, ignoring Jerry.

"Lou brought me pretzels and bottled water," I said. "The only other water here is out of the tap. Sometimes I . . . that water . . . it's gross. I think . . . I think I can lose some weight this week." I was dizzy and I could hear myself rambling.

"You're loopy enough on that medicine," she said. "You don't need low blood sugar, too. Can I bring you a burger or something? Would they let me? What about magazines?"

I shook my head. We were all quiet.

"Seriously," she said, "Are we being bad friends leaving you here? I feel like a good friend would get you out."

"No, I'm OK."

I didn't know what else to say to them and it scared me. I felt disconnected from my best friends, even more so than when I was lying to them night and day. Two days earlier, they hadn't known that anything was wrong with me. Now, they were visiting me in a detox tank, a place where every staff member had been charged with turning me into a different person.

"Do the Asian nurses give you sponge baths?" Jerry asked, jolting me back into the moment.

"OK, that's it," Devon said standing up. "Li, we'll let you get back to bed. Call me if I can do anything. And check in with me before Shirl and Harv get you on Friday."

"Yo, I'm going upstairs," Jerry said, giving me a hug. I could smell the smoke on him and suddenly felt desperate for a cigarette. Then I realized that it was the first time since taking Librium that I'd even thought about cigarettes.

"Yeah, good idea. You belong in a gown," Devon said. She hugged me hard and then the two of them were on their way.

Were they going to get drinks and talk about me now? They would probably head to Coconut Grill, just a couple of blocks away and order vodka sodas. I knew they were scared for me, and I ached to go with them where I could drink and smoke—show them that I was still here. But at that moment, dizzy, hungry, and still exhausted, I just needed to lie down.

• • •

Time passed quickly over those few days, mostly because I spent the vast majority of it sleeping. My body had been worn out, abused, and now wiped out with Librium. Unless I was forced to go to a meeting or a meal, for those few days I was a detoxing slug, finally able to just lie down and rest like one of those raindrops on the window of the Russian's car.

My intention hadn't been to be antisocial, but in fact I was. A later review of my records from Gracie Square turned up notes from nurses stating, "She remained depressed and irritable. Stayed in her room most of the time." When a nurse came by "for 1:1 interaction" she received "superficial smiling." I was "encouraged to interact with others in the dayroom," but refused to do so. Apparently, there was bingo.

On Thursday morning, I had my first visit from Annie, a social worker. *Great*, I thought. *Just how many attendants do I appear to need?* I smiled and motioned for Annie to take a seat on the wooden chair at the foot of my bed, as if we were in my office high above Times Square.

Annie was young, maybe in her midtwenties, with rich olive skin and long black hair that she kept pulled back in a low, professional ponytail. Empathy emanated from her warm brown eyes as she smiled with her lips closed and slowly sat down. She carried a clipboard and wore an identification lanyard around her neck. Underneath the clipboard was a folder that appeared to be full of pamphlets.

Right away I envied her. She'd chosen a career in the helping arts. I wondered if doing meaningful work could keep a person safe from the horrors of addiction. If I'd chosen a different career—one that fulfilled me, gave back to the world, brought people happiness—would I have ended up here? Back when I made my career decisions, what fulfilled me was having a nice apartment in the city and a shitload of money to party with.

"So, Lisa," Annie began, "I'm here to talk with you about what happens after you leave tomorrow. First, though, how are you feeling? Do you feel ready to leave?"

I had developed two positions in my hospital bed: lying on my side in a fetal curve when I was alone, and sitting up hugging my knees when I had to speak to people. What did this body language say about my readiness to leave? I sat up and hugged my knees.

"Yes, I'm ready."

At that moment, I realized that this was my third consecutive day without a drink. Such a stretch hadn't happened since college when I was trying to lose weight. I didn't know if it was the Librium, but I felt like a different human being, physically. It was as if my insides had been removed, run through a car wash, and then dropped back into my body. I was still shaky but less so. I also noticed that the shooting pains and constant aches were gone, and what I found fascinating was that I couldn't recall when the pains had gone away. But just now in this moment, I realized that I was pain free. For the first time in years, my body felt good. It reminded me of how I felt right after my breast reduction, finally free of the two giant burdens I'd been lugging around. Alcohol had been a similar burden.

"I see that you live in the city," Annie said, flipping through my file. "Do you live alone?"

"Yes."

"Do you have family or friends nearby in case you need anything or have any problems when you first get home? A lot of people struggle at the beginning. It's normal." I wanted to be Annie. She seemed so *good*. Her parents must be proud. Then I thought about my parents at home worrying about me.

"Yes, plenty. And a good friend lives in my building," I said.

"OK. Good. Dr. Landry recommends that you continue treatment after you leave here. I brought information on several places you might think about. You'd have to check with your insurance, but it's likely you'd be covered for a full twenty-eight day stay at most of them."

"Wait, what? What are you talking about? No one said anything about a twenty-eight day anything. I'm not doing that. I have to go back to work on Monday." I felt a heat rush through my body all the way up into my cheeks and I sat up straight. Could they *make* me go somewhere for twenty-eight days?

Annie looked disappointed but not entirely discouraged. "Well, if you can't go away, there are excellent intensive out-patient programs right here in the city. Most meet five days a week for different amounts of time. I can give you that information, too." Aha, I wasn't obligated to do anything when I left. I felt back in control, so I became bitchy.

"No, Annie. Did you hear what I said? I have to go back to work *on Monday*. I told them I'd be out for a week having a procedure. I can't all of a sudden say I'm gone for a month or be in and out all the time. I can't tell them what really happened." I felt the tears welling up in my eyes.

"OK. I understand," Annie said. "I'll talk to Dr. Landry."

Immediately I felt bad for being nasty. "Thank you. Just please make sure he understands that I have to go back to work on Monday."

"I will. I'm going to leave these brochures with you," she said, handing me a small pile of pastel colored papers that had been folded twice to form rectangular pamphlets. "Just general information on 12-step programs. Help in figuring out what might be right for you and your family."

I decided to keep my next tirade to myself. *My family? I'm not dragging them any deeper into this! Why can't you people do your jobs in the time we agreed to? What is this, some bullshit system with a hundred "steps" where you all make money from the same person?* "OK, thanks," I said. We shook hands and she left.

I stuffed the pamphlets into my bag and climbed under the scratchy sheet to try to nap, but my racing thoughts wouldn't let me sleep. Pamphlets, meetings, twelve steps, happy hours, prescription drugs, tattooed addicts, nosy colleagues, retirement parties, holidays, people watching me for slipups . . . I thrashed around in the bed, my mind swirling. I'd checked into this place on a desperate impulse, and soon I'd have to leave the building and head out into the consequences.

• • •

My Librium dosage was tapered in preparation for my release the next day. I would get my final dose on Friday morning, meet with Dr. Landry, and then be handed over to my family for reintroduction to the outside world. I agreed to continue taking the Lexapro indefinitely. I liked Dr. Landry's explanation: I had a chemical imbalance in my brain that drove my depression and anxiety. For decades I'd been self-medicating—numbing it with alcohol and cocaine—but that had made my condition much worse. That was the story, and now I was supposed to start treating my mental imbalance with the right medication. It sounded simple enough.

When Friday morning arrived, I went through my final appointed rounds of breakfast, physical exam, and meds line. At about ten o'clock Dr. Landry appeared in my doorway. "Did you know your parents and brother have been waiting in the lobby for about a half hour?" he asked.

"No, but that sounds right," I said, smiling.

"They've been very supportive. That's good. Let them help you."

"I will," I said. My mother's idea of help would be snatching a drink out of my hand as if I were a four-year-old trying to lick rat poison. My father and brother would be more subtle. They'd talk about work—my successes, my goals—and then they'd offer to bring me hot tea and fruit smoothies.

I saw my discharge papers on Dr. Landry's clipboard. Sitting across desks from partners in a law firm for years had taught me to read upside down. I saw the diagnosis of "Major Depressive Disorder" and a prescription for Lexapro.

"So, how are you feeling? Are you ready to leave?" he asked.

"Yes. Ready to leave," I said. I patted the packed and zipped duffle bag at my feet to confirm it.

"Annie tells me that you're refusing to go to a twenty-eight-day program from here. Or even a daily intensive outpatient program. I had hoped that after our talk you would understand the critical importance of immediate, focused aftercare."

"I do understand," I said. "I didn't say that I wasn't willing to do *anything*. I just have to go back to work on Monday. They don't know where I am and I can't let them know."

"Why not?" he asked. "You told me that you spend a significant amount of your time at work. Don't you think it will be better if the people you're with every day know that you're in the earliest stages of recovery? There's nothing to be ashamed of. It's a disease, not a personal failing."

"Yeah, I get that, but no. It's not OK in a big law firm. We talk about alcoholics behind their backs." His expression didn't change, but I still felt like a jerk. "I know that sounds bad, but . . . well, nobody cares if it's a disease. It's considered a weakness, and they always find a way to cut the weak from the herd. I'll come clean anywhere but at work."

"I understand what you're saying, but Lisa, that's just wrong," he said. "The only way you're going to get healthy and stay sober is if you start to live your life honestly. Lying to the people you spend the most time with is not the way to do it." I was pretty sure that my expression didn't change. "Do you want to stay sober, Lisa?"

"Yes. I think I do. I feel a lot better, and I'd like to not drink for a while at least. And see what happens." Did he have any idea what "staying sober" was going to do to my life? I couldn't promise him forever, but I could promise him for now.

"Well then, you really need to attend an outpatient program that meets two or three times a week in the evenings. Is that something you'd consider?"

"Yeah, sure. I'm happy to do that," I said.

"I must tell you, Lisa, if you want to stay sober out there, you're going to have to work really hard. It will be the most difficult thing you've ever done. Right now, your sobriety couldn't be more fragile. And you haven't even been away for the recommended twenty-eight days. You should do more than the outpatient program a couple of nights a week. You really should go to 12-step meetings every day."

Meetings. Every day. You're killin' me, Doc. "OK," I lied. "I'll do that."

It was my fourth day without an unprescribed substance in my body. My hair hadn't been washed in over a week and my face was covered in an oil film, but I felt ten years younger. Still, *daily* 12-step meetings? This had been a huge week, and I needed a break from all this crap. I just wanted my life back.

"Good. I'm glad you'll attend meetings. What you're doing isn't the best next step or what I would recommend, but if you commit to sobriety and take the suggestions you're given, you'll be able to do it, one day at a time," he said. "Just remember there's always support out there. I'll set you up for a Monday morning appointment at HopeCare, the outpatient rehab facility. You can go back to work Tuesday."

He handed me the forms I needed to sign for official release. I decided not to fight him on going to HopeCare on Monday. I had one foot out the door and didn't want to blow it.

Ashley showed up as I was signing the last documents. Then Dr. Landry shook my hand. "Good luck, Lisa. We're here if you need us." *Please God no*, I thought.

"Thank you for everything. I really appreciate it," I said, trying to look like a mature, sober person.

Ashley gave me copies of the forms and all of the contraband that Vivian had confiscated when I arrived. The sight of the gold and white Marlboro Lights pack sent an adrenaline surge through my body. No one had said I couldn't smoke when I got out of here. But wait, what did that mean the sight of a bottle of Yellow Tail was going to do to me?

"OK! Let's go downstairs and see your family," Ashley said.

Before I followed her, I took a hard look at my room, the nurses' station, and everything else I could see on the floor. Maybe if I seared the memory of it into my brain, I could bring the worst images to mind every time I thought about having a drink or a line of coke. *Take a deep breath*, I thought. *What have you learned here?*

I thought that I could control my drinking by myself. I was wrong.

I believed that the alcoholic way I was living was just "who I was." I was wrong.

I believed that I would never consider quitting drinking entirely. I was wrong.

The week gave me hope, but walking past those hospital doors and back into the wild city was going to make me feel like a lamb on the Serengeti. I no longer felt like the ass-kicking corporate lawyer who looked a CEO in the eyes while firmly shaking hands or the independent New York broad who would walk twenty blocks alone at 3:00 a.m. I felt frail, like someone who's just survived a vicious round of stomach flu, and nothing sounded more comforting than sliding back onto my barstool at Kenny's and dialing Henry.

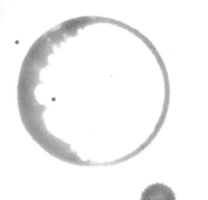

19

As soon as Ashley and I made it down to the lobby, my mother rushed me with a bear hug. The intensity of it reminded me of when she would nearly tackle me at the Newark Airport when I came home during college breaks.

For several seconds, she held me with both hands at a "let me look at you" length, and then she hugged me again. Without a bloodstream full of booze, I found the scent of her cologne comforting. A week earlier it would have been nauseating.

As was his custom, my dad gave me a peck of a kiss and rubbed my head. I thought I could see relief behind his eyeglasses, as if all was better now that I was in their custody. After Lou hugged me and kissed my cheek, he nodded at my dad, as if to say, "We're OK." I sprouted more tears, this time at the memory of how I turned a car around for coke on the day my brother's baby was born.

This was awkward. I was a successful, independent thirty-eight-year-old woman, and my parents were retrieving me from a locked down psychiatric ward. Was there etiquette to govern such an occasion? Should I apologize? Make a joke? Should I tell them about the merits of the Asian floor relative to the detox floor? I didn't know so I stayed quiet.

"You look good, kid," my dad said, nodding.

"Good one, Dad," I said. "But thanks. I actually feel pretty good."

The four of us walked out the front door of Gracie Square into the sunny April morning. I was wearing the same grubby jeans and sweater as when I walked in Monday night. Having not seen the sun, the moon, or anything else outdoors since Monday, I turned my face toward the light. The day was cool, but the sun shot a bolt of warmth through my body.

As we walked up the block toward the car, my mother linked her arm through mine. "So, your father got the tuna fish from Ronnie's and a fresh pumpernickel rye bagel for you. Does that sound good? You'll stay until Sunday?"

"Yeah, great."

"That's good," she said.

My father and my brother walked in front of us discussing my brother's latest case. I appreciated that no one asked me about what went on inside the hospital, and I was profoundly relieved that they didn't ask about what had gone on to land me there. Were we all going to try to move forward without discussing it? Maybe the questions would come later. Certainly, I owed them some explanations, but for that moment, we were just a regular family walking down a city street. I tipped my head back, closed my eyes, and took deep breaths of the cool air. I wasn't exactly Andy Dufresne just finished tunneling my way out of Shawshank, but in the sunshine of that New York morning, I felt free and full of hope.

My dad gave his ticket to the parking lot cashier and I watched the bustle along First Avenue. People carried Starbucks cups while walking little dogs on long leashes. Pairs of fluffed and manicured mothers around my age pushed baby strollers. I looked down at the Gracie Square hospital bracelet on my wrist and felt a little sick about the differences in our lives. According to my teenage master plan, I was supposed to have been one of them by now. My successful New York husband and I were going to have two deliriously happy children thriving in their exclusive, super-smart-kid academies. They would come home each day to healthful after-school snacks prepared with love in our kitchen with its granite counter tops and Viking stove. I couldn't rip off the bracelet so I covered it with my sleeve.

One day at a time, Lisa. Don't compare yourself to other people—some of those women probably have Starbucks cups full of cranberry and vodka.

"Let it go." "Easy does it." "Live and let live." I was determined to try out these new slogans; maybe that would help quiet the racket that was already revving back up in my addled brain. My insides were calling for drinks, drinks. For me, morning in New York meant "time for drinks." Oh to feel icy cold vodka oozing down my throat right now. Or warm red wine or even a light white pinot. Fuck. It was brutal. How was I going to make it? I reached under my sleeve and rubbed the hospital bracelet as if it had super powers.

On the ride into northern New Jersey, I sat behind the driver's seat with my head tilted against the window. Mom sat next to me, holding my hand the whole way. Her skin was soft, mine felt scaly. Maybe this new start would bring new grooming habits, and I would moisturize every day as Mom had always preached.

As soon as we arrived at my parents' townhouse, I dashed upstairs to the shower. I peeled off the clothes that I would never wear again and threw them into a heap on the carpeted floor of the guest bedroom. I walked naked past my Cabbage Patch doll and the stuffed panda I'd bought during an eighth-grade class trip to DC. They just sat there smiling at me like silly-faced old ladies offering encouragement behind frozen faces that masked their disgust. I gave them the finger.

The shower felt miraculous. I stood under the spray for a long time, letting the water run over me while I swayed back and forth with my eyes closed. This was what it was like to stand up straight in a shower. My God, how long had it been since I'd been able to stand, turn, or bend forward in a shower without the risk of falling over and cracking my head on porcelain? How many times had I vomited while showering? To think that most people go their entire lives without vomiting in a shower.

My thoughts began to whirl again. Why did I abuse myself with alcohol and drugs for so long? Why could other people shut themselves off after a few? What was it that made me decide to check into Gracie Square? What the hell did sober people do with their time?? *Stop focusing on negative things— none of the answers are going to appear in the shower. Focus on the shower. "Let it go."*

After two shampoos and a thorough scrubbing, I emerged from the bathroom feeling clean for the first time in a week. I grabbed a pair of my mother's soft cotton pajamas and a pair of my dad's oversized, padded socks from their bedroom, combed out my hair and went downstairs. Lou had taken the day off of work, so he was planted in the den with my parents.

"Better?" my mom asked, looking up over her reading glasses.

"Much. Thanks," I said. They were watching a Bogart movie on the big screen television that Lou and I had bought for our dad's seventy-fifth birthday. I lay down next to my mom on the long couch and rested my head on her lap. I wanted a cigarette, but I was too tired to move. With a system still full of Librium, I feel asleep in minutes.

When I woke up, it was five o'clock, and my head was on a pillow instead of on my mother's lap. "Hey, look who's up," Lou said from the couch across the room.

"Yessss! Sleeping Beauty rises," my dad said from his recliner. He removed the giant headphones he wore over his ears. At seventy-five, Dad had pretty bad hearing, but the headphone system allowed the rest of us to watch television with him.

"You hungry?" Lou asked. "We were just talking about dinner."

"Yeah, definitely," I said, without raising my head from the pillow. "I think my stomach might be completely empty. But I'm not taking off these pajamas."

"OK, we'll order Chinese," my mom said. "I'll grab the menu." She trotted up the stairs to the kitchen.

Given my recent release from the all-Asian-all-the-time floor at Gracie Square, I would have preferred pizza, but I was committed to no longer being a pain in everyone's ass—starting right now—so I didn't say anything.

Not five minutes later, I learned that the world was not about to start revolving around me. "Are we drinking?" my dad asked my mother and brother, slightly tentatively. After all, it was cocktail hour and everyone had had a rough day. "We know *you're* not," he said to me with laugh. Then all three of them looked at me for a response.

I looked back at them blankly. Of course, my first thought was that if I couldn't drink, nobody else should. So much for not being a pain in everyone's ass. No one at Gracie Square had told me what to do in this situation, but Dr. Landry had said that staying sober would be the hardest thing I'd ever do. This must have been what he meant.

Buck up, Lisa. Welcome to your new life. "You guys go ahead," I said. "It's OK. I'm going to have to get used to it," I said. I dug my fingernails into the palm of my hand.

"Are you sure?" my mother asked.

"Yeah, I'm sure . . . I guess. I can't tell everyone around me not to drink because I'm an alcoholic, right?"

For ten years I'd known that I was addicted, but right then I was amazed at how easily the words, "I'm an alcoholic," breezed from my mouth in front of my family.

"OK, as long as you're sure," my dad said as he headed up the stairs toward the booze. Minutes later he came back down with two glasses of Dewar's and a Heineken.

"I need a cigarette," I announced loudly in a small act of revenge.

"Really??" my mom asked. Her forehead was scrunched in distress. "You smoke? Like a regular smoker?"

Time for me to launch another ugly truth about her little pink daughter. "Well, not like a *regular* smoker. I always just smoked when I drank," I said. "But then I started drinking all the time, so . . ."

"Just do it outside," she said.

"What? You're going to make her go outside?" my father asked.

"She's not smoking cigarettes *in the house.*"

"Dad, it's fine. I'm happy to go outside. The fresh air will be good."

"I'll go with you," Lou said. He popped up from the couch and slid on his leather loafers. I pulled on my crummy Nikes.

Cigarettes and lighter in hand, I opened the sliding glass door of the den and took a seat outside on one of the cement steps leading to the patio. I felt my parents' eyes on me as I moved. Lou sat next to me.

"So unreal," I said. "I can't believe I did this." I lit my cigarette and took a long drag. It tasted like home. I blew the smoke away from Lou and took another greedy drag then rocked my head back and exhaled, "Ahhh."

"Hey, you did the right thing. The guy at Gracie Square told us that people don't end up there unless they need to be there. He said you really have to try to stay sober now."

Wow, if I did decide to go back to drinking, I was going to have to become an even better liar. "Well, my plan is to try it. I can't make any promises, though. Everyone I hang out with drinks, and I'm not going to get rid of my friends. But I have to say, this is the first time in years that I haven't felt close to barfing or passing out."

"Well, that should tell you something. You know we'll all do whatever we can for you. Seriously."

"Yeah, I know," I said. "As long as it doesn't mean not having a drink at cocktail hour," I laughed a little and elbowed him in the ribs.

"Oh, no! Seriously, we don't have to drink. Oh man, we should have known better."

Then came more guilt. Was I ever going to get any of this right? "No, no, it's fine," I said. "Really! I have to get used to being around people who can drink. I mean, I'd love a drink, but they kept saying that for me alcohol is like poison, poison that kills over time. So I'm going to have to try the 'one day at a time' stuff."

"One day at a time?" Lou laughed. "You've always mapped things out a week in advance."

"I know!" I smiled. "Now time is going to move in slow motion. Anyway, how are Mom and Dad doing with this?" I asked.

"They're OK. We all feel bad that we didn't know."

"There's no way you could have known," I said. "The things I was hiding, you wouldn't believe. I became a great liar. Apparently it's a thing alcoholics do. It's how they, we, keep going." I shrugged and stared at the sky, watching the trail of my exhaled smoke.

"If it was so bad, why didn't you come to us? We wouldn't have judged you. Why didn't you let anybody help you?"

"I didn't want to stop." I gave him a moment to let that sink in. "Lou, if you'd had any idea of what I was putting into my body, you would have done everything you could to make me stop."

"That's true." He thought about it for a moment. "So what changed?"

"Honestly, I don't really know. I guess I realized that I couldn't get it under control and that it was going to kill me." I stubbed the cigarette out in one of my mother's plants and said, "I don't want to die."

He reached over and held my hand, and I began to cry. "Thank God." he said. "I can't even imagine that." I cried harder. Then I thought again about his baby's birthday and the choice I made. I covered my face with my free hand and wept, wondering if that memory would ever stop hurting.

When we went back inside, it was clear that cocktail hour at my parents' place had taken a big hit. The glasses were still filled, but there were no joyful clinks of glasses and no toasts to each other's health, just quiet sips between hunks of Jarlsberg cheese on Carr's Water Crackers. Stuffing my face with food comforted me in my strange new life. If I had to be the only person not drinking, I'd certainly let myself enjoy eating. But would I get fat? *Oh God, please don't let my addiction transfer to food.*

230

What it would be like to have a rocks glass full of vodka with a splash of soda right now? It would taste strong but soothing going down. A shudder ran through my body. *Shit.*

I decided that rather than indulge booze fantasies, as fast as possible I'd change my mental channel. When I began to dream of wine in my bloodstream, I'd flip to the little Latin guy blasting us at my first group meeting: "You *do not pick up a drink or a drug.* One day at a time. Just for today, YOU DO NOT DRINK, NO MATTER WHAT." So I decided to not drink that day, just for that day.

By the time I went to bed that night, the Librium had worn off. Lou had long since left for his normal home, normal baby, and normal wife. My parents and I had made our way upstairs at about nine o'clock. They weren't going to leave me alone until they saw me all the way through to the end of this momentous day. I wondered, *are they worried that I'll sneak downstairs and bust into their liquor cabinet? They should be.*

As I brushed my teeth, I looked at the toilet and remembered doing coke off its lid just a few weeks earlier as my parents watched TV. I felt a shudder of disgust, and I knew that a drink would nicely numb my guilt. But then the living hell timer would start again because I never had "a" drink. I'd finish the bottle. *Remember that, remember that. You do not drink no matter what. You do not pick up no matter what.*

Maybe it was the lighting, but in this mirror I looked less sickly than I had the week before. Bags still puffed under my eyes and my face was blotchy, but my skin no longer looked gray. Some of the bloat was gone and I could see my cheekbones.

With a fresh mouth and scrubbed skin, I climbed between the clean sheets of the guest room bed. Maybe I should grab a book from the bookcase, I thought, maybe reread my favorite:

A Prayer for Owen Meany. But my eyelids were heavy. Turning off the light, I did theatrical stretch across the bed and settled into the soft mattress. *Just go to sleep,* I thought, *just as people all around the world do every night. You don't need drugs to make you sleep. You don't need to pass out. One night at a time. Just fall asleep like a fucking normal person.*

20

I spent the rest of the weekend lying around my parents' house, overeating and subjecting them to my constant trips to the patio to smoke cigarettes. My mom even sat out there with me a few times.

"You know, I've never even tried a cigarette," she said, watching me smoke on Saturday afternoon. It had been a constant refrain since the first time she discovered a pack of Merits in my underwear drawer when I was fifteen.

"You're welcome to try one of mine anytime. They're delicious," I said, popping a few smoke rings out of my mouth.

"Yuck. How do you do that?" she asked.

"Practice."

"That's terrible, Lisa. I hope you don't plan to smoke forever."

"Who knows? I'm not making long-term plans. I'm just trying to not drink for this one day." Wow, listen to me *getting with the program.* I hoped I wasn't going to become one of those platitude preachers. "They said in the hospital that if you smoke now, you shouldn't try to quit while you're trying to quit drinking, not for the first year."

"First *year*?" She looked at me with wide eyes. "OK," she said, with a sigh and a shrug. "I guess whatever it takes to stop drinking is what you need to do."

"Exactly." I put my arm around her and gave her a squeeze. She returned the gesture with a full body embrace.

As full of questions as my parents must have been, all I heard all weekend was, "Are you OK?" and "Do you need anything?" At some point we'd have to talk about the lie I had been living for so long, but that weekend was all about making sure that I was okay and nowhere near the liquor cabinet.

On Sunday morning I came downstairs early. Mom was working on the *New York Times* crossword puzzle and Dad was unpacking fresh bagels and lox. "We're up?" my dad asked.

"Yeah, we're up." I grabbed a giant mug from above the sink. "But we need coffee."

"Good, good. We made a full pot," he said. They watched me pour the coffee and their eyes followed me from the coffee-maker to the refrigerator for milk and then to the cabinet with the Splenda in it.

I sprinkled and stirred in the sweetener, and without looking up I asked, "What's going on? You're staring at me."

"Nothing!" my mom said. "We were just wondering about today."

"What about today?" I asked.

"Well, you're supposed to go back to the city. But we were thinking maybe you could stay here tonight and then Daddy can drive you into the city before your appointment at that place."

"Yeah," my dad said. "We can do the early morning run, before traffic." He used to do "the early morning run" for me when I was practicing law and would come home to New Jersey for the weekend. They loved when I stayed over on Sunday night, and he would get up at five-thirty on Monday to take me into Manhattan. Dad would be awake and chirpy, and I'd be brutally hungover from having sucked down another bottle of wine after they'd gone to sleep the night before.

"Thanks," I said. "But I'm kind of anxious to get home. And I'm going to have to do it soon anyway."

They looked at each other with resignation. My dad said, "OK. Then we'll take you in today."

"Will anyone be there with you?" my mom asked.

"No, but if I need anyone I have plenty of babysitters available. And you don't have to drive me in! I'll just call a car service. I'm sick of inconveniencing everyone."

"You're not inconveniencing us!" my mother said. "Just let us take you in, check out the apartment with you."

• • •

When I opened my apartment door a couple of hours later my mother said, "Wow! You left the place in good shape!"

"Uh, no. I didn't. Russell and Devon must have been here." I knew they had planned to come over and remove any contraband, but I hadn't expected a full cleaning. The shades were up, the curtains were open, and the sun blazed into the living room. The drug cave had been transformed.

I kicked off my shoes, dropped my bag, and expected a flood of memories of parties and laughing and drinking. But there was no flood. Strange, I thought. The good memories had long been blackened by the year of self-poisoning misery. But in that moment, none of those thoughts came back either. I just felt "here."

"OK, you guys don't need to stick around. I'm fine," I said to my parents. They hadn't been inside my apartment in years. I had always gone to New Jersey, or if they came into the city we met at a restaurant. All the truth in that made me feel guilty again.

"What about food?" my mother asked as she stood in front of the refrigerator. "There's nothing but water and soy sauce in here."

"Yeah, don't worry. I'll go up the street to the market and get some stuff. Maybe I'll order in sushi for dinner."

"You're going to go out and walk around?" she asked.

"Yes, Mom. Don't worry. It's Sunday. The liquor stores are closed."

"Oh, that's good," she said, inspecting the contents of my pantry.

She really had no idea what "needing to drink" meant. The liquor stores were closed, but the bars were open, and I could have named five restaurants in a three-block radius that would have sold me a bottle or three of wine that day, even delivered them.

"Shirley, let her be. She'll be fine. She's doing great. Let's leave her alone and let's get out of here," my dad said.

"All right, all right," Mom said.

"Thank you so much for everything," I said. "I couldn't have gotten through this without you." My eyes welled up and my face grew hot. I felt ready, and yet the thought of being left alone roiled my stomach with fear. It had never ended well before.

As soon as I shut the door behind them, I pounded my head against it and stood there with my hand still on the knob. Once I had no doubt that they were gone, I knew it would be easy to run over to the Belgian restaurant on the corner for a fast martini. Who would know? Mark didn't know I was home yet, and if I used the stairs and went out the basement door, there was almost no chance he would see me. I could put on a hat and sunglasses and keep my head down. Or I could call the Italian restaurant that was fast on delivery and order a couple bottles of red wine with my penne arrabiata. If I was really lucky, Russell and Devon missed a bag of coke in my closet.

"AAAHHHHH!" I screamed, banging my fist against the door while I kicked it. I shook my head and blinked hard. I was terrified. *Don't do it*, I thought. But how do I not do it?

I reverted to the one thing I knew would stop me before I could start. I called Mark.

"Hey! What's up? You're back!" he said.

"Yeah, are you home? Can you come up?"

"Yeah, sure. Let me finish something up for school. I'll come up in half an hour."

"Can you finish what you're doing up here? I think I need someone else here. Like now." My voice cracked.

"No problem. I'll be right there." *Thank God*, I thought, hanging up.

Two minutes later Mark was at the door. Tears started running down my face when I saw him, and I immediately pressed the extra set of keys into his hands. "Take these," I said. "I need to know that you might walk in any minute."

"OK," he said, dropping the keys into his bag. "Lisa, are you all right?"

I fell onto the couch and started sobbing. "I think so. I don't know," I said between gulps of breath. "I'm scared. Just give me a minute." Mark waited quietly. When I'd calmed down, I said, "I'm sorry. It's just, normally I'd pour a drink right now, but I can't. I mean, I can't if I don't want to throw away what I just did last week. I don't want to do that, but, fuuuck I want to do that so badly."

"I think I get it. My friend's mother said it would be hard when you got home."

"Fuck your friend's mother! Will you please stop talking to her about me?" I screamed.

"OK, OK. What did they tell you to do when you wanted to drink?"

"Go to one of those meetings. But I don't want to do that right now." I sounded like a confused three-year-old. *This is too much,* I thought. *I can't do this. If Mark weren't here, I would have slammed a drink by now.* Going to detox had been a mistake. It was too much too fast. I started chewing my fingernails to see if that would help. Maybe I could focus on a new habit. Fuck. Fuck. Fuck. How was I going to live this kind of life?

"Are you hungry? Want to eat?" Mark asked.

"Yes! Yes! Food! Let's get food." Food would make me feel better. Of course, food! I jumped up to grab the delivery menus from my kitchen drawer.

"Pizza?" he asked. "Can we get pizza?"

"Yes, pizza, great. Call them now!" I squealed.

"Excellent," Mark said, already dialing.

After I was full, the desperate craving for a drink passed. We flipped around television shows for a while and then Mark asked, "Do you want me to stay over tonight?"

"No, I want to do this on my own tonight." He looked warily at me, which was irritating. I didn't need the people in my life treating me like a child. *Dammit,* I thought. *I'm not a child! And I don't want to live like a prisoner!* FUCK, why wasn't there someone else to blame! There was certainly no reason to take it out on Mark. "I promise I'll call if I start going sideways," I said.

He took one last inspection through the kitchen. "You sure you're OK?"

"Yes, I can do this." *Really?* I thought. *Can you?* I hugged Mark goodbye and bolted the door behind him. Then I stopped and looked at myself in the old "I hate you" mirror/coke plate hanging by the door. This time I broke into a big cheesy smile and said, "Yes, I can do this! One day at a time!"

Then I screamed, "FUCK!!"

• • •

It was very early the next morning when my eyes popped open. 5:30 a.m. I sat up and grabbed the glass of clear liquid from my nightstand and drank. For a blurred second I expected the taste of vodka to hit my tongue, but then *wait!* I thought, *that's the water I left there last night. I didn't drink alcohol or use coke yesterday. Oh my God, I'm still sober! I stayed overnight by myself without drinking! HOLY SHIT!* I kicked off the covers and pumped my fists in the air like an eight-year-old who had just scored her first soccer goal.

OK, now what? What the hell do sober people do at five-thirty in the morning? It was such a miracle to feel human in the morning, that I wanted to be awake for it. For the first time in memory I woke up without hating myself. It was the most profound relief I can ever remember feeling. Not even the mosquito could mess with me today.

I made a pot of coffee and while watching morning news drank ten of the twelve cups. What if I became a coffee addict and start walking around the city with a white paper cup in my hand? I'd have to get oversized sunglasses and a tiny purse dog to complete the look. I could do that!

Small things meant a lot that morning. Not throwing up within thirty minutes of waking up, being able to stand upright in the shower, and having a coherent early phone conversation with my parents to assure them that I was OK. These were all things I'd never expected to do again. I felt fortunate.

I arrived early for my 9:00 a.m. appointment at HopeCare. The location was ideal, just a few blocks north of my apartment and to the west, which was on my way home from work. Hope-Care itself was located in the basement. A large white sign with the facility's heart-emblazoned logo greeted me and directed me "DOWNSTAIRS." It looked about right—like the crappy old church basement I'd predicted.

Two young receptionists sat in a large cubicle just inside glass double doors. There were a couple of oversized, stuffed faux leather chairs, along with a few folding metal chairs lining the wall. A small water cooler sat in the corner. Seedy as it was, it was a big step up from Gracie Square.

"Hi. I'm Lisa Smith! I have a nine o'clock appointment with Teddy Minter," I barked like a cheerleader. In trying so hard to demonstrate to these strangers that I was not fucked up on that morning, my greeting might have had the opposite effect.

"Sure, sweetie, that's great. I'm Tracy," said one of the receptionists. "You haven't been here before?" She looked at her computer screen and chomped a piece of gum.

"No, this is my first time."

As Tracy searched her computer, I leaned over on the counter and unsuccessfully tried to see what was popping up on the screen. Clearly, they knew where I'd been and why. What did they have on me? Tracy hurried to hand me a clipboard and said, "Why don't you have a seat over there and fill out these forms?"

I filled out the forms, handed them back to Tracy, and then surveyed the room. The half-empty vending machine was from another era and looked to be filled with its original Mars Bars and bags of Skittles. Next to it stood a more modern looking soda machine with a sign that read "THIRSTY?" I let out a half-hearted laugh and thought, if I hadn't been so fucking thirsty all my life I wouldn't be here.

"He's ready to see you," Tracy said, leading me to Teddy's office. She knocked on the door.

"C'mon in," a calm, low male voice said. Teddy was seated at his desk, an old built-in that ran along a side wall and was almost completely covered in papers. Bookshelves were fitted around the desk and rose almost to the ceiling. Teddy pushed his rolling chair back and stood up. He was a tall, ruddy-faced man, stocky but not fat, graying around the temples, and slightly sluggish. In the way that he nodded slowly to me, I sensed that he'd had some life experiences similar to mine. He sized me up from under droopy eyelids.

We shook hands, and I sat in the metal chair at the end of his desk. I pulled my knees up to my chest and hugged them as I waited for him to begin.

"OK, Lisa, how are you doing? Have you been OK since you left Gracie Square?"

I assumed that he was asking whether I was still sober. "Yes," I said. "I'm OK. I've been doing OK." My elation of the early morning was gradually darkening as I realized that I had an entire day to get through without drinking.

"Great. Then let me give you some information," he said. "I recommend that you start in our Early Recovery group. It meets on Mondays and Thursdays from 7:15 p.m. until 8:45 p.m. I am the counselor for the group and act as its discussion facilitator. We talk about issues that people like you face on a day-to-day basis."

"Sounds great," I said. I had no idea what "people like me" faced, so I was interested.

"Good, good." He started writing notes.

"I have a few questions, though," I said. "Are all of the people in the group alcoholics? Or are there drug addicts, too?"

"Lisa, you probably heard this at Gracie Square, but an addict is an addict. Whether the person was addicted to alcohol or cocaine or heroin or painkillers, it's all the same disease.

The group includes people with the full range of substance abuse issues."

"Will there be celebrities in Group?" I couldn't resist. Teddy furrowed his brow.

"I can't answer that," he said. "Client confidentiality is strictly maintained here at HopeCare. Absolutely no exceptions." I switched to a serious face and signed the required forms.

As I walked back out onto the street and lit a cigarette, a surreal sensation came over me. It was as if I'd spent a month in a foreign country only to return home and find that English no longer sounded familiar. I felt more clear-headed than ever, but my dominant thought was *what happened to me*?

Passing several liquor stores, I looked longingly into the windows, my heart swelling at the lineup of beautiful glass bottles that I knew so well. I longed for them in the way that normal people ache for puppies in a pet shop.

I tried to find the upside. Well, the idea of being in a rehab program did sound kind of badass. And then there was the part about surviving a near-death experience—that might earn me a few cool points. But oh, hell. I could try to dress it up however I liked. I was still going to be sitting in a dingy basement next to some toothless guy named Clyde.

21

I'd been counseled strongly against going back to work too soon. Dr. Landry advised against it. My father advised against it. I think the falafel guy on the corner of 45th and 6th might have advised against it. But I felt that I had no choice. I had to stick with my story of having been out "for a minor procedure," so now it was time to march my imperceptibly repaired self back onto the battlefield. Of course, if anyone noticed that I looked just a little fresher, stepped just a little lighter, that would be fine with me.

I was awake again at 5:30 a.m. on Tuesday. It was way too early to go into the office, so I sat on my living room couch, drank a pot of coffee, smoked a few breakfast cigarettes, and watched the sun rise outside my windows. I couldn't remember the last time I had seen a sunrise without despising it. When coke and booze had kept me up all night, there was no joy in the dawning of a new day. Of course I took it out on the day, not on the drugs or the booze.

At about eight thirty, I rode down the elevator of my building with a few other people heading for work. They all looked clear-eyed and ready for the day, briefcases and newspapers at their sides. My hand instinctively covered my mouth, and I smiled, remembering that there had been no booze to cause booze breath. I could put my hand down. Incredible.

Outside my apartment building, the mid-April morning in New York was bright and filled with the normal sounds of kids squealing, cabs honking, and jackhammers rattling. I lit a cigarette. Making my way west to the Union Square subway station felt like a new route. As always, I noticed the dogs with their owners walking them. But this time I didn't think the dogs had it better than I did.

Union Square station's oddly low ceiling amplified the wail of trains screeching in and out as a crush of people proceeded along its stairways and catwalk platforms. I walked calmly toward my train, still not believing that I was moving among normal people on a normal commute on a normal Tuesday morning. Just taking public transportation to my job, not racing uptown in a cab because I was late again, not choreographing my gestures to hide my trembling hands, not sweating on a frigid winter day.

I slipped into my office on the twenty-third floor overlooking the flashing billboards of Times Square and closed the door behind me. Even though it was after nine o'clock, the firm was still relatively quiet.

As my computer booted up, I glanced around my office. *What a disaster.* Piles of paper lay everywhere. They littered my desk, the shelves, and the windowsill. As if in tribute to the trees they had once been, the paper piles seem to be growing. Taken alone, these piles wouldn't have been enough to alert anyone that there was something very wrong with the occupant of this office; many a lawyer's office looked as if the cops had torn it apart looking for stolen jewels.

But the Post-it notes—they were a giveaway.

Covered in scribble resembling a child's first attempt at the alphabet, they were everywhere—sticking out of folders, nestled inside legal pads, hanging limply from my computer monitor, and huddled in odd shaped piles next to my telephone. Above my desk, they lined up like a short order cook's tickets. They even formed illogical patterns across the floor, like the work of some kind of psychotic board game designer.

As my addiction had grown more severe, my memory had become less and less reliable, so I made detailed notes on legal pads to keep track of just about everything. What information do I have to track down? Who do I need to coordinate? What's due? And when? But in short time, I began to lose track of which notes were on which pads. So I turned to the Post-it. Electric yellow and easy to position with trembling hands, they helped me keep the most important information organized. And when my notes became incomprehensible, I'd just add more Post-its. Now looking at the hundreds of little yellow slips of paper around the room, I could only shake my head.

Disgusted with the scene, I threw myself into a thorough cleaning of my office. After a half hour, I was exhausted, frustrated, and angry—thoroughly pissed off at the old me. I hadn't consumed any booze this morning, so I felt entitled to a bright, shiny new work space. *Why should I have to be the one to clean up this scene of wreckage?*

Just as I was about to recklessly start dumping files into the giant recycling bin, my friend Rick from down the hall knocked on the door. All wrapped up in his barn jacket and ready to smoke, he squinted his sharp blue eyes at me as if to assess my condition. "Hey, man. Welcome back. You OK? Go smoke?" he asked.

"Yeah, definitely. Let's go." I grabbed my jacket off the hook on the wall.

"So, how are you doing? Did you have an operation?" he asked, as we stood smoking just east of Times Square.

"No, no operation," I said. I was ready for the questions. "Just had some shit going on with my stomach. I'm much better." I'd considered being honest with Rick. I even thought he might have guessed, given our occasional drunken nights after work in Rosie O'Grady's across the street. But I decided that if I was going to tell him the real story, it wasn't going to be today.

"OK, as long as you're all right. It's good to have you back, man," he said. He flicked his cigarette into a puddle on 46th Street. Rick always smoked faster than I did.

"Thanks. Believe it or not, I'm glad to be back."

"So, you want to hit the bar after work?"

The words sent an electrical charge through every part of my body. I tried not to change my expression.

"I can catch you up on all the shit that went down while you were out. You're not going to believe the stories I have about that client event last week," he said, shaking his head and laughing.

"I'd love to, but I can't. I'm on medication for at least thirty days, and I can't drink while I'm taking it. It totally sucks." I liked this story because it was mostly true. I was on Lexapro and certainly not supposed to drink.

"You can't drink? For thirty days? Holy shit," Rick said. "I can't imagine going a month without a drink. How long has it been?" he asked.

"Eight days," I said, way too fast. "It's not so easy. You'd be surprised."

"No, I wouldn't. You could just come to the bar and drink Diet Coke or something."

"Nah, that would be depressing," I said. I knew I wouldn't see nine days sober if I went anywhere near a barstool.

"Well, you'll save a lot of cash." We looked at each other and laughed. A couple of weeks earlier, we had hit the bar after work and stayed for two bottles of wine past our plan. Rick charged the bill but he couldn't find the receipt the next day, and neither of us could remember how much we'd spent. When he called the bar and found out that our bar tab had been $200, we laughed like idiots.

"Yeah, so will you," I laughed as I shoved him and we walked back into the building.

• • •

That night I emerged from the Union Square subway station and stood face-to-face with Shades of Green, a dark, smoky Irish bar across the street. It was a beer and shots kind of dive, perfect to duck into and throw down a few quick drinks before I had to be someplace in the neighborhood. I wondered if I was the only person to order a glass of white wine in that bar. I pictured myself in there, slugging cheap chardonnay at eleven in the morning, right after they opened.

That was just the first challenge on the walk home. I also had to pass the other bars and restaurants in Gramercy Park where I used to drink: Sal Anthony's, Verbena, Yama, and of course the granddaddy, Pete's Tavern.

It was painful peering into that long front window. Now Pete's looked like an aquarium full of exotic fish gliding past each other. It would be so easy for me to slide up to that bar, grab a quick glass of wine, and be on my way. I could get away with it. Nobody would know.

Gracie Square, jackass. You just got out of Gracie fucking Square.

My craving began to feel dangerous, so I tried to negotiate with myself. *Look at them*, I thought. *Poor guys, chained to that*

247

bar. They have no choice. They have to drink. And they hate themselves for it and wish they could stop. That's not me anymore. I'm sober.

That didn't work for shit. There were plenty of people in Pete's Tavern who had a drink or two with friends and called it a night. They weren't obsessed with their next drink; they could take it or leave it. This truth was almost unbearable to me. *Why, why, why wasn't I born with that ability?*

Overwhelmed with resentment, I resolved to change my walking route, so for the next three months, I didn't walk past my beloved Pete's Tavern. It was a small change, but it made a big difference to me. I had to practice trying to avoid reminders of the good part of drinking, all the joy that being in bars had brought me: my friends and me singing along to our favorite songs, feeling the night rev up at around eleven, clinking glasses like high fives after someone said something hilarious, just being part of the crowd, that uninhibited crowd bouncing with happy energy. Sigh. Would I find the same joy in a pot of coffee at five thirty in the morning?

Every time those happy drinking memories popped into my head, I would visualize my room at Gracie Square. I had become my own psych experiment, presenting positive and negative reinforcements to alter the subject's thinking. *No, you will not drink today. But you may get up, get dressed, and get with the program. Fuck.*

22

When Thursday arrived, I watched the clock, excited and a little nervous about my first meeting with my new Group. The meeting didn't start until 7:15 p.m, but having had an extremely productive workday, I had finished up in the office by five thirty. It was astonishing to discover what a sober person can accomplish in a day. Afraid to walk around in the wilds of bars and liquor stores, I put my feet up on my desk and called Devon. During the first few days of my ordeal, everyone had checked in with me daily, but now that the drama was over they were back to their own lives and we were back to a more normal routine.

She answered her cell phone while riding a bus from her office on Wall Street to her apartment on the Upper East Side. "Hey, what's up?" I asked.

"Hey you," she said. "What's going on?"

"Oh, everything and nothing. Coming back to work has been OK—weird though, because of the phantom procedure bullshit I've been giving everyone. But OK. And I have my first Group thing at the rehab tonight."

"Oh my God," she laughed. "That's right. You have to tell me if there are any celebrities or cute guys there," she said.

Devon wasn't letting go of her fantasy that a trip to detox could land you on the cover of *InStyle: Celebrity Weddings*.

"Well, I'm not supposed to talk about the people, but I'll keep my eyes open. I can't date anyone there or they'll kick me out. But I can pass them along to you!"

"Mmm, I don't know if that's a good idea. I'm not looking for an alcoholic or a drug addict," she said.

"That's pretty much who you meet every Saturday night," I said. "Besides, if I meet them at rehab, that means they're getting their life together. That beats the hell out of dating some knucklehead who's hungover every weekend." Why did I feel the need to defend these people?

"You know what," she said, "You're right. Keep your eyes open. I bet you meet some of those Wall Street guys who shoot up at lunch. No, screw that. I'll take an ex-drinker. Or coke . . . booze or coke. No heroin. Are you getting all this down?" she laughed.

I laughed with her. "Noted," I said. "And shall I assume you wouldn't mind a sex addict?"

"Is that a trick question?"

"What are you doing this weekend?" I asked, purely out of habit. Of course I had a pretty good idea of the answer.

"Tomorrow probably just meet up with Peter, David, and whoever else wants to come along for some drinks and maybe dinner after work." We both paused, then Devon added, "Um, do you want to join us? Can you do that?"

"I guess I could. It's not like there's anywhere I'm not allowed to go. But they do tell you to stay away from situations where you used to drink, so I probably shouldn't. Maybe not this soon." My face felt hot and my throat clenched as if I might cry. How strange it was, talking about my new sober life with one of my best drinking buddies. I could feel an awkward distance between us, like when a girlfriend has a baby and then forgets how to talk to her single friends.

"So then what are you going to do all weekend?" she asked. "Do you want me to come over instead?" I knew she'd be happy to give up her plans and sit with me if I wanted it.

"No, no. That's OK, but thanks. Mark's around, so we'll probably order some food and watch a movie," I said.

And there it was. My new normal. After almost fifteen years of tearing it up from Friday to Sunday with my dearest, happiest, funniest friends, I would now watch and wave from the shore of a Friday afternoon as they sailed away on the Good Ship Party time. What had I done to deserve this?

Devon said, "Well, I'm really proud of you. This has to be *really* tough. Let's try to have dinner one night next week, if that works for you."

"Thanks. Yeah, dinner next week would be great," I said and we hung up.

I put my elbows on my desk and my face in my hands and thought, *how much did that suck*? I couldn't remember ever being on a phone call with Devon that ended with my feeling angry. But I was angry. I was angry about feeling left out, left out because of a *disease*. I was angry that the fun wasn't about to slow down without me. I was angry about feeling like damaged goods.

I decided to dump all of this on the Group.

I arrived at HopeCare about twenty minutes before the meeting started, which gave me time to size up my new compatriots in the decrepit waiting area. There were about twenty of them, a mix of the same types of men and women I'd seen on the 6 train during rush hour. All sizes and colors, many were around my age give or take ten years. Some were dressed professionally, but the majority came in jeans. Feeling like a sausage after twelve hours in my tight, black pencil skirt at the end of the day, I made a mental note to bring jeans and a sweater to the office on Meeting days.

Tracy was at the reception desk. "Hey, Lisa, how are you doing? Welcome back," she smiled. She seemed surprised to see me. I wondered how many people signed on for help from HopeCare and then never showed up again.

"Hey, Tracy. Anything I need to do?" People were walking back and forth across the room and checking in at different tables.

"Yeah, honey, first take this," she handed me a strip of thin, clear plastic with a bright orange rectangular sticker affixed to it. I tipped my head like a confused puppy. "It's to show which group you're in because a couple of them start around the same time. You can put it on your jacket or wherever ... "

Already I was annoyed. What kind of dumb process was this? They can't just point me to my Group's room? We have to be color coded? Were these addicts a bunch of nitwits? Were the staff? I slid the orange sticker into one of my pockets and zipped my coat.

All the chairs were taken, so I looked for a spot on the floor where I could sit and work on a crossword puzzle. Apparently I had broken my first rule because a woman seated behind a desk called out to me. "Young lady. Excuse me." Her reading glasses were sliding down her nose. "I don't think you've checked in with me yet."

I approached her desk and saw that her nametag read "Alice." There were all kinds of medical-looking containers and plastic bags strewn around her area. "Um, no, I haven't. Is there something I need to do?" I asked.

"Is this your first time, sweetheart?" Alice asked me kindly.

"Yes, it is. Lisa Smith."

"OK." She ran her pen down a column of names on a sheet of paper. "Here you are. Welcome to HopeCare, dear." She handed me a clear plastic cup with a green lid and a blank sticker attached to it. "Please urinate in this and then bring it back to me."

"What?" I asked, picking up the cup and looking at it as if I'd never seen anything like it. "Where? Here? Or do I take this home?"

"Here, of course!" she laughed. "How could we let you take that home? The bathroom is at the end of the hall straight through the reception area."

I looked down the hall and saw a guy in a flannel shirt, jeans, and work boots walking toward us and holding a plastic cup half full of yellow liquid. He looked younger than me and a bit disheveled, and he held his pee cup as casually as I'd hold a glass of Chablis. Good grief, this place was all class. I knew I was going to be expected to pee in a cup, but what about a *little* privacy!

I lowered my head and carried the cup toward the bathroom. No one in the packed waiting area showed any interest in me or what I was doing. Maybe that was their version of privacy: nobody gave a shit.

The ladies' room had a sign taped to the swinging entry door that declared "ONLY ONE CLIENT IN BATHROOM AT A TIME." I supposed that was meant to prevent the swapping of urine, but the bathroom had a private stall and room for at least two people to stand near the sink. This system was completely breachable. *They really must believe in the honor code,* I thought. *With addicts?*

I was beginning to get a feeling that there were lessons to be found in all aspects of this journey. So far this evening

I'd learned, "If you prefer to urinate with privacy, don't become an alcoholic."

I made a mental note that if I ever decided to use again, I'd need to get some clean pee from Jessica or Devon before Group. Then I remembered what I heard at Gracie Square: staying sober is up to the addict. HopeCare could set up all kinds of rules and threats, but if I decided to drink again or pass off someone else's urine as mine, the awful consequences would ultimately be mine. And I had no difficulty recalling some of those grisly consequences, many of them involving horrific bodily functions on all fours in my bathroom. In that moment I felt grateful for being offered this help to never again experience those kinds of consequences.

Teddy's Group met in an office that didn't belong to him, in the basement, just off the reception area. I walked a few steps in and stopped abruptly. We'd been assigned to the office of a crazy cat lady. There were cat images everywhere. Cat wall posters, cat desk calendar, cat birthday cards, cat coffee mug, cat clock with a ticking tail. I had hoped that the women of HopeCare might be models of growth for me. The cat menagerie was a discouraging discovery. I thought to myself, *what a "cat-tastrophe,"* and then had to fight back the giggles. That was a pretty clear sign of how emotionally worn out I was—my humor had been reduced to puns.

The room held about a dozen chairs arranged in a circle. On one of them, there was a clipboard marking it as Teddy's seat. I watched the group file in as if they were a jury that had reached its verdict. I studied their faces, but there was no reading this crowd. Blacks, whites, Latinos, women, men, twentysomethings, fiftysomethings—it was as if a random smattering of subjects had been sent from the Census Bureau.

Once we started, I got into the rhythm of Group quickly. Teddy passed his clipboard around so we could all sign in and note our days, "C&S." The meth addict next to me explained that it meant, "Clean and Sober."

Teddy introduced me as, "our new Group member," and asked me how I was doing.

"I'm fine," I said, still clinging to my favorite answer. "Well, of course I'm dying for a drink. But I get it. If I start up drinking the way I was, it will kill me. So, I'm not going to drink today." *Spoken like an actual sober person. Huh.*

I saw heads nodding all around the circle. Then they started talking. I heard things like, "I missed my mother's funeral because I was out on a tear." "I'd been sober for five years. Then I picked up a drink, and two weeks later I woke up in a motel surrounded by empty half-gallons of Jack Daniels." "I got knifed in a bar fight and don't remember a thing." It all reminded me of a scene in *The Sopranos* that I'd thought was completely farfetched, but listening to these stories, I could easily imagine Christopher Moltisanti on one of these chairs talking about how he shot heroin and nodded out on his girlfriend's couch, accidentally crushing her dog to death underneath him.

Everyone had the same intense mental obsession with drugs and alcohol. It was all they thought about, and it made them do awful things that they never would have done sober. They were exactly like me. They knew all about that thing in my brain, the faulty "STOP" button. They understood what the days and nights were like, how with every day that passes you find yourself willing to do something more awful than the day before. They had all done the awful things. My God, were *these* my people?

When the session ended, I stood outside with a few people to have a cigarette. Jack, a homicide cop from Queens who

255

loved whiskey and hookers, said to me, "Funny, you don't look like a cokehead. Thought you'd be all white wine at the dinner table."

I laughed. "Yeah, there was white wine at the dinner table. But it was also at the lunch table and the breakfast table, along with a shitload of coke." He laughed back. *Aww, look at that*, I thought. *I've made my first rehab friend.*

In another session, we were asked to write a "goodbye" letter to our "drug of our choice." Timothy, a young, black haired, chisel-cheeked heroin addict, was a stand-out with his simple, "Fuck you, heroin, you motherfucker." I'd never before heard anything so beautifully written.

The exercise was difficult for me. First, I had a problem with the idea of a "drug of choice." Was it alcohol? Was it cocaine? Was there a "choice"?

And how to say goodbye to them? Did it need to be forever? Where Timothy was succinct and direct with his message to his drug, I tended toward negotiation and ambivalence. "Why couldn't you let me stop when the party was over? Why did you have to keep pawing at me after everyone else had gone home? And why do you have to be so intense that this goodbye needs to be final? Can't I still see you on New Year's Eve, birthdays, and maybe every other Saturday night?"

• • •

After a few weeks of staying clean, I felt mentally and physically fantastic. I felt rested after sleep, I felt energetic throughout the day, and I was even beginning to feel good about myself. That's when I became terrified of relapse. It started to feel as if this was all some sick joke perpetrated by a puppeteer who had made me alcoholic in the first place. He was bored, and this is how he entertained himself—by letting his puppets go through the agony of getting clean, then handing them a bottle of scotch and watching the show.

In Group I was told that until now I'd been riding a "pink cloud," the puffy glow that we newly clean addicts float around in because we're just so damned happy to have been released from Hell. But what happens when the novelty wears off?

My friend Calvin from Group knew something about that. A preppy looking guy in his late thirties, he'd been using coke since he was a teenager, and after first trying to get clean more than ten years ago, he'd gone through relapse after relapse after relapse, each time starting the process all over again full of regret and self-hatred. A successful journalist for a financial magazine, Calvin seemed so insightful when he spoke about his addiction that I just couldn't understand why he kept choosing to use drugs.

One night as Calvin and I smoked outside of HopeCare, I decided to find out. "So, what happened? Why'd you pick up again?" I asked, using the vernacular that came naturally to me now.

"You know, it's funny," he said, careful not to blow smoke in my face, "I knew it was going to happen. I actually celebrated my ninety days sober with a call to my dealer followed by a whole lot of coke." He ran a hand through his hair and shook his head.

"What do you mean you *knew* it was going to happen? How did you know?"

"My buddy Bill emailed me on Thursday and asked if I wanted to get together Friday night. I said 'OK.'"

"That's it? That's all it took? Does Bill have some kind of devil power?"

"It's not Bill's fault. It's on me. He doesn't understand. He doesn't have to understand. But I know that if I'm planning to connect with Bill on a Friday, that I might use, that I'll *probably* use. So, if I don't want to pick up, I don't go out with Bill on Friday night. It's that simple."

I wondered what that meant about my friends and me. "So, do you think it's just a matter of time before you can hang out with Bill again on a Friday?"

"I can't go out with Bill on a Friday. Period. It's like that dumb line we keep hearing, 'If you hang around a barbershop long enough, you're gonna get a haircut.' As silly as that sounds, it's true. Maybe *you* can hang out with your friends on weekend nights, just going along and drinking Diet Coke, but I can't." I didn't think I could either. Not today.

We stood there for a while watching cabs go by. Then I said, "I'm terrified of relapse."

"That's good, you should be. A healthy fear of relapse is an excellent thing. I wish I had more of it. I'll tell you, once you give sobriety a serious shot, the joy of going out and using is over for you. There's no going back to thinking 'it's just a party, just a good time' you know? If you can say out loud that this stuff is killing you and yet you still go back to it . . . " He took a drag from his cigarette and exhaled toward the sky. "I don't wish that feeling on anyone."

I felt myself nodding as he spoke. I wanted to store his words so I could tap them if I ever needed them.

When I got home, Mark was sitting in front of the television watching financial news. After Gracie Square our relationship was only platonic, but he still hung around my apartment and supported me however he could.

"That guy I'm friends with at Group relapsed again," I told Mark that night.

Mark was always interested in my Group stories, but without his having any emotional connection to the people, the bad news never distressed him. "Isn't that like the third time he's relapsed since you met him?" he asked.

"Yeah, it's terrible." I plopped down next to him on the couch and lit a cigarette. "He keeps trying to quit and then BOOM! He's high again."

"That doesn't make any sense," he said.

"Addiction doesn't make any sense. That scares the shit out of me. Am I going to end up getting drunk in the mornings again?"

"It's already been a few weeks and you're doing great. You're not going to blow it."

"Are you kidding?" I said. "If it were that easy, no alcoholic would ever drink again."

Mark rested his hand on my shoulder. "If you drink again, it will be a disaster."

"Yeah," I said. I took a long drag of my cigarette and exhaled slowly. "Except for the drinking part."

23

During the last couple of years of addiction, I lied to everyone in my life and cut myself off from a lot of friends. Managing a demanding job while I had a ravenous monkey clinging to my back narrowed my world dramatically, and frequent isolation helped keep my secret. Anyone allowed long looks might have seen the problem.

Then there was the issue of friends in other cities, friends so far away that the lying had been effortless. Now it was time to start cleaning those messes.

My dear high school friend Randi had moved to Los Angeles in her early thirties, and our lives had diverged profoundly. While I was crawling around my closet floor hoping to find a dropped bag of coke at sunrise, Randi was teaching yoga and performing sun salutations in the Santa Monica mountains. We spoke often, but the relationship had changed. From her side of the conversation came truth. From my side, it was all bullshit.

Two months before Gracie Square, all wound up on coke, I had called Randi at two in the morning to tell her about a business trip I'd be taking to San Francisco in May. We decided that after San Francisco I should visit her in LA and that turned into,

261

"Let's go to Paris together!" The trip became even more exciting when Randi read that during our time in France, Sting would be performing in a small, converted movie theater in Paris. If Sting had asked her to, Randi would have launched herself off the side of those Santa Monica mountains. Then to make the plan even more delicious, one of Randi's yoga students offered us her apartment in Paris's Marais district. Suddenly, we were two girlfriends headed for a thrilling vacation. The wine! The nightclubs! The wine!

But then I sent myself to detox, and now I had to tell Randi not only that I wasn't drinking anymore but that I was an addict. "Randi, I'm a cokehead." No, that didn't sound right. "Sweetie, you know how I've always liked to tip a few cocktails?" Not quite. "Hey girl, I have some good news and some bad news..."

Not long before, I would have prepared for an uncomfortable phone call by taking a deep breath and downing half a bottle of merlot. Now it was just me and deep breaths. In the first two minutes of the call, I blurted it in one rambling sentence.

"...I'm an alcoholic and was also abusing cocaine, but two weeks ago I checked myself into rehab, got myself clean, and now I take meds and go to meetings and it's working... I feel really good about it... my life looks completely different now and I—"

As always, Randi responded like a burst of sunshine and rainbows.

"Oh, Lisa, that's so cool! I'm so happy!" Randi squealed. Well maybe not all rainbows. "But what the fuck happened?" she added.

"I just kind of broke. It got so far out of hand. I thought I could control it but I couldn't. One day I just decided that it had to stop, and I checked myself into rehab."

"I'm so glad you did it. I was hoping—"

I bristled. "Hoping?"

"I mean, for a long time I've thought you had a problem. I don't know . . . there were signs. For one, you only called me when it was late, really late your time. And you'd ramble. You'd repeat things two or three times."

Once again, talking to a dear friend was making my face flush and my eyes wet with tears. But I didn't want to look backward, so I directed the conversation to the future, the future that scared the hell out of me. I'd been sober for less than two weeks. How the fuck was I was going to travel and handle work meetings and then have to mingle through social receptions in San Francisco? And *how the fuck* was I going to survive vacations in Los Angeles and Paris without either alcohol or Group?

"You're going to have to help me out on this trip," I told her. "I mean, Paris! I'm going to feel like the kid at Disneyland who's too short to go on the good rides."

• • •

On the morning of my flight to San Francisco, I arrived at JFK with a pulsing skull and a sour milk stomach. I came very close to canceling the whole plan and going home to the new pajamas I had finally bought myself.

Airports had never been good places for me. To me, a terminal was just one giant pub crawl with a convenient hallway to guide the way. Traditionally, I would arrive early enough to get through security and have plenty of drinking time before that dead zone of pre-boarding time at the gate. I wasn't nervous about air travel, but that was my script before boarding and after takeoff. Who would begrudge a nervous flier six or seven calm-down cocktails? In-flight drinking required its own strategy. Those tiny bottles were useless, so I'd order two at a time, and after a couple rounds of that, I'd make my way to the back of the plane and ask a different flight attendant for two more.

Everything about this trip needed to be different. Even though I'd already spent six weeks avoiding the pitfalls that would threaten my new life, somehow those seemed like child's play compared to a six-hour plane ride followed by cocktail receptions, nights out in LA, a transatlantic flight to Europe, and then Paris! I was as nervous as a first-grader who'd been sent away to military school.

Following "Fake it 'til you make it," a tenet popular among Group members, I decided to pretend that I was something other than a traveler who would have traded her diamond necklace for a glass of warm champagne. Like a horse wearing blinders, I lowered my head and focused on the hallway as I walked through the terminal. My gate was directly across from a neon sign that announced, "COCKTAILS," in the shape of a tilted martini glass, so sitting there was out of the question. I found an unpopulated gate nearby, read the latest *People*, and distracted myself with food.

The time dragged, and I was running out of distractions. I really needed to get on that plane and away from airport bars. *I wonder if I qualify as someone needing special assistance.*

One flight at a time. One flight at a time.

The flight attendant called my row, and within minutes of boarding the plane, I stuffed my carry-on into the overhead, buckled my seatbelt, inserted my iPod earphones, and cranked the volume on my workout playlist. Two Twix bars, a large bag of pretzels, three Diet Sprites, a second "reading" of *People*, and a thorough examination of every unnecessary gadget in the Sky Mall got me through the flight. After the plane landed I put the blinders back on and made my way to baggage claim.

Arriving at my San Francisco hotel sober, I felt as if I'd broken the tape in the New York City Marathon.

"OK, one person, checking in for three nights," the receptionist said as the bellman loaded my bags onto a cart.

"Yes, thanks. And can you please double-check that it's a smoking room?"

"Let me confirm," she said politely, but I was sure I could hear what she was thinking: *you realize you're in California, right?*

I tapped a drum line with my foot until she confirmed that my remaining vice was allowed. I wasn't going to make it through this challenge without nicotine, lots of nicotine, any time I wanted it.

She slid a tiny manila folder toward me and pulled out two keys. "Here's your room key and this one's for the minibar."

"I won't be needing this one," I said, sliding the smaller key back across the reception desk.

"Are you sure?" she asked. "You might want something late at night."

I can promise you I'll want something late at night, dumbass. Spare me the upsell and keep your key to the gates of fucking Hell. "I'm sure."

I was barely settled into my room before I had to be downstairs for the first cocktail hour of the conference. I grabbed two of every hors d'oeuvre that passed by without even asking what they were.

"Hi. Club soda with a splash of cranberry juice and a lime, please," I said to the bartender.

From behind me I heard a familiar voice. "Club soda?! Who are you and what have you done with Lisa Smith?" It was Lara, one of my colleagues based in another office. She was younger than I and had been a good party buddy at past conferences after the lightweights had headed off to sleep. Her straight black hair had been expertly blown out, and she wore an expensive dark blue fitted suit. A glass of red wine dangled from her hand.

"Yeah, I know," I fake laughed, kissing her cheek. "I had a stomach problem taken care of recently. I'm still on the medication. Can't drink."

"What? You mean you're not drinking this whole trip? That's *bullshit*! We have a suite upstairs for after parties! You'll still come, right?" Lara said, taking a long sip of wine. She was already rocking back and forth in her high heels which offered a preview of the hours to come.

"Probably not. This medicine really wipes me out."

"Come on! Are you sure you can't drink? I was really looking forward to partying with you! Just *one*?"

Wow, I thought. Is this what I was like for *ten years of professional functions*, hectoring people to drink with me like a Cuervo-soaked coed?

Back in my room, I flopped backwards onto the bed, kicked off my high heels, and threw my arms over my head. I wanted a drink badly, very badly. Oh that gorgeous crimson wine in Lara's glass. Or a frosty cold martini just poured, its layer of sparkling ice flecks dancing around plump bleu cheese olives. Or a Long Island Iced Tea, all five white liquors joining forces and sliding down my throat to deliver a merciful blast of blood warmth and nerve cell ecstasy! Oh God, anything. A quick hit of whiskey, cheap tequila. I didn't care. All I'd have to do is call down for that little key.

"FUUUUCK!" I screamed into a pillow.

STOP, I thought. *Gracie Square, Gracie Square. YOU DO NOT PICK UP, NO MATTER WHAT.* I scurried down to the lobby store and bought a Hershey bar. Thanks to the chocolate and three quick cigarettes, the urge passed. The booze cravings were like everything I'd ever heard about labor pains— they came on fast and hard, and if I could breathe and distract my way through a few excruciating minutes, they would pass.

Until the next one.

By the time I got to Los Angeles, I was both relieved to be with Randi and proud of myself for making it through a conference without a drink. Randi looked like a poster girl for the good life. Her skin was peanut butter brown, and blonde streaks brightened her wavy, brown hair. She had developed one of those yoga bodies that meant never dressing to hide. Wearing denim shorts and a tiny t-shirt with a Buddhist symbol, she looked as if she'd stepped right out of college. I hugged her hard. In my arms she felt like a ballet dancer—somehow both delicate as a baby bird and strong as a linebacker.

We drove up the Pacific Coast Highway in her bouncy Subaru. The LA sun was brighter than I had remembered, and the ocean surface glittered like a billion pieces of magical glass. We chattered and laughed like the high school friends we had once been.

Then I said what was really on my mind. "You know, it's fine for you to drink while I'm around." I kept my eyes on the glittery glass.

Randi whipped her head toward me and then back to the road. "What are you talking about? I'm not drinking while you're here."

"Hey, I don't want to wreck this trip for you. Not drinking wine in Paris or getting buzzed for the Sting show? It's a vacation."

"I don't care. Drinking doesn't mean anything to me," she said. "I maybe have a drink once a month if I go to a party, and I don't even feel good after one. Anyway, I'm not about to drink while you're still going through rehab."

"That's really sweet of you." I said. "I just don't want anyone acting different because of me."

"Don't be a dope," she said. "You just got out of detox. If it's
better for you to have people around you not drink, just say it."

She was right. This was all new to me, and I didn't know
how things were supposed to work. What should I expect from
people? What could I ask for without being a social pain in the
ass? I felt like a new vegetarian who doesn't want to miss the
barbecue and also doesn't want anybody making special food
for her but sure as hell doesn't want to come home with a belly
full of beef trying to slog its way through her intestines.

I had taken several trips to Paris, but I'd spent very little of my time there even remotely sober. Why would anyone
choose to stroll and eat and dance their way through Paris
nights sober? On previous trips, I'd been on the Parisian Party
Program: eat in world-class restaurants, drink fabulous wine,
kiss French men, and troll for drugs in hip nightclubs. Don't
worry about tours or galleries or learning the history—daytime
was all about sleeping off what I'd done the night before. Headaches, dehydration, street noise, and a shortage of ice kept me
complaining as I tried to sleep through the world's most beautiful city.

But this time I saw Paris, actually saw it. Up early each
morning, I would buy a copy of the *International Tribune* and
work the crossword puzzle at a café as I wired myself up on crois-
sants and café au lait. This time I kept my eyes open and reveled
in my time with Randi as well as my time alone. Many times I
stopped and let myself enjoy a feeling of profound gratitude.

My Internet search turned up several English-speaking
12-step meetings in Paris, and I decided to try one at the American Church on the Quai d'Orsay. The next morning, I navi-
gated the Metro from the Marais to the Invalides stop, and as

soon as I stepped outside the Metro station, I knew I was lost. At that early hour, there was almost no one around to ask for help, and anyway I wanted a break from seeing pained expressions on Parisian faces when I tripped over my clunky high school French. So I tried to find my own way to the church and ended up turning a five-minute walk into a forty-five minute labyrinth. Before long, as I stood on a corner trying not to look like a lost American, frustration and self-doubt joined the outing. *I'm not an adventurer. I'm not self-sufficient. I have no sense of direction. Where the hell is this church? Forget it, I don't need this meeting. Ugh, I look helpless. Why haven't I kept up with French? What the hell was the point of taking it if I was only going to abandon it? Why is everything so fucking hard for me??*

And with feelings of insecurity came the need for a drink. *Does anybody drink in the morning around here? They have 12-step meetings—they must have morning drinkers.* What if I found a nice café and started by ordering a coffee? Then I could say something like, "Hey, I'm on vacation, let's make it a Café Calva, heavy on the brandy. What's that, barman? You're a master of the espresso martini? C'est magnifique! I'll try one!"

Wait. How the hell did I switch so quickly from gratitude to coffee boozing? I had to get control of this head of mine. If I couldn't switch off the static altogether, at least I could try to change the channel, so I repeated that Gracie Square wall mantra: "Get up. Get dressed. Get with the program." And I visualized the day room. The memory of that cold, barren cell lined with the smell of sweat, piss, and disinfectant offered a dramatic contrast to France's blooming spring trees and centuries-old architecture. So I reminded myself that on that lovely Paris morning, I'd gotten up and had gotten dressed. Now, I'd better get with le fucking programme.

I refocused on finding the meeting and feeling grateful again. It was during that walk that I realized something enlightening about gratitude: I could make myself feel it by thinking about what's good *or* by thinking about what isn't bad. Yes, I was aware that it was a stunning day and that I was walking along La Seine, the one and only river right in the heart of the city of a thousand dreams. And I was conscious of my good luck to feel healthy enough to walk it and to be well off enough to pay for the trip. But the flash of awareness that really perked my mood was actually about what I was missing.

On that morning, I *wasn't* face down in a pillow soaked in saliva groaning as I negotiated with my stomach to please hold back the vomit because I just couldn't bear to drag my wretched body to a toilet where I'd lie there, face on the seat, mouth breathing until another nausea wave passed. None of that was happening. I was lost in a foreign city, but I was standing up straight. Could I ever need anything more than that?

I found the church, a Gothic-style structure with a soaring green spire and joined my fellow sober folk under the high ceilings of the room inside. What could a 12-step meeting possibly be like in Paris? In fact, it looked like a 12-step meeting in New York. The big difference was the chic. *Man,* I thought looking around at my fellow group members. *Parisians roll out of bed looking more stylish than I do in my best black-tie dress.* But in the meeting we were all very much the same, sharing similar stories and repeating the familiar expressions that illustrate what we deal with in recovery: "I'm struggling today," "I feel so fortunate to be alive," and "My worst day sober is better than my best day on drugs." I knew these people and they knew me. What a revelation: 12-step meetings were like McDonald's, you could find them just about anywhere in the world, and they always served just what you expected.

270

The night before we left France, Randi and I stood front row center at the intimate Olympia Theater. With nobody between us and Sting, he sang to us and no one else. Randi cried like a teenager watching the Beatles step off their plane in 1964. I cried because I couldn't believe that this could be my life.

• • •

After the Paris trip, I began attending Group twice a week and 12-step meetings every other day. I was no longer including the "if" in my thoughts about staying sober. It had become all about "how." I heard story after story about people who had almost drunk themselves dead but who were now living fulfilling lives as long as they didn't pick up a drink. I wanted to be those people, decades deep into sobriety, my drunk days far behind, my time spent trying to help the next girl to shuffle in from Gracie Square. So I linked arms with Lexapro, and we put one foot in front of the other.

It was time I chose a sponsor—she should be another woman who had been sober longer than I had and who was living the kind of sobriety I wanted for myself. If she agreed to become my sponsor, she would be like a sober coach and guide me through the 12-steps. After some scouting, I chose Jennifer, a manufacturing executive with long blonde hair and perfectly painted nails. She looked so much like Natasha Richardson it seemed strange to me that when she opened her mouth, American English came out. Jennifer worked a stressful job, just as I did. She loved booze and coke, as I did. And she got sober when her self-poisoning began to threaten her career, as I did. Jennifer also had a marriage at stake, and she wasn't willing to trash it. Now she was the picture of calm in the midst of New York nuttiness and an endless wave of corporate shit storms. I could see us in each other and I liked it.

One Wednesday afternoon I called Jennifer from my office. "So I'm having dinner with my friends tonight, but I won't stay out late."

"The friends you used to drink with?" she asked.

"Yes," I said.

"I thought you were keeping it to breakfasts and lunches with them?"

"I have been. But it's been three months. I'm sure it'll be fine." It was quiet for a moment.

"Have you ever, in the fifteen years you've been friends with these people, ever, not had a drink when you all went out to dinner?" she asked.

"No," I said with a sigh, my eyes turning toward the ceiling.

"But after just three months of sobriety you're *sure* it'll be fine?" Ugh. She was a tough broad and dammit, she was right.

"I guess it could be hard," I said.

"That's an understatement," she said. "If you want to go, go. But I think you're putting yourself at risk without good reason."

She was right. She was right. She was right. It had been only three months. I had a tremendous amount to lose, and I just didn't know if I was stronger than a 1999 Far Niente.

"Hey, it's me," I said when Devon picked up her office phone a few minutes later.

"Hey, you."

"Listen," I said. "I'm not going to make it tonight." I felt my throat choke up.

"What? Why?" she asked.

"I'm not ready. It's that simple. Fuck! I'm not ready. I'm afraid of drinking."

"I completely understand. You have to do whatever's best for you. We'll miss you, though."

Fuck me.

• • •

A few months later, some of my friends started turning forty. That meant parties. I'd gotten good at sidestepping out of weeknight hangs, and the occasional brunches were easy to manage—even normal people didn't always order booze to go with their eggs Benedict—but these milestones presented a much bigger hurdle. These were my people and my people were turning forty.

"Baby, you're still coming to the party, right?" Jerry had asked me early in the week.

"You know I wouldn't miss the night you step into real adulthood," I said, as if I hadn't spent the past ten days trying to craft an excuse.

"I don't know about that," he laughed. "You know it might get a little out of hand, so. . ."

"I know. But it's a big night. I want to be there."

Jerry's fortieth party was held on a Saturday night at The Palm, a steakhouse in the Theater District. It was a classic party establishment with dark brown walls lined with color caricatures of the restaurant's most famous and biggest-spending customers. Everything at The Palm was thick and meaty, from the heavy wooden tables to the steaks to most of the patrons. As in so many other New York restaurants, Jerry had buddied up to the bartender, so the drinks flowed whenever we showed up. That night, twenty of us took over the private dining room, and all through the night, full bottles of wine were marched into the room as fast at the empty ones were marched out.

At the dinner, Jessica and Devon hovered around me as if I were a diabetic in a Godiva store.

"Does the seltzer have enough cranberry for you?" Jessica asked when my mocktail arrived.

Devon handed me a plate, "Here, Li, have a plate of fried calamari—all tentacles attached, just the way you like it."

"It's cold out tonight. We want to call you a car when you're ready," Jessica said.

By the time dessert was served, I had breathed in countless wine fumes, heard countless glasses clink, and heard countless happy old stories about Jerry and the gang. I had made it through my first post-rehab party, the kind of energetic drinking romp that had dominated almost all of my thirties. I was tired, sober, and happy to go home.

In clean pajamas, I stood in front of the bathroom mirror washing my face and thinking about the night. I'd left a party while it was still rumbling, and something about that made me feel left out. Someone in Group had said that it's helpful to "play the tape through," to think about what the scene would look like if I'd said "yes" to alcohol after months of hard fought sobriety. That was an easy exercise. Even if I could have made my friends believe that I could drink "just one, maybe two and then call it a night," in the best-case scenario I would have drunk more than anyone realized, passed out in my own bed, and awakened the next day dehydrated, aching, vomiting, and wanting to die of self-hatred. In the worst-case scenario, I would have blacked out somewhere dangerous or called Henry for a bunch of coke. That is, if I hadn't already stepped blindly in front of a speeding truck and been smeared across 50th Street.

● ● ●

I awoke feeling the simple tiredness of having gone to bed late. That was all, just a little Sunday morning laziness. I thought, *I'll spend a couple of hours drinking coffee and reading the paper in my pajamas.* I couldn't help smiling as I padded into the kitchen and poured water into the back of the coffeemaker that I no longer neglected. I looked forward to talking through the party post-game with my friends hours later after they'd already been up once for Advil and water and had thrown themselves back onto the mercy of their mattresses.

Curled on my couch with a big cup of expensive coffee warming my hands, I looked around my bright living room, so pleasant when the curtains were pulled wide, and thought about the night before. Things had changed and forever. From now on, the memories I created with my friends would simply not look like the memories we had built up to now. From my sober station the night before, I had watched as the personalities expanded and volume boomed with every refilled glass. And for every single second of the party, I was completely aware that I was the sober one, the one who wasn't like everybody else.

Sitting there in the morning sunshine, I felt content and even a little bit proud. But it wasn't until many years later when I realized that my choice on the night of Jerry's fortieth birthday was the most extraordinary accomplishment of my life.

Epilogue

It's been twelve years since I got sober...

I've apologized to people I hurt when I was drinking and using drugs. They haven't all forgiven me.

I hold a job I would have lost in a week if I were drinking. Twice during presentations I've suffered anxiety attacks so vicious that I've had to halt the meeting and lower my head into deep breaths as partners handed me glasses of water.

I married a wonderful man in the Santa Fe home that we bought together. I wore pale blue because white would have felt ridiculous.

I held my father's hand and gave him morphine as he lay dying. Then I pulled myself together and delivered a eulogy that I hope was worthy of him.

I've watched friends I met in recovery jam onstage with rock gods and act in the hottest HBO television shows. I've built friendships with people who came to a 12-step meeting one day and relapsed the next.

I buried a best friend. I still can't accept his death.

I regularly call sober friends from 12-step programs who help me stay clean. In turn, I help incredible people to stand up straight, salvage their careers, save their marriages, and anchor their families.

I now have a niece and a nephew, and I made it to the hospital the day Ben was born. I'm the aunt who shows up for sleepovers.

On many mornings, I haven't wanted to get out of bed. On most mornings, I've gotten out of bed.

On more than 4,000 mornings, I have awakened and made a decision:

"Just for today, I will not drink."

About the Author

Photo by Rod Goodman

Lisa Smith is a writer and a lawyer in New York City. Sober for more than ten years, she is passionate about breaking the stigma of drug and alcohol addiction, particularly for professional women.

Lisa's writing has been published in *The Washington Post*, *Chicago Tribune*, AfterPartyMagazine, and Addiction.com. She is on the Board of Directors of the NY Writers Coalition and The Writers Room in Greenwich Village.

Prior to working for more than fifteen years in legal marketing, she practiced corporate finance law at a leading international law firm.

After attending Northwestern University, Lisa received a JD from Rutgers School of Law, where she served on the editorial board of the *Rutgers Law Review*.